HAIG

FIELD-MARSHAL EARL HAIG, VISCOUNT DAWICK AND BARON HAIG, AND 29TH LAIRD OF BEMERSYDE, O.M., K.T., G.C.B., G.C.V.O., K.C.I.E.

HAIG

By DUFF COOPER

Garden City, N. Y.
DOUBLEDAY, DORAN
& Company, Incorporated
MCMXXXVI

PRINTED AT THE *Country Life Press*, GARDEN CITY, N. Y., U. S. A.

FIRST EDITION

TO

THE MEMORY

OF THE MEN WHO SERVED WITH HIM

THIS BIOGRAPHY

OF

EARL HAIG OF BEMERSYDE

IS DEDICATED

AS HE WOULD HAVE WISHED

PREFACE

THE executors of the late Lord Haig, who invited me to write this book, have placed at my disposal all the relevant documents in their possession. The most important of these is the diary that he kept throughout the war. The average entry for each day amounts to two or three typewritten foolscap pages. With it is incorporated a large number of other papers—letters, received and dispatched, official records of important meetings, telegrams, orders of the day, maps, etc. The copy which is housed in the office of the committee of Imperial Defence is contained in thirty-six folio volumes.

I am deeply indebted to many relatives, friends and brother officers of the late Field Marshal for the assistance that they have given me. If I were to mention their names the list would be too long, but I must express particular gratitude to Brigadier General Sir James Edmonds, the official historian, who has not only read the proofs but has helped me with his advice and unrivalled knowledge of the Western Front.

DUFF COOPER

Contents

CONTENTS

Illustrations

Maps

CHAPTER I

From Oxford to the Army

[illegible]

CHAPTER I

From Oxford to the Army

On the 19th of June in the year 1861 Douglas Haig was born at 24 Charlotte Square, Edinburgh, the last of a large family. Scotsmen take a greater interest in their forbears than do the English, and the Haigs can boast of genealogical trees with their roots in the dim ages. John Haig, however, the father of Douglas, was a distiller of whisky, and in the performance of that useful function he had acquired considerable wealth. Nevertheless he was accounted fortunate when he secured as his bride the beautiful Miss Veitch of Elrock, who was his junior by nineteen years. The Veitches belonged to that section of society who in the middle of the nineteenth century were still able to look down on the trading community, and they considered that they had conferred a favour on the Haigs by consigning a dowerless daughter to their care.

The marriage, despite the disparity of ages and the suggestion of misalliance, proved eminently successful. The young wife, with a devotion commoner, perhaps, in those days than in these, gave up her whole life to the care of her home, the duties of her religion and the welfare of her children. She took no part in society, either in Edinburgh or at her husband's country house in Fife. Every morning at four o'clock she would rise from her bed in order to visit the rooms where her children were sleeping, and the religious faith which she implanted in their minds remained with them when she was no longer there to remind them of it.

The family increased with almost mechanical regularity. The marriage took place in 1839, and during the twenty-two years that followed eleven children were born at intervals of two years between each. Nine survived; and the fact that the two who were born in 1853 and 1855 died young emphasized the gap between the six elder and the three younger children. Douglas' eldest brother was twenty years older, and his youngest sister was ten years older than himself. It was therefore natural that their relations toward him should be those rather of uncle and aunt than of brother and sister, and they showed themselves fully sensible of the responsibility that such circumstances imposed, especially after the deaths of their father and mother which occurred in 1878 and 1879.

Like Wellington before him, he was considered the dunce of the family, and like his contemporary Henry Wilson, who failed three times to pass into Sandhurst, Douglas Haig gave no precocious evidence of intellectual ability. He was first sent to a day school in Edinburgh and later to a preparatory school at Rugby, with a view to passing thence into the public school which Dr Arnold had made famous. But he proved a backward scholar, it was feared that he would fail in the entrance examination, and he was eventually sent to Clifton College, where apparently at that time the standard of education expected of novices was less exacting.

He remained at Clifton for four years, from 1875 to 1879. He was a popular and handsome boy, but did not distinguish himself either at work or at athletics. He was a member of the School House, for which he eventually played both at cricket and at football, but he never played for the school.

When he left school he was eighteen years of age, possessed of a fortune which assured him independence, and he was an orphan. The first use that he made of his liberty was to accompany one of his elder brothers, Hugo, on a visit to America. They travelled as far as California, and during the journey he decided that he would go to Oxford on his return. He accordingly became an undergraduate of Brasenose in the autumn of 1880.

His reception by the principal of that College was reminiscent of an earlier Oxford that was rapidly passing, if it had not already passed, away. Dr Cradock had held his position for twenty-seven years. To the young undergraduate at their first interview he exclaimed, "Ride, sir, ride—I like to see the gentlemen of Brasenose in top boots";—and to the future Lord Askwith, who joined the college on the same day, he said, "Drink plenty of port, sir, you want port in this damp climate."

Haig was not slow to act upon the suggestion tendered to him by so high an authority. Although he spent much of his first year in rowing, and achieved considerable success on the river, he subsequently devoted all his leisure and most of his attention to riding, which he realized was an accomplishment likely to prove of greater value in his future career; and it was at Oxford that he acquired that skill in horsemanship which distinguished him for the rest of his life. It was here, also, that he learned to play polo, the only game at which he ever excelled.

But he learned more at Oxford than to ride and to play polo. Many boys who have not risen to the highest places in their public schools, nor exercised that influence which is reserved for those who distinguish themselves at either of the two games that are there considered of importance, suffer, when they come to the university, from a consciousness of inferiority, which may impair their development. They are fortunate, therefore, if they quickly appreciate the new scale of values that obtains in University life, where cricket and football are not the only games, nor athletics the only criterion of merit.

Haig, with his good looks, his experience of travel, his sufficiency of means and his fine horsemanship, soon became a person of some importance in a certain sphere. He was elected to the most fashionable clubs, the Vampyres, a Brasenose Sunday luncheon club, the Phoenix, Vincent's and the Bullingdon. He became an intimate friend of the most prominent, that is to say the wealthiest and the gayest, of the undergraduates.

It would not have been surprising if the young Scotsman had had his head turned by success so easily achieved. He was under no necessity of earning his living; he had to fear neither a father's frown nor a mother's reproaches; he was well equipped for appreciating the cup of pleasure that was offered to him, and it would be hard to blame him if he had drained it to the dregs. But in his veins there ran the blood of the Covenanters, and in his heart there remained the teachings of the Presbyterian religion which he had learned at his mother's knee. And Oxford, which gave him a sense of his own importance, filled him also with the determination to do himself justice, and to succeed in the career that he had decided to adopt. "No dinner and no club", writes Lord Askwith, "deterred Haig if he was not prepared for a particular lecture or essay. As to wine and cards, he was more than abstemious. His object was to pass his schools, and to pass them quickly, and he cut or left a social gathering for his books with singular tenacity of purpose."

The same witness asserts that Haig informed him on the evening of his arrival at Brasenose that he intended to go into the army. It appears somewhat curious that if he had formed this decision so early he should have thought it necessary to go to the university, instead of going straight to Sandhurst; and there are some who hold that he had seriously contemplated the Diplomatic Service as a career, in which his character, as it subsequently developed, makes it doubtful whether he would have achieved great distinction. But however this may be, there is no doubt that while he was at Oxford he drew up the plans for his future career and that, having done so, he never wavered in carrying them out.

It was during his last year at Oxford that he first kept a diary. It begins in January and ends in May, and there are many gaps in its continuity. But the virus had entered into his blood, and for the rest of his life, although with intermissions, he retained the diary-keeping habit.

In February, 1883, he opens the volume as follows:

"Having oftentimes heard of the advantages to be derived from keeping a diary, I determined to keep one. The difficulty is to have a good day to begin upon. I think it as well to start from the nineteenth day of last June, upon which day I was twenty-one, and put down as many events as I can remember with accuracy which happened from this day."

The diary is a cheerful chronicle of Oxford life from the point of view of one whose principal interests are hunting and polo, who enjoys the club life of the university and plays his part in club politics, but who is determined to combine with this easygoing existence that modicum of work which will enable him to satisfy the examiners.

"We had a very good champagne lunch afterward," he wrote one Sunday, "I sat between Macpherson-Grant and Phusia. I had promised to lunch with Brassey in Balliol but could not go owing to the meeting. I went however about 2.30 and found Brassey and Collingwood finished. He did not mind when I told him he had been elected to Bullingdon."

He retained through life the habit of recording who

sat upon either side of him at a meal, although his later diaries until the Great War hold less of human interest than this first one.

Comments on his fellow undergraduates are interesting in retrospect, and reveal as much of the writer as they do of the subject. The present Bishop of Exeter, then Lord William Cecil, is described as follows: "The Fish seems a clever chap and can talk away most amusingly. His clothes, poor fellow, are not of the most swagger! In fact very seedy resembling the garb of a scholar." Later on when the younger brother, Lord Robert, appears on the scene—— "This Cecil like his brother does not waste much money on his clothes. He is long and thin, stoops somewhat and plays real tennis. Riding he does not care for." The occasion of this meeting was a dinner at Pom Macdonnell's, and the diary continues: "I had a great argument with T. Hitchcock on the merit of backhand strokes at polo, as against turning the ball. I maintained that the backhand stroke was the game for the Oxford team to play on account of the ponies not being very good."

Throughout his life Haig was not disposed to think evil of his fellowmen. In this first diary criticisms and character sketches are invariably kind and tolerant. The harshest judgment that he passes on anybody is "he seems to be rather a snob and talks a heap of rubbish; I could almost fancy him unscrupulous".

When Douglas Haig came down from Oxford in the summer of 1883, he had passed the examinations, known as Groups, which entitled him to a degree, but, as he had missed one term out of his three years owing to illness, he was debarred from actually taking the degree until he should have completed, by coming up for another term, the required period of residence. He had no intention, however, of wasting any more time and, apart from a short holiday in France, he spent the interval between Oxford and Sandhurst at a crammer's, a Mr Litchfield of Hampton Court, where he prepared himself for the entrance examination.

In those days a university graduate could present himself for the Sandhurst examination up to the age of twenty-two. Haig was more than halfway through his twenty-third year when in February, 1884, he entered the Royal Military College.

The system which thus permitted army candidates to avail themselves both of a university education and of the technical training provided by the War Department had one important advantage. At the age at which cadets now enter Sandhurst or Woolwich, seventeen or eighteen, they retain to some extent the irresponsibility of boyhood; they come straight from school; they are avid of pleasure in all its forms and they have a natural and healthy disinclination for concentrated study. But if a man is ever going to take his life seriously he will be prepared to do so at the age of twenty-two after having spent three comparatively easy years at the university. This was certainly the case with Haig. He now set himself with all the determination of his earnest nature to the task of rendering himself an efficient officer. His contemporaries at Sandhurst can still remember the sensation, almost of awe, with which they regarded such an appetite and capacity for hard work in one of their companions.

The diary ceases during this period. The leisure necessary for its continuance was lacking, but we may be sure that there were no more luncheon or dinner parties to be recorded. Polo was now his sole form of relaxation and polo, after all, as an aid to horsemanship, is of direct assistance in the training of a cavalry officer. It was here at Sandhurst that the legend of Haig, as of a man who must one day rise to the highest command, originated. Such labours were not without their reward. At the end of the year, in December, 1884, he passed out first in order of merit, and he was awarded the Anson Memorial Sword as senior under-officer, the highest honour which Sandhurst has to offer. On February 7, 1885, he received his commission in the Seventh Hussars.

The years that followed were uneventful. They were years of profound peace both in Europe and throughout the world.

In August, 1886, Haig was one of a team selected to play polo for England against the United States, and in consequence paid his second visit to America. The first match was played at Newport on August twenty-fifth, and the second three days later. His old Oxford friend, Tommy Hitchcock, was one of the opposing team but, despite his prowess, the Americans were easily defeated by ten goals to four and fourteen goals to two. These were indeed the days of England's greatness.

In 1888 he became adjutant of the regiment and henceforth entries in the diary become less concerned with sport and more with military training. In 1889 and again in 1890 he enjoyed short periods of European leave, the greater part of which was spent in London, although on each occasion he paused in Paris on his way from Marseilles, and in 1890 he visited Monte Carlo, where he gambled with characteristic caution, coming away neither a winner nor a loser.

In 1891 he took no leave to Europe but visited instead the two extremes of the Indian Empire, Ceylon and the Northwest Frontier. In this year also he was specially selected by the inspector general of cavalry to act as brigade major at the cavalry camp at Aligarh. In January, 1892, he was again selected for special duty, at the Poona camp, and was attached to the headquarters staff of the Bombay Army. This year he travelled still farther afield, paying a visit to Australia. He was most hospitably entertained wherever he went, and thoroughly enjoyed the visit. But during these long holidays and living the leisurely life of a regimental officer, his ambition to obtain complete mastery of his profession remained unsatisfied. He was very popular with his brother officers, but his mind was occupied with thoughts that they could not share. "Take Beresford and Toby Liebert out at 6.30 A.M.," he writes one day, "to show them how to use a plane table and make a sketch. Fancy two officers so long in the service to be ignorant of such small matters." These things were always surprising him.

The year 1893 brought to Haig a severe disappointment and the only setback that he ever received in his military career. He had spent in serious study the greater part of the interval between his arrival in England in the previous September and the staff college examination in June. He had lived for some time with a German family at Düsseldorf in order to improve his knowledge of that language. But in spite of all his efforts he failed. Not only did he fall short by eighteen marks in mathematics, which was one of the obligatory subjects, but he was also rejected—and this was far more serious—on the ground that he was suffering from colour blindness. He protested against this decision and adduced the testimony of a certain Professor Mohren, whom he described as "the great German oculist", who had certified him as free from this defect. As he succeeded in getting into staff college three years later, we must assume that the professor's word was accepted. It was a subject upon which he always felt extremely sensitive, and with regard to which no jokes were permitted. Years afterward, when he was riding with his aide-de-camp across the plains of Flanders, he pointed to a field in the middle distance and commented on the beauty of the scarlet poppies that were growing there. The discreet aide-de-camp murmured his agreement, but looking where the commander in chief was pointing, he could see nothing but the rich brown earth recently turned by the plough.

There is no diary for the year 1893, nor for the year that follows. It is possible that he destroyed anything that he wrote during those years. He must have been suffering from that sense of frustration and wasted effort which overcomes all men who devote their lives to the public service and who, after years of conscientious labour, see others, whom they know to be their inferiors, soaring above them. By entering the army through Oxford, he had already lost seniority, and his equals in rank were by several years his juniors in age. He had now to return to his regiment in India with the bitterness of failure in his heart.

He returned to England in order to act as aide-de-camp to General Sir Keith Fraser during the autumn manœuvres. Fraser was then inspector general of cavalry, and was fully aware of the extent to which the cavalry required bringing up to date in order to render them efficient for modern warfare. Haig, therefore, could learn much from him both in the theory, and, during manœuvres, in the practice of war. He did not, however, confine his study of cavalry methods to those which were followed in his own country. In the autumn of 1893, while on leave in Europe, and again in the autumn of 1894, he paid visits to France which proved of great value to himself and to the Intelligence Division of the War Office. In September, 1893, he attended the cavalry manœuvres in Touraine. His report, which runs to some forty folio pages, was transmitted to the War Office by the military attaché in Paris with a covering note to the effect that "by the courtesy of the French officers, Captain Haig was afforded unusually favourable opportunities of seeing and judging all that was done".

In the spring of 1895, he paid a visit to Berlin, where he was received with the greatest courtesy in German military circles. Every facility was placed at his disposal; nothing in the way of hospitality was omitted. He made many friends during his stay, and retained a favourable impression of the German people which even the fever of the War never obliterated.

His visit to Germany was brought to an abrupt conclusion when he learned that Sir Evelyn Wood was about to conduct a "staff tour" in England, beginning on June twenty-first; that Colonel French was to command the cavalry on one side and that he had been invited to act as French's staff officer. He therefore returned with all speed, and it was as well that he did so, for these manœuvres proved of some importance to his future career. Not only did they mark the beginning of his connection with French, but they also were the occasion of his first meeting with Sir Evelyn Wood, who then held the position of quartermaster general, and who was to prove a loyal and useful friend.

In the following month he went to Kissingen for the cure, whence he wrote to his sister:

"I received a civil letter from Sir Evelyn Wood mentioning something he wished me to tell him about connected with the German Army. His last sentence was as follows—— 'It gave me much pleasure to meet you and have a talk, and the more so because I knew you pretty well on paper before. I think I may honestly say of you, what we cannot always say, that the expectation, though great, was even less than the pleasure you gave me by your conversation.' I told you that we got on very well together. Sir E. W. is a capital fellow to have upon one's side as he always gets his own way."

The new *Cavalry Drill Book* which French had begun but had left unfinished on his promotion to the position of assistant adjutant general, was completed by Haig in 1895. That such a task should have been entrusted to so junior an officer is evidence of the high opinion generally held of his attainments. When this was finished he devoted the rest of the winter to hunting until he entered staff college in January of 1896.

During the twenty-two months that he spent at the staff college no diary was kept, and few letters of this period survive. There were many among his fellow students who afterward acquired celebrity, Lord Allenby, Sir Richard Haking, Sir Thompson Capper, Sir William Furse, Sir George Macdonogh and Sir J. E. Edmonds, the official historian of the war. It is the more surprising in view of the amount of talent there collected that Haig's superiority should have been sufficiently outstanding to lead the chief instructor, Colonel G. F. R. Henderson, the author of *Stonewall Jackson,* to prophesy that he would one day be commander in chief of the British Army. Nor was this one of those prophecies which are only remembered after they are fulfilled. General Edmonds never forgot it, and when Haig was given the Aldershot command in 1911 he wrote to remind him of it, pointing out that even then the fulfilment of the prophecy was incomplete. To which Haig replied on August 31, 1911: "I think that dear old Henderson must have been talking very much through his hat when he said that he thought I would ever be commander in chief of the British Army. I only wish to be of some use somewhere."

CHAPTER II

The Soudan and South Africa

BEFORE SETTING FORTH for the Soudan in 1898, Haig received an invitation to spend from Saturday to Monday at Sandringham with the Prince and Princess of Wales. His brother-in-law, Mr Jameson, was the link between him and the Court and this was not the first occasion on which Haig had met his future sovereign. An extract from the diary:

Sunday, January 23. Princess and some go to church about 11.30. The prince, Holford, Sykes and self go in at 12. *Excellent* sermon from the bishop on Gordon—Hebrews, Ch. XI., verse 8. "And he went out, not knowing whither he went."

Before lunch see dogs York Cottage. After lunch walk round with princess and see the gardens, yearlings, mares in foal, etc. After dinner discuss cavalry organization, Indian frontier, etc. with H.R.H. Difficulty in finding a good map of Central Asia! H.R.H. desires me to "write regularly" to him from Egypt.

He left early the next morning and on February third arrived at Cairo, where he remained for a few days. He signed an agreement to serve with the Egyptian Army for two years, receiving at the same time a comforting assurance that there would be no difficulty about terminating his contract earlier should he desire to do so.

He mentions both in his diary and his letters the kindness and cordiality with which he was received by Lord Kitchener, although these were qualities which Kitchener did not always display to junior officers on first acquaintance. But Haig's reputation had evidently gone before him.

In the ensuing months the young officer distinguished himself in actions against the Dervishes, particularly in the decisive battle of Omdurman, after which he returned to England. On September 14, 1899, he received instructions to act as chief staff officer to Sir John French, who had been selected to command the cavalry in Natal.

Of everything that took place during the crowded days at Ladysmith, Haig kept a most careful record. Of every order that he sent out and, so far as possible, of every order received he retained a copy. These orders, together with a summary of the events of each day, carefully put together, with the original documents preserved when available, are bound together in four volumes, which for long were exhibited at the staff college as models of what such things should be. For the professional soldier, anxious to study his profession, these volumes possess a lasting value, for although all the weapons of war change and are ever changing, the main principles remain the same. One of the first of these is that a soldier should be prepared to learn something new from every practical experience of warfare. Haig's experience of this war was, so far, limited to a fortnight, but although he had not much leisure at Cape Town nor interval for quiet thought—he had to share with French a bedroom at the Mount Nelson Hotel—he availed himself of such opportunity as existed for setting down on paper the lessons he had learned.

The early military disasters had aroused in the people and government of Great Britain the determination to make further efforts. To Lord Roberts, who was then commanding in Ireland, was handed over the supreme command in

South Africa, and Lord Kitchener, who was still in the Soudan completing his work of the previous year, was appointed chief of staff. Meanwhile the dawn of the twentieth century broke red and threatening for the British Empire. While her two greatest generals were in mid ocean, her three defeated armies licking their wounds, the Great Powers of the world, among whom Great Britain counted not a single ally nor a single friend, stood expectantly round the arena watching with undisguised delight the fierce mauling to which the old lion was being subjected by the claws of so diminutive an antagonist.

French protested the decision to replace his chief of staff by Lord Erroll, who was a full colonel, but who had only just arrived from England, and he telegraphed to the chief of staff on January eighteenth, "May I point out that appointment of A.A.G. to cavalry division was promised by Sir Redvers Buller to Major Haig with local rank of lieutenant colonel. . . . I earnestly beg that Field Marshal will be pleased to confirm this. Major Haig has performed duty of chief staff officer to a division since landing in Natal. He has acted in this capacity under my command in three general engagements and many smaller fights. I have several times mentioned him in despatches. His services have been invaluable."

The answer came, "Field Marshal Commander in Chief fully realizes the very excellent services rendered by Major Haig and much regrets not being able to meet your views as regards his taking position of A.A.G. of the cavalry division. That position, however, the field marshal thinks must be filled by the appointment of a senior officer, and he feels sure you will find Colonel the Earl of Erroll an efficient officer."

When Haig paid a visit to Cape Town at the beginning of February, he wrote to his sister, "Everyone here condoles with me at being superseded by Erroll, so I expect the field marshal has discovered that he has done the wrong thing. As a matter of fact I think less about this appointment than my friends. But, of course, it is gratifying to find one's work has been appreciated in the division."

It was as D.A.A.G., therefore, that Haig took part in the relief of Kimberley, but whatever his official post he remained in fact the right-hand man of General French, who scored upon this occasion one of the outstanding successes of the war.

On February 22, 1900, Haig wrote to his sister: "I was appointed lieutenant colonel last night and today take over command of the Third Cavalry Brigade. . . . It is a great piece of good luck being given the command of this brigade, for of course we have any number of old fossils about—full colonels, etc. Kitchener has supportd us cavalry well and French has quite a free hand now. I think you will agree with me that I have not been mistaken as to the power of cavalry when led with determination even in spite of modern guns." But before closing the letter he wrote as a postscript: "Since writing above I have been appointed chief staff officer of the division (that is A.A.G.), Lord Erroll being moved to Roberts' staff as staff officer for mounted infantry. This will suit me very well."

The relief of Kimberley was followed by the surrender of Cronje at Paardeberg on February twenty-ninth, and the almost simultaneous relief of Ladysmith. Bloemfontein, the capital of the Orange Free State, was taken in March. The relief of Mafeking took place in May, and when in June Pretoria was captured many people believed that the war was over. It had still two years to run. Officers, however, began to think of their futures, and in August Haig wrote from Middleburg:

By the way, French had a letter from Evelyn Wood this morning about me, stating briefly that the cavalry had not

HAIG IN SOUTH AFRICA

done well in this campaign except under French, and suggesting that the cause was a difficulty in cavalry leaders. So in his opinion it was to the interests of the service to put me soon in command of a regiment and he directs him to take what action he (French) thinks fit in the matter. French is replying that I had once been appointed to a brigade, and that I might now be in command of one were it not to the interests of the service that I should remain on in my present billet. My present appointment of chief staff officer of a cavalry division of four cavalry brigades is superior to any regimental appointment. . . . French is anxious to have me made an A.D.C. to the Queen because that at once gives me the rank of a full colonel. At present I am a lieutenant colonel in South Africa. Personally I don't care much what happens to me in the way of reward, for I despise those who only work when they hope to get something in return! Many thanks for the shaving soap. It arrived at the right time. I always shave and I was getting a bit short. I hear our staff is considered well dressed and clean; this has a good effect on all ranks.

In the following month he wrote:

It is a necessary thing to command a regiment and I should like to do so if I was given command of a good one in a good station. French is only too anxious to help me on, but I think in remaining on as his chief staff officer I did the best for the cavalry division, for him and for myself. One did not foresee this war lasting so long, otherwise I might have taken some skallywag corps or other. So don't make a fuss about my being now in the same position as I started in. Recollect also many have gone lower down. And as to rewards, if you only knew what duffers will get and do get H.M.'s decorations and are promoted, you would realize how little I value them. Everything comes in time, and decorations come in abundance with declining years and imbecility. No one yet on this staff, fortunately, has got a decoration of any kind, otherwise we might have achieved disaster like the other *décorés*.

The last stages of the South African War make dull reading, and must have made dull fighting for those engaged in it. Guerrilla warfare is from the point of view of the bigger battalions as tedious as it is inglorious. The rounding up of the elusive commandos proved a far longer business than anyone had anticipated. Early in 1901 Haig was given an independent command in Cape Colony, and had three, and later six columns under his orders. His difficulties were increased by the uncertainty as to who might be friend or foe. "It is more difficult," he wrote, "hunting the Boers in this colony where all the farmers are secretly their friends, and the government almost seems to assist the invader, than in the Free State or Transvaal where we can treat everyone as the enemy. . . . My chief difficulty now is to find horses for the six columns under my command independently of the remount department. So I have people all over the colony commandeering what horses they can find. . . . I am having the inmates of each farmhouse registered and a ticket pasted on the front door giving a description of each man. Then our patrols pay surprise visits at night and arrest anyone not on the list and note the absentees as rebels. We have already caught several in this way."

One of the regiments serving under him was the Seventeenth Lancers, of which he was at this time given the command. From henceforward the Seventeenth Lancers remained his regiment, whose fortunes, whether he was with them or not, he always followed with loyal and paternal care. It so happened that this regiment sustained one of the few comparatively serious reverses which befell the British Army in South Africa in the year 1901.

Haig's letters contain several references to misunderstandings which were already occurring between Lord Kitchener and General French. "Lord K. seems to meddle rather," he writes in September, "and does not give French quite a free hand. Personally when I was in command directly under K. I did not find this the case. Indeed, I did just whatever I thought fit and never asked him what he wanted but merely told him what I had done."

That Haig's independence of mind and frankness of speech had been noticed, not without misgiving, in the highest quarters, is proved by the following extract from a letter to a friend written at about this time.

You ask me too for my opinions on certain commanders and on their actions. Curiously enough Henrietta writes me a second edition of advice which the Prince of Wales was good enough to give to Willie Jameson for my benefit. The same advice was administered to me by Holford after the Soudan campaign—namely, that I am too fond of criticizing my superior officers. My "criticisms" says H.R.H. "may be correct, but it does not do." Now I never criticize people except privately, and what a stupid letter it would be if I did not express an opinion. Besides, I think we would have better generals in the higher ranks and the country would not have had to pass through such a period of anxiety had honest criticism, based on sound reasoning, been more general in reference to military affairs during the last twenty years. But whether I am right or wrong, I like to let my pen have a free run when I write to you, so I trust you won't give me away and say I consider our worthy authorities are old stupids, ignorant even of the first principles of the game of war. Still I never go as far as that and make general statements of such a sweeping nature: I always give particular instances—chapter and verse in fact.

Peace came at last, at the end of May in 1902. It seemed to Haig and to many another soldier, who had been fighting so long, that the terms were much too lenient and that the enemy should have been taught a sterner lesson. As usual on such occasions, the blame was vaguely cast upon the politicians by those who were ignorant of the true facts, and were unaware that it was the soldier, Lord Kitchener, who had firmly supported the generous terms that were offered to the enemy, whereas Lord Milner, the politician, had been in favour of severer measures.

The conclusion of peace did not mean the immediate return of Haig to England. He was given command of a large number of troops and placed in charge of a vast territory, "a triangle of about six hundred miles each side which includes the main line from Capetown to Kimberley". It was known as the Western Sub-district of Cape Colony, and it was his duty to secure the restoration of peaceful conditions and the maintenance of order.

French left South Africa in June. The two soldiers, who had been through so much together, and for both of whom fate still held so much in store, took an affectionate farewell. "The little man", wrote Haig, "was almost in tears bidding goodbye, and I was sorry to part with him. He had a much warmer welcome from the people and soldiers on the ship than Lord K. French is most popular. By the way, when I come home there must be no nonsense—meet me just as you sent me away; no crowd of relations—just yourself and a friend."

Twice again in subsequent letters he reverts to this latter theme—"I suppose you will be back in England before then, but if you are not intending to be back so soon I trust you will not alter any of your plans on my account, because I dislike any fuss having reference to myself. So don't let on to anyone when I am likely to be back. They will see me quite soon enough." And once more, when he informs his sister of the ship on which he is sailing, he adds, "But I trust you will not make any fuss or put yourself or anyone else out in any way because of my arrival."

There is no false modesty in these injunctions contained in private letters which were never intended for other eyes than those of the woman to whom they were addressed, there is no mawkish desire to escape publicity, but only the genuine distaste of a reserved but sensitive man for anything in the nature of public acclamation.

It was not until September that he sailed for England. Having left before the declaration of war, he did not return until after the conclusion and realization of peace. He was not exaggerating his right to expect "a good spell of leave" when he wrote: "for three years straight away, on active service against a well-armed and active enemy like the Boers, entails a considerable amount of hard work upon all ranks and much anxiety at times upon those responsible for giving and transmitting orders. So though very fit and well I am anxious to do something else as a change."

In that war when so many reputations had been lost, his had been firmly established, and he came home at the age of forty-one with the certainty of a distinguished military career before him.

CHAPTER III

Before the World War

HAVING RETURNED from the Boer War as a colonel, Haig was appointed about a year later inspector general of cavalry in India, where Lord Kitchener was commander in chief. A few years earlier Haig had lent a considerable sum of money to a senior officer who would otherwise have been compelled to leave the service. He had done so, as he explained to his sister at the time, not only out of friendship for the officer concerned, but also in the belief that his retirement would be a loss to the army. Some difficulty had arisen about the repayment, and he learned that his trustees had been taking action in the matter. He immediately wrote to Mrs Jameson, "I would prefer to lose the money rather than that General —— should be pressed for it. . . . With my present pay I can live in luxury out here. I cannot stand the 'bunya' class. You know the bunya of course. How he sits round his bags of grain and flour and foodstuffs and ghee and, fat and greasy, gloats over every pice, and grinds the wretched tiller of the soil down by usury and close dealings."

A few months later he wrote again, "Please thank Percy" (an American friend, Percy Chubb) "for his kindly wishes 'to make a pile for me', but I believe I have as much money as is good for me. I have some good ponies and horses and enjoy myself pretty well without feeling the want of money.

Too much luxury is ruining the country (I mean England), and also the Yankees!"

The enthusiasm with which Haig threw himself into this work communicated itself to others, and before he left India he was happy to notice a distinct improvement in the tactical ideas held by officers, which he knew was attributable to his training. He was a firm believer in the system of staff rides which had recently been introduced into India and which henceforth became an accepted method of training, and after his return to England he published under the title of *Cavalry Studies* accounts of the five staff rides carried out under his supervision, and of the experience gained by them.

The work reveals deep study, wide reading and the clear thought that comes of prolonged reflection. He does not fall into the common error of judging military competence entirely by results. "The success," he writes, "which everywhere followed the Germans in the campaign of 1870, has blinded many soldiers to the errors which were often committed and passed unpunished." He criticizes particularly the German use of their cavalry, which was all distributed in comparatively small contingents among the various army corps. There should have been an independent cavalry body or reserve such as Napoleon always retained under his own command for special purposes. The Germans never learned this lesson, and long afterward it was Haig's opinion that, had they possessed sufficient available cavalry to follow up the pursuit in March, 1918, events would have gone more hardly for the allies.

He sailed to England in April, 1905. This visit was to prove an important one in his private life. He was now approaching the end of his forty-fourth year, and if he ever intended to marry the decision should not be much longer postponed.

From the time of their first meeting King Edward had

been deeply interested in Haig's career, and when he heard that he was on leave in England he caused him to be invited to Windsor Castle for Ascot races. It so happened that the Maid of Honour who should have been in attendance on Queen Alexandra was unwell, and her place was therefore taken by Miss Dorothy Vivian.

The guests arrived on the Monday, but it was not until Thursday that Miss Vivian and General Haig were introduced. After the races Haig was to have played golf with the Prince of Wales, but owing to the Prince having been detained a foursome was made up in which Miss Vivian and Haig played as partners. He invited her to play again the next morning, which she did, spent most of his time at the races with her that day and took her in to dinner in the evening. The guests were to leave the castle on Saturday morning, but Haig suggested to Miss Vivian that they should play another game of golf before he went.

When she met him, however, on the course next morning she was surprised to see him immediately dismiss the caddies and make it plain that he had no intention of playing. He suggested that they should sit down somewhere, but after a short search being unable to find a seat he blurted out "Then I must propose to you standing." The proposal was unexpected, but it was not refused.

After Haig was appointed director of military training in 1906 the services he rendered during the next three years were not particularly conspicuous to the public, but would suffice in themselves to entitle him to the lasting gratitude of his fellow countrymen. It was a period of preparation. At long last, and not too late, a secretary of state had arrived at the War Office who was determined to prepare for war. The two principal difficulties that faced him were the objections of the powerful left wing of the Liberal party to any increase in expenditure on the forces, and the obscurantism of highly placed officers who hated the idea of reform.

It was of vital importance and proved of inestimable value to the British Empire that there should have been at this crucial moment two clear brains and powerful minds working at the great military problem. Two more different types it would be difficult to conceive than Haldane, the subtle-minded philosopher with the smooth flow of words, and the ponderous ungainly body, and Haig, the man of action, alert and vigorous physically and mentally, swift in decision, almost tongue-tied in debate. Two things they had in common, the vision of what was coming, and the determination to be prepared for it. One evening, after they had been dining alone together, Haig entered in his diary, "We discussed objects for which army and expeditionary force exist. He in no doubt—viz. to organize to support France and Russia against Germany, and perhaps Austria. By organizing war may be prevented."

The work of army reorganization was more arduous and fatiguing than any to which Haig had been accustomed. Long hours at his desk in the War Office were interrupted by luncheons and followed by dinners at Haldane's house in Queen Anne's Gate, sometimes alone with his chief and sometimes attended by other workers from the War Office or colleagues from the Cabinet. Too often also, when the dinners were over and the guests had left, a further consultation would take place in the secretary of state's study, and the weary director would not get home until the small hours. To Haldane such work was the breath of life, such hours were habitual and the discussion of difficult problems to the accompaniment of continual cigars was the pleasantest way of passing the time. But Haig did not talk easily and did not smoke at all. He was accustomed to early hours, fresh air and much exercise. It is not surprising, therefore, that after a year and a half of such strenuous labour his health gave way and during April and May of 1908 he was seriously ill.

He made, however, a quick recovery and was at work again by the middle of June. These were happy years, despite the intensity of the work. There was no time for hunting or polo, but there were visits to Windsor, Sandringham and Balmoral, as well as to the houses of his relatives in Scotland. In London there was always a home for him and his wife at 23 Prince's Gate, the house of Mr and Mrs Jameson, but he preferred to live in the country as much as possible, and therefore took a house in Farnborough from which he could travel to and fro. In March, 1907, his first child, a daughter, was born, and a second daughter was born in November, 1908.

His sister Henrietta was keenly interested in spiritualism, and on more than one occasion persuaded him to accompany her to a *séance*. He gravely set down in his diary what occurred without comment, and without offering an opinion as to the reliability of the participants. At his first visit, on being introduced to the lady with psychic powers and encouraged to consult the spirits with whom she was in communication, he asked which would be the better system for the expansion of the territorial army, a company or a battalion basis. It is possible to sympathize with the medium, who can hardly have been expecting an enquiry of this nature, and had certainly never been asked such a question before. The spirits favoured a company basis.

The interview continued, "When under control by a little native girl called Sunshine, she said that I was influenced by several spirits—notably a small man named Napoleon, who aided me. That it was in my power to be helped by him for good affairs, but I might repel him if his influence was for bad, though he had become changed for the better in the spirit world. I was destined to do much good and benefit my country. Asked by me how to ensure the territorial army scheme being a success, she said thought governed the world. Think out the scheme thoroughly, one's thoughts would then be put in such a convincing manner that the people would respond, without any compulsion, and the national army would be a reality. She could not bring Napoleon to me, but I must think of him and try and get his aid as he was always near me."

The creation of the territorial army was not the only work that occupied Haig's time and attention. He was one of Haldane's most intimate advisers, more intimate than some whose positions were superior to his, and he was, as Haldane recognized in his book, *Before the War,* closely connected with all the important reforms carried out at this period.

The following is Haig's account of the coming into being of the Imperial General Staff:

I had a most interesting forenoon yesterday. I met Mr Haldane at the colonial office a little before eleven o'clock and attended the colonial conference with him. The chief of general staff and the Q.M.G. and Director of Operations were also there. At eleven o'clock Mr Haldane took his seat on Lord Elgin's right. The latter presided. The premiers were sitting at a horseshoe table on each side of him in order of seniority of the colonies. Deakin, who made the good speech on Friday night, was on Elgin's left with his defence minister—latter very ugly with a goat-like beard and spectacles—on the whole like old Kruger. Next was Dr Jim, then Moor from Natal, then Botha and his interpreter Dr Smartt (of Cape Colony). On Haldane's right came Sir W. Laurier and Borden (of Canada), then, representatives of New Zealand and Newfoundland and assistants farther down the table—two shorthand writers in the centre of the horseshoe, but at a small table apart. Secretaries at tables round the walls of the room. We four had chairs placed for us behind Haldane. The latter made a short speech of twenty minutes explaining our organization, and ended with a motion for the Conference to adopt. All the premiers then spoke in turn—all very patriotic. Mr Haldane's speech was very well received and all asked that it should be published. His motion was also agreed to. The latter practically creates the Imperial General Staff and so puts 50 per cent onto the value of the general staff. It was nearly two before I got away, so I only caught the 3 P.M. train.

Haig's interest in questions of defence was not confined to military matters. He drew up about this time a lengthy memorandum dealing with the need of improved staff methods in the navy. He had been deeply shocked to discover that "the leading naval power should have no textbooks on the art of naval war, and no naval records in an available form for the use of officers; and that Mr Julian Corbett (a civilian) should be the only individual at present qualified to lecture on naval history."

The memorandum produced no immediate effect, but it was read by the Cabinet and effected a lasting impression on the mind of Winston Churchill. When the latter became First Lord of the Admiralty a few years later he immediately set about the organization of a general staff and the creation of a naval war college. He remembered what Haig had written and turned to him for advice. "The general", he writes in the first volume of *The World Crisis,* "furnished me with a masterly paper setting forth the military doctrine of staff organization, and constituting in many respects a formidable commentary on existing naval methods."

In November, 1907, Haig was transferred from the post of director of military training to that of director of staff duties. Henceforward questions of policy and war organization were dealt with by the director of staff duties, who therefore laid down the policy which the director of military training had merely to carry out.

On April 15, 1909, Sir O'Moore Creagh, who had been

HAIG IN INDIA, 1911

appointed commander in chief in India, called at the War Office and invited Haig to go out with him as his chief of the staff. At first Haig declined, but he finally decided to go. No reason is given in his diary for this decision. He doubtless felt that, interesting as his work had been, he had now had enough of it, that the Indian appointment would provide him with a new field of activity, and a new source of experience, and he was probably glad of a change from the long hours of office life.

In India he was anxious to impress upon everybody an imperial outlook upon military affairs. He persistently combated the idea that there was one army of Great Britain and another of India and that the latter was concerned only with the affairs of that subcontinent. His opinion on this matter, the wisdom of which became, in the light of after events, so plainly apparent, did not recommend itself to the higher authorities at the time. When it was discovered by Lord Morley, secretary of state for India, that the chief of the staff in India had carefully worked out a scheme for the utilization of the Indian Army outside the frontiers of India in the emergency of a world war, orders were peremptorily sent out from home and transmitted to Haig by the viceroy, that not only were all studies of this nature to be abandoned forthwith, but that also, incredible as it may seem, any plans of this nature that had been drawn up were to be destroyed.

Haig gave the necessary instructions, in accordance with his bounden duty, to the senior officer concerned, General Hamilton Gordon, who, however, declared later that there was at the time "a look in Haig's eye which made me realize that he would not regard any deviation from rigid adherence to orders with undue severity". Instead of being destroyed as commanded the plan was carefully preserved, and in the fulness of time when the need for it was felt it was brought forth from its hiding place, so that in 1914 troops were conveyed from India to Europe according to the very scheme that Haig had been reprimanded for preparing.

Nor was it only with regard to the transfer of troops from India to Europe that Haig's mind was busy during these years. He further worked out in detail schemes for military operations directed from India both against Mesopotamia and German East Africa, and these schemes were actually adopted during the war.

Early in 1911 the Crown Prince of Germany paid a visit to India, but Haig, although present at all the official festivities, does not appear to have had any private conversation with the royal visitor, and there is no record in the diary of the impression that he produced.

For two years and a half Haig held the position of commander in chief at Aldershot. He actually took over the command on March 1, 1912, and he remained there until August, 1914. No sensational events so far as he and his command were concerned took place during this period. It was the lull before the storm.

CHAPTER IV

Against Overpowering Odds

When at last the war broke out, Haig greeted it in no spirit of enthusiasm. It was the moment for which he had been preparing, but to which he had not looked forward with any emotions save those of awe and dread. He knew how fierce and how long a struggle lay before his country, and how tremendous were the issues which were at stake.

On the afternoon of Wednesday, July 29, 1914, he received a telegram from the secretary of state for war, instructing him to adopt "precautionary measures" as detailed in the defence scheme. "All our arrangements were ready," he writes in his diary, "even to the extent of having the telegrams written out. These merely had to be dated and despatched." Six days later, at five in the evening, he received a telegraphic message containing the one word "Mobilize". Every detail had been so well thought out and foreseen that on the receipt of these momentous instructions it was unnecessary for the general officer commanding at Aldershot to take a single decision. "I had thus", he writes, "all my time free to make arrangements for my own departure for the front, to visit Field Marshal French's G.H.Q. now established at the Hotel Metropole in London, and to ponder over the terribly critical military situation as it gradually developed day by day."

Fourteen years had passed since French and Haig had

planned and led the great ride to the relief of Kimberley. In the days of peace they had seen little of one another. In private life they had neither friends nor pursuits in common, and Haig, who had so sternly devoted these years to acquiring further proficiency in his profession, could not believe that French, who took life more easily, possessed either the military knowledge or the gifts of character demanded by the great position which he had been called upon to fill. "In my own heart", he wrote in his diary on August eleventh, "I know that French is quite unfit for this great command at a time of crisis in our nation's history."

"In all my dreams I have never been so bold as to imagine that, when that war did break out, I should hold one of the most important commands in the British Army," he wrote later. "I feel very pleased at receiving command of the First Army Corps, and I also feel the greatest confidence that we will give a good account of ourselves, *if only* our higher command give us a reasonable chance! . . . I am determined to behave as I did in the South African War, namely, to be thoroughly loyal and do my duty as a subordinate should, trying all the time to see Sir John's good qualities and not his weak ones. For most certainly French and Murray (French's chief of staff) have much to commend them, although neither in my opinion is at all fitted for the appointment which he now holds at this moment of crisis in our country's history."

He arrived at Havre on August fifteenth, the birthday of Napoleon. The British Expeditionary Force which, according to plans carefully drawn up beforehand, was conveyed from England to France between August twelfth and August seventeenth, consisted of about one hundred thousand men. It was divided into two army corps, the first commanded by Sir Douglas Haig, the second by Sir James Grierson, who died on the way to the battle front and was succeeded by Sir Horace Smith-Dorrien. In each army corps there were two divisions. The First and Second divisions belonged to the First Army Corps, and they were commanded by General Lomax and General Monro respectively. In each division there were three brigades and in each brigade there were four battalions. The strength of a division was about eighteen thousand men. In addition to these four infantry divisions there was one cavalry division under the command of General Allenby. It is important, with a view to maintaining a sense of proportion, to remember that as against these five British divisions there were seventy French and seventy-two German divisions on the Western Front.

Haig spent the night of August fifteenth at Tortoni's Hotel in Havre, and on the following morning went to call on the French general in command of the town. "After talking platitudes for a few minutes, we were asked to drink a glass of sweet champagne to the health of the two armies."

On Friday, August twenty-first, the advance of the British Army into Belgium began. On August twenty-third the First and Second divisions of Haig's corps were distributed in villages southeast of Mons, and west of Binche, the most advanced positions they were to hold for many years.

In order to appreciate the full significance of the events that were taking place, it is necessary to look at the map of Europe and to understand the German plan of campaign. There was nothing new about this plan. It had been drawn up many years before, and had lain hidden in the archives of the German War Ministry, while its outlines had been imprinted on the minds of those who held the highest commands. Its author was Count Alfred Schlieffen, and in its strength and its simplicity it bears the stamp of military genius.

The portion of France between Switzerland and Belgium was believed, and was later proved, to be impregnable.

The gap in the fortifications between Toul and Epinal was too obvious a lure to deceive the meanest intelligence. In order, therefore, to invade France, neutrality must be violated and there could be no hesitation in choosing between the Swiss mountains and the Belgian plains. Schlieffen himself had contemplated the invasion of both Holland and Belgium. He had anticipated that the violation of Dutch neutrality by Germany might bring about an immediate violation of Belgian neutrality by France, and that, in this manner, the political discredit attaching to a treaty breaker would be equally shared between the two countries. The original plan had undergone some modification at the hands of Moltke, but the outline of it remained.

When, therefore, the vast colossus of the German Army, far larger than the best information had reported it could possibly be, rolled up against the impenetrable barrier of the Franco-German frontier, there took place a gesture which, curiously enough, had been foreseen by British writers, had been foretold to the Cabinet by Lord Kitchener, had been explained as probable in the staff college for twenty years, but for which the French General Staff was entirely unprepared. From Thionville, in the northeast corner of France, the German Army suddenly thrust out a terrible right arm. With this right arm it sought to accomplish a vast encircling movement, sweeping away in the first few days the loyal but pitiful resistance of Belgium, encompassing in its vast stretch a line from Ghent through Amiens to the southwest of Paris, and so encircling the whole of the French Army and driving it back to its own destruction against its eastern frontier, where it would find the remainder of the German forces waiting eagerly to receive it and complete its annihilation.

The reports which had been disturbing Haig all these days, and of which he had thought too little notice was taken at General Headquarters, were those which told of

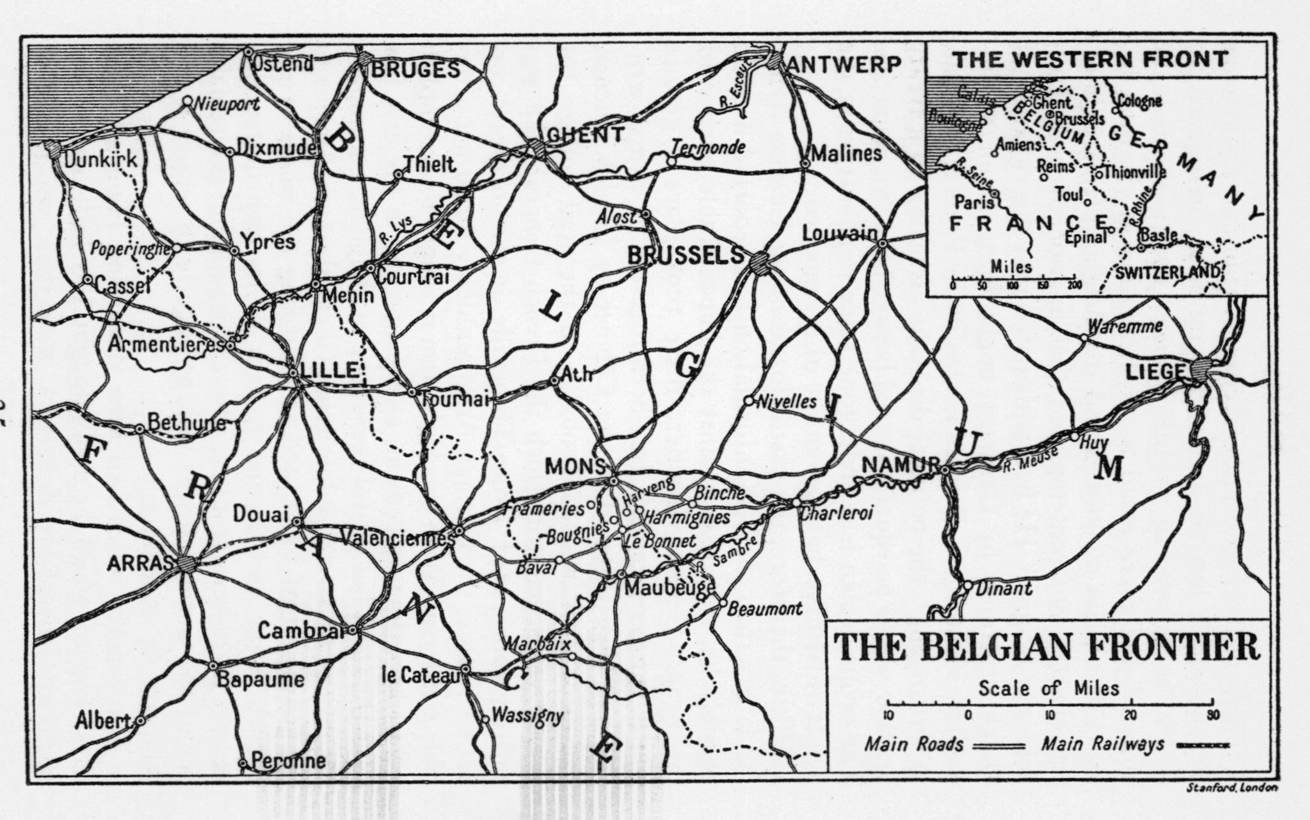
THE BELGIAN FRONTIER
Scale of Miles
10 0 10 20 30
Main Roads
Main Railways
Stanford, London
THE WESTERN FRONT
Calais
Boulogne
Ghent
Brussels
Cologne
BELGIUM
GERMANY
Amiens
Reims
Thionville
R. Seine
Toul
R. Rhine
Paris
FRANCE
Epinal
Basle
SWITZERLAND
Miles
0 50 100 150 200
Ostend
BRUGES
ANTWERP
R. Escaut
Nieuport
GHENT
Termonde
Malines
Dunkirk
Dixmude
Thielt
Alost
Louvain
R. Lys
Poperinghe
Ypres
BRUSSELS
Cassel
Courtrai
Menin
Waremme
Armentieres
LILLE
Ath
LIEGE
Tournai
Nivelles
Bethune
Huy
MONS
NAMUR
R. Meuse
Harveng
Binche
Frameries
Harmignies
Charleroi
Douai
Bougnies
Le Bonnet
Valenciennes
R. Sambre
ARRAS
Bavai
Maubeuge
Dinant
Beaumont
Cambrai
Marbaix
Bapaume
le Cateau
Wassigny
Albert
Peronne
B E L G I U M
F R A N C E

German troops still pouring westward and threatening both the Channel ports and the left flank of the allied armies. These troops formed, in fact, the extended and ever-extending right hand of the encircling enemy, and when they were compelled by the British advance to pause, to contract and to fight, it was nothing less than the clenched fist of the huge German army that struck the five divisions of the Expeditionary Force full in the face.

Nor was it only the strength of that fist and the reserve of force lying behind it that rendered it so formidable. A graver danger lay in the fact that the arm was not yet extended to its full length. It was capable of stretching farther and, in doing so, of turning the flank of its opponents. An army with its flank turned is lost.

Meanwhile the French offensive, of which Henry Wilson had spoken so optimistically, had already taken place while he was speaking. Schlieffen had foreseen this attack, and had welcomed it as warmly as a boxer with his right arm free would welcome the head of his opponent under his left shoulder. In the event, however, this attack had proved even less successful than Schlieffen had anticipated. The advance of the French centre, consisting of their Third and Fourth armies, would have rendered the withdrawal of their left wing, the Fifth Army and the British Expeditionary Force, even more disastrous. But they had attacked and been defeated on August twenty-first. They were now in retreat, and it was their retreat and the retreat of the Fifth Army combined with the encircling movement of the First and Second German armies on the left of our line which had placed the British forces in such fearful jeopardy when Haig was awakened at two o'clock in the morning of Monday, August twenty-fourth, and received orders to retreat at once.

"I spent the morning at Le Bonnet", reads his diary entry. "Sir John French came to see me there, evidently very anxious, but was reassured at seeing the orderly way in which the retreat of my troops was proceeding. I took him to some rising ground about one-half mile northwest of Le Bonnet whence the enemy's shelling was plainly visible. The attack to the north seemed also very heavy."

The retreat continued, and the Haig Corps passed in comparative calm the day of August twenty-sixth, during which the Second Corps was fighting for its life at Le Cateau, and so it happened that the small British Army was cut into two halves, and that for a whole week the one half had no knowledge of what the other half was doing. Yet both were in communication with G.H.Q. At 8.30 on that same evening of August twenty-sixth Haig telegraphed to G.H.Q. "No news of Second Corps except sound of guns from direction of Le Cateau and Beaumont. Can First Corps be of any assistance?" To this message G.H.Q. sent no reply, so that Haig telegraphed again, sending his message to the Second Corps through G.H.Q., as the most rapid means of transmission, "Please let me know your situation and news. We are well able to co-operate with you today, we could hear the sound of your battle, but could get no information as to its progress, and could form no idea how we could assist you." Again there was no reply. As the official historian justly observes, "At this hour G.H.Q. seem to have given up the Second Corps as lost." But, in fact, the Second Corps had fought on that day, the anniversary of Crécy, a battle not less remarkable as a feat of arms nor less important in its effect upon history.

The morning of August twenty-seventh broke grey and gloomy. Heavy storms of rain fell at intervals throughout the day while the melancholy retreat of the First Corps continued. The soldiers knew nothing of the heroic battle that their comrades had fought the day before, they had never heard of the Schlieffen plan, nor could they understand the vast implications of the strategical situation; they only knew that they were weary to death, footsore and sleepless, and that they had still to retreat before the enemy, whom they longed to fight and who were pressing relentlessly on their heels. On this day a battalion of the Munster Fusiliers, acting as part of the rear guard, became detached from the main body of the First (Guards) Brigade, and after fighting for nearly twelve hours against overwhelming odds perished almost to a man.

It was anticipated that the Germans would make a great effort on September first to commemorate in a suitable manner the victory of Sedan. In point of fact, although the fighting was severe and the losses of the Fourth (Guards) Brigade in a heroic rearguard action were very heavy, the end of the day, during which a further stage in the retreat had been accomplished, seemed to leave the situation materially unaltered. But three events of first-class importance for the future conduct of the war had actually taken place.

French had reached a state of mind in which he could think only of the preservation of his own force. He had abandoned any immediate intention of further co-operation with his allies and decided to retire altogether from the fighting line, to retreat to the south of the Seine and with his base at La Rochelle to await future developments.

Kitchener was horrified at French's decision, and the British Cabinet shared his dismay. In the very early morning, therefore, of September first, he left London for Paris where he met French in the course of the day. The result of their conversation was that French abandoned his previously declared purpose of quitting the fighting line, and agreed to conform to the best of his ability to the wishes of Joffre and the movements of the French Army.

On the previous day the extreme right wing of the invading host, the First German Army, under Kluck, definitely altered the line of their advance from a southern to a south-easterly direction. It is said that Schlieffen, the originator of the plan of campaign, exclaimed on his death bed, "It must come to a fight. Only make the right wing strong," and we have seen how strong it was when the British Army first encountered it on the twenty-third August. But Moltke, the German commander in chief, instead of strengthening had weakened it. In spite of the victory at Tannenberg on August twenty-eighth, no troops had been transferred from the Eastern to the Western Front; in spite of the failure of the First and Second French armies in their attacks on the left of the German line, no reinforcements had been sent to the right. The result was that that strong right fist was no longer so firmly clenched. The fingers were becoming looser, at any moment they might begin to flap, and the consciousness of weakness naturally produced a tendency to draw in toward the central body as being the fountain of strength. And so the original grand conception of the vast sweeping movement that was to have brought the extreme right to the south of the Seine, and to have included Paris in its huge embrace, was abandoned in favour of a little stab that seemed for the moment to promise an easier and swifter victory.

A further important decision was taken on the first of September which was to have some influence on the events to come. Joffre decided to reinforce the troops defending Paris, and in order to do so he incorporated the whole of the Sixth Army and one corps of the Third Army with its garrison. At the same time he advised the government to leave for Bordeaux. They did so on the following day. The result was that on the second September, General Galliéni, the military governor of Paris, had fewer politicians at his elbow and more troops under his command.

For four more days the long retreat continued. Each morning the corps marched before daybreak always with the knowledge that the enemy were at their heels and frequently exposed to shell fire. When they arrived at their destination the heavy labours of the staff began, making arrangements for the next day's move and distributing billets for the next night's rest. On the second Haig slept at Meaux which was "like a city of the dead—no one moving in the streets except some aged men and women". The next night he stayed at La Fringale—"a shooting box, evidently used by a syndicate of sportsmen from Paris." Thence still farther south to a château at Faremoutiers, three miles southwest of Coulommiers.

There the "night passed quietly except for attack by troops of Uhlans on an outpost of the Black Watch near Aulnoy. Canny Scots, they had stretched a strand of barbed wire across the main road so that, when the German horsemen charged down and tried to gallop through the picket in the dark, the horses tripped up, eight Uhlans were killed and the officer was captured."

On September fifth troops marched as usual at 3 A.M. in a southwesterly direction toward Melun. The day was cooler and there was more life in the men. At the village of Marles Haig paused for breakfast which he had with his staff in an orchard adjoining the church. It was while he was sitting there under the trees that Major Dawnay arrived with a message from the commander in chief. It contained the information, long desired, that on the morrow the allied forces were to turn on their pursuers. "The army on the sixth September will advance eastward with a view to attacking."

"No words", wrote Haig, "could have been more welcome to the troops. For thirteen days, broken only by a short rest at St Gobain, the First Corps had retreated without a check and had fought a continuous series of rearguard actions, some of them serious. The total distance covered was not less than 160 miles, and there was not a man in the force who had not covered considerably more than this distance. The total losses in action throughout this period were 81 officers and 2180 noncommissioned officers and men. These figures, however, give no idea of the demands which were made upon the force under my command. The actual fighting was the least of our difficulties."

CHAPTER V

Marne and Aisne

IT IS UNNECESSARY here to revive the controversy as to whether it was Joffre or Galliéni who first appreciated the value of the opportunity which the German movement had given to the allied armies. Suffice it to say that little time was lost in coming to the decision that the moment had arrived to turn on the pursuers, and on September sixth the whole of the allied line advanced.

Haig used sometimes to say that he never knew there had been a battle of the Marne, and on this, the first day of it, the First Corps certainly experienced very little serious fighting.

The corps bivouacked that night, September seventh, along the south bank of the Grand Morin, a tributary of the Marne. Haig slept in a house at Choisy where German officers had been billeted a few nights before. "A German general slept in my room. Before he left he put his foot through the looking-glass in the wardrobe—hardly a manly act! The poor woman in charge was much upset."

The advance was resumed at 6 A.M. on September eighth. Having crossed the Grand Morin without difficulty the corps was confronted by a more formidable obstacle in the Petit Morin, another small river flowing between steep and high banks, where the enemy put up a more determined resistance. The German superiority in numbers of machine guns and the use they made of them provided the British Army with a useful lesson. "The enemy's guns and cavalry", wrote Haig, "did not long remain in action, but the machine guns were handled with great skill and resolution. In the closely wooded valley they afforded no target to our artillery and, whenever our infantry advanced, fire was opened from some unexpected direction, sometimes from the woods, sometimes from windows."

After the difficulty which the First Corps had experienced in crossing the Petit Morin they naturally anticipated that the Marne would prove a far more formidable obstacle. A broad river with few bridges and many houses on its banks, it offered to a retreating army ideal opportunities for fighting rearguard actions. But when the First Corps reached the bridges they found that the enemy had disappeared and, although elaborate barricades had been erected which took as long as two hours to remove, the advance guard of the First Division had crossed the Marne at Nogent by 7.30 A.M. on September ninth. Soon afterward the Second Division effected a crossing farther west at Charly.

For three more days the pursuit of the rapidly retreating German Army continued. On September eleventh the whole of the British Expeditionary Force wheeled in a north-easterly direction. The First Corps being on the right had therefore a comparatively short march. This action was taken in accordance with a request received from General Joffre.

"Personally," wrote Haig, "I think it is a mistake to have changed direction now, because the enemy on our front was close to us last night and was much exhausted. Had we advanced today on Soissons, with cavalry on both flanks, large captures seemed likely."

All the evidence that has subsequently come to light confirms the view that Haig's appreciation of the position was the correct one. We know now from narratives such as

Captain Bloem's *Advance from Mons* how utterly worn-out were the German troops; we know from official reports how wide was the gap between the First and the Second German Armies and how lightly it was defended; and it is impossible, in light of the facts that are now available, to avoid the conclusion that an opportunity was missed which might have brought the war to a sudden and dramatic conclusion. From the moment that the German advance was turned into a retreat, those in Germany who properly understood the situation realized that the great plan had failed. It had depended for its success upon swiftness of execution. If the war of rapid action were to become a war of slow attrition the superior resources of the allies must tell in the end. If the retreat from the Marne, difficult as it was to explain, had been followed by a spectacular defeat, it is not impossible that in Germany the voice of sanity would have prevailed and peace would have been negotiated, for the Germans had no more envisaged and were no more prepared for four years of trench warfare than were the allies.

But this was not to be. The Germans were accorded on September eleventh and twelfth that short but vital breathing space which enabled them to cross the Aisne, to recover their morale, and to adopt a strong position from which they could hold their ground and beat back their pursuers.

"The evening of the twelfth September", runs the diary, "marks the close of the second phase of this campaign. That phase comprises the sudden check of the enemy's forward movement toward Paris on the sixth September, followed by our advance which drove him back to the Aisne. During the seven days from the sixth to the twelfth of September the First Corps acting in co-operation with the rest of the British force on its left and with the French Fifth Army on its right, covered a distance of seventy miles, fought two important engagements—at the Petit Morin on the eighth and Hautevesnes and Courchamps on the tenth, captured one thousand prisoners, two field guns, six machine guns and other material. When it is remembered that these feats followed immediately on a long and exhausting retreat, it will be realized that the short-service regular army of today has nothing to fear from comparison with the long-service army of the last century."

The obstacles which now presented themselves to the advancing British Army consisted not only of the swiftly running river Aisne with its steep and wooded banks and the greater part of its bridges broken, but also a formidable ridge of rising ground beyond it along which there stretched a road which was to prove memorable in the history of the war, Le Chemin des Dames.

The following is from Haig's description of the situation of the First Corps after the fighting of September the fourteenth:

The idea of an immediate northward advance of the allied forces was gradually abandoned, and the line which had been gained by the First Corps as the result of an offensive battle had to be adapted for purposes of defence. The total length of this line from the right of the Second Brigade to point 166 north of Chavonne was not less than twelve thousand yards, a very extended front to be held by a force of only two divisions, reduced by casualties against an active German enemy with large reserves to draw upon. The result was that until the arrival of some troops of the Fifth Division on the eighteenth September only small local reserves could be kept in hand. It was, therefore, almost impossible to relieve the men in the trenches where, even when not attacked, they were subjected by night as well as day to high-explosive shell fire.

An additional difficulty was that, with the right of my line thrust forward, the trenches held just south of the Chemin des Dames by the Second Brigade—as well as those held by the French left—were subjected to a very troublesome enfilade fire, both from rifle and artillery, which caused us many casualties. This point in my line was always rather vulnerable and caused some anxiety. The north end of the Paissy ridge could be, and constantly was, swept by artillery fire from three directions—east, north and west. The Tirailleurs (from Morocco) on my right were almost without officers, so that I could not be quite certain of them, and artillery positions from which to reply to the German fire were not easy to find. I therefore regarded this as my most vulnerable point, and for that reason I kept the bulk of the cavalry on the right flank, and also placed my corps reserve at Oeuilly and Bourg, when the arrival of the Sixth Division enabled me to form one. The Ostel ridge was also always a dangerous point, but there, with the assistance of the guns of the Third Division, a cross fire from east and south could be brought to bear upon any hostile infantry advancing to attack.

In other respects, as soon as there had been time to dig proper trenches, the position was stronger than might have been expected. On the high ground our trenches were on the reverse slopes so that they received some protection from artillery fire—the field for infantry fire was, though comparatively short when judged by text-book standards, very open, and the enemy's infantry soon showed that they had no inclination to face our musketry and shrapnel. In the Chivy and Braye valleys an effective artillery fire could be brought to bear against any attack. However, a reverse at either of these points would not have been so serious a matter as on the ridge, and any ground lost could probably have been quickly recovered.

Although temporarily thrown on to the defensive on this line, we were not prevented from undertaking local offensive action at every opportunity. The fight of the 14th gave our men increased confidence in their officers, in themselves, and in their weapons; and in the fighting which followed, the British soldier soon established a moral superiority over the German.

September 14, 1914, is a date in the history of the Great War more important than any of those who were engaged in the fighting could have anticipated, for from that day we may date the beginning of the long and tragic story of trench warfare, for which no army was prepared, and which no high military authority in any country had foreseen. On the same day also, General von Falkenhayn succeeded General von Moltke as chief of staff of the German Army; but in order that the change of command might not discourage the troops the latter, though deprived of his position, was ordered to remain at his post.

Haig was aroused a little after midnight on the morning of September fifteenth by John Gough, who had just returned from a visit to G.H.Q. He brought the information that French was very anxious with regard to the situation. He feared lest a vigorous offensive by the enemy might drive our troops back into the Aisne.

"There was nothing for it but to hold on to our present position and make it as strong as possible by means of entrenchments."

In the course of the day, Haig received a letter from French in which he wrote, "I feel very strongly that the favourable position we are in (on the whole), and the good chance we have of ultimately throwing the enemy back, are due to the splendid advance and stand which has been made by you and the First Army Corps."

On the same day he telegraphed to Lord Kitchener: "Owing chiefly to the fine advance made yesterday by Sir Douglas Haig and the First Corps, we are in a favourable position on our right."

During the month that followed, the British Army passed through their apprenticeship to the trade of trench warfare.

Many of the older officers, who had been slow to appreciate the importance of the air arm, were still reluctant to make full use of the invention, but Haig's mind was never stereotyped, and from the first he had given the greatest encouragement to the pioneers in military aviation, and he was eager to discover fresh ways of utilizing their prowess.

The effect of their co-operation with the artillery was soon noticeable, for a few days later he writes, "Much use has been made of observers in aeroplanes to locate the enemy's guns and trenches, as well as to direct the fire of our own artillery. The observers, who in this case are also the pilots, in machines fitted with wireless, have been particularly successful, and each day has shown improved results as experience has been gained. These good results are apparent. Our guns now daily attack the German guns with success, while latterly the Germans appear to have failed to locate our guns, and have expended ammunition in searching areas with but little effect."

The relations between the First Corps and their French allies on their right, whom they now had some opportunity of getting to know, were extremely satisfactory. Hearing that the Moroccan troops were short of rations, Haig immediately ordered ten thousand British rations, which were available, to be conveyed to them with his best wishes. The following letter of thanks from General de Maud'huy shows the effect produced by this act of comradeship.

Maizy. September 19th.
Headquarters of the Eighteenth Corps.

DEAR SIR DOUGLAS,

Nothing could touch me more deeply than your kindness toward my half-starved soldiers, and those ten thousand rations are a gift which I shall always remember.

With my warmest thanks and hoping that, one day or another to be useful to you, believe me your very respectful and devoted DE MAUD'HUY.

"On the first October," Haig wrote in his diary, "both sides were occupying practically the same lines as those which they held on the night of the fourteenth September. The First Corps has voluntarily given up some ground at the head of the Chivy valley, elsewhere it is very firmly established in trenches which could be held against greatly superior numbers."

If Haig himself had written the history of the war, he would not have closed the account of this phase of the campaign without reminding his readers of the important part that had been played by the cavalry until the initiation of trench warfare. He was well aware of it himself at the time, as is shown by the following entry in his diary:

"I wrote to General Allenby commanding cavalry division this evening, to thank him for the very effective support which the First Corps had received from the cavalry. On the fourteenth when my left flank was uncovered owing to the retirement of the Third Division, two cavalry brigades rapidly prolonged my left near Chavonne, and these held the trenches day and night on the left of the Fourth (Guards) Brigade in the same part of the field. Also on the flank a brigade was on duty all day. Sometimes the men were put in the trenches to give the infantry a rest. Altogether our cavalry have shown a splendid spirit and have helped us in a way I shall never forget."

CHAPTER VI

Ypres to Loos, 1914–15

AFTER THE BATTLES of the Marne and Aisne the war settled down to the stalemate of trench fighting which was to last four years. While Haig was one of the foreseeing generals who anticipated a long struggle there were periods when the war seemed nearing a climax—great battles, victories, defeats. To the public of that time the news from the front was vital in every detail; so far as the censorship permitted each engagement was followed as eagerly as if it were the final act in the long drama. Ypres, Neuve Chapelle, Aubers Ridge, Festubert and Loos are names graven on the memories of the war generation, though for their children these terrible combats may seem but vague incidents in the ups and downs of the entrenched armies, swaying backward and forward without either side gaining more than a temporary advantage.

The British Expeditionary Force, grown to three corps in the autumn of 1914, had moved toward the Channel and taken up its position as the extreme left wing of the allies before October twenty-second. After the failure of Sir John French's attempt to outflank the German right at La Bassée came a series of desperate encounters culminating in the first battle of Ypres.

In the accounts which Haig gives of these days of bitter warfare, accounts which were written either at the time or immediately afterward, it is noticeable that he never fails to pay tribute to the gallantry of the foe, that there is not a line to suggest that he is infected by the then fashionable spirit of hatred, nor does he ever employ, when writing of the Germans, the opprobrious terms "Hun" and "Boche" which were in almost universal use among the allies.

Describing the recovery of some trenches lost to the enemy on October twenty-third, he writes, "The attack was very strongly opposed and the bayonet had to be used. The Germans resisted until the very end and gave way only when machine guns were enfilading their trenches at very close range, and when they were threatened by cold steel."

On the twenty-fifth, "The Germans, quite young fellows, came on with great gallantry. One mounted officer kept encouraging his men to go forward, until within four hundred yards of our firing line, when he was killed."

The mood of the German High Command at this time may be judged from the terms of the following Order of the Day:

"The break-through" (which was to take place on the following day) "will be of decisive importance. We must and therefore will conquer, settle for ever the centuries-long struggle, end the war and strike the decisive blow against our most detested enemy. We will finish with the British, Indians, Canadians, Moroccans and other trash, feeble adversaries who surrender in mass if they are attacked with vigour."

The First Division had been heavily engaged since dawn on October third. Hopelessly outnumbered by the enemy, they had been fighting with desperate tenacity. As an example of their depleted strength, it may be recorded that when the First Battalion of the Scots Guards captured fifty-eight Bavarians they could not spare the men to act as an escort to the prisoners. But all the time the bombardment of the British trenches was increasing in violence and accuracy. By 9.30 A.M. the Welsh Regiment, says the official historian, had been literally "blown out of their trenches." At 10 A.M. the report reached Haig's headquarters that the "situation in the trenches south and southeast of Gheluvelt was serious." This statement certainly did not err on the side of exaggeration. It was indeed difficult for those behind the line to learn how the battle was progressing. Such telephonic communication as had existed had long broken down. Every runner who left the trenches was killed before his message could be delivered. It has been reckoned that the British were outnumbered by six to one, and the proportion of German superiority in artillery was far greater. The enemy's accounts of the fighting are those which reflect the greatest credit upon their opponents. They tell of the "maze of obstacles that were encountered and of the fresh troops continually being hurled into the fray." There were, in fact, no obstacles save the trenches, and such defences as had been hastily designed and strengthened in the few hours that had been available. Nor were there any fresh troops engaged on the British side that day. The men who defended the village of Gheluvelt were all that remained of that First Division who in the last six weeks had spent nearly a fortnight in continual retreat, nearly another fortnight in continual advance, who had lain a month in the trenches under ceaseless fire, who had been hastily transferred from one scene of warfare to another, only to be plunged immediately into fiercer fighting; they had fought actions which in other ages would have marked epochs, and they had taken them with a grumble and a smile as a part of their daily work; these were the remnant of that mercenary army, termed by their enemies contemptible, men whose names should be enshrined for ever in the hearts of Englishmen, saints and martyrs of their race.

Haig had moved his reporting centre back to the white

château in order that General Lomax might "make himself comfortable in Hooge Château". It was in Hooge Château, therefore, that Lomax and Monro, together with their highest staff officers, were now engaged in earnest council of war. When a low-flying enemy aeroplane flew over the château, they did not heed it, when a shell fell in the château garden they continued their work. The next shell fell on the entrance to the council chamber itself. Six staff officers were killed in an instant, Monro, the commander of the Second Division, was stunned, and Lomax the calm, resourceful, utterly reliable commander of the heroic First Division, received his death wound. The news of this tragedy reached Haig about 2 P.M., and once more he prepared to visit the front line himself in order to form his own opinion and possibly to take command himself of the First Division.

At that moment Sir John French arrived. Such was the congestion of traffic on the road that he had been obliged to walk part of the way. When he was informed of the desperate condition of affairs, he "was full of sympathy and expressed his gratitude for what the corps, as well as I myself had done since we landed in France. No one could have been nicer at such a time of crisis. But he had no reinforcements to send me, and viewed the situation with the utmost gravity."

There seems to have been something almost valedictory in the words which the commander in chief addressed to his corps commander before he sadly turned to retrace his steps towards his car. Once again Haig mounted his horse, and the thought can hardly have been absent from his mind that he might be doing so for the last time. Nor would he have greatly cared to live if the British Army had been defeated and the war lost. But in the very gateway of the Château he encountered General Rice, galloping, breathless. "Gheluvelt has been recaptured! The First Division has rallied."

This is not the place to tell again the hardly credible story of how the fortunes of the day had been restored, how one battalion of the Worcestershire together with any stragglers, batmen or crooks who could be hastily collected, under the guidance and inspiration of General C. Fitzclarence, under the leadership of Major E. B. Hankey, advanced over ground that meant certain death for the majority, and charged into the blazing village of Gheluvelt, so that the astonished enemy turned and fled.

Haig heard the good news as calmly as he had heard the bad. He despatched an aide-de-camp to catch the commander in chief if possible before he reached his car, and himself "rode forward to be in closer touch with the situation, and see if I could do anything to organize stragglers and push them forward to help in checking the enemy. I rode to Veldhoek and saw Generals Landon, Capper and Fitzclarence, and found that Rice's report was true"—it was not unnatural that he should have doubted it—"Gheluvelt has been retaken by the Worcesters and the situation has been restored."

The white château itself was heavily shelled on November second. Three men were killed and a large chandelier in Haig's office crashed on to the table. He accordingly moved his headquarters and slept that night at Ypres in "a fine old house with some good old furniture in it. Its present owner went to England last week, but his housekeeper and cook, two old people, looked after us with great care, and I was sorry to see the place so upset. They gave us dinner, and some good claret in spite of the shelling." A direct hit was scored on this house the next day, and Haig's reporting centre was hit the day after, when Colonel Marker, his quartermaster general, was mortally wounded. "Enemy had evidently some spies about to help him to direct his fire so accurately, this being the third time my headquarters have been shelled in the last few days."

On November fifth, Haig motored to Bailleul to see Sir John French and lunched with him.

"The table was laid in a room at the back of a chemist's shop. The corps commanders were present at the meeting, viz. Smith-Dorrien, Pulteney, Sir James Willcocks and Allenby. The Second Corps (Smith-Dorrien) is to relieve my first corps as soon as possible, so that my divisions may have a rest in which to refit. I was very astonished to find that the point which attracted most interest was, 'Winter leave' for the army! Personally, my one thought was how soon I could get my battle-worn troops relieved and given a few days' rest out of the trenches and shell fire!"

The days that followed were always anxious and often critical. Hardly for a moment did the pressure from the enemy cease or slacken. Almost nightly Haig had to be roused in the middle of his short sleep to be presented with some urgent and disturbing intelligence. His officers marvelled at the manner in which he would immediately recover consciousness and the complete possession of all his faculties, would appreciate instantly the new situation, give his instructions and fall asleep again almost before they had left the room.

The Germans, after continued repulses, determined to make one more terrific effort to win their way through Ypres to the channel ports. At 3 A.M. on November eleventh, Haig was roused by an urgent message from the French General d'Urbal asking for the return of two battalions of Zouaves who had been placed under his command.

"The night had been a quiet one, but at 9.30 A.M. a heavy attack, preceded by extremely heavy shelling by a large number of guns along the whole front of the First and Second Divisions, suddenly devloped. The line which we held was pierced just north of the Menin road and consequently the Royal Fusiliers, whose trenches were immediately south of the road, were enfiladed and this regiment lost very heavily. Its colonel, McMahon, was killed, and the strength of the regiment was reduced to two subalterns and about one hundred men."

A counterattack by the Royal Scots Fusiliers was launched, which after very heavy casualties succeeded in re-establishing the line. It had, however, been broken in another place, south of Polygon Wood, and toward noon Lord Cavan, who was commanding on the right wing of the First Corps, reported that the French, who were on his right, were giving way under heavy shell fire. "The situation, therefore, at this point was extremely critical, most of the Divisional and Corps reserves had been used up to re-establish the position in the vicinity of the Menin road. . . . By this time it had been ascertained from prisoners of war that we were opposed by regiments of the Prussian Guard, an entirely new body of troops which had been able to concentrate in this area without any information of the movement being received by G.Q.G. of the allied forces."

Once again fresh troops, the flower of the Prussian Army, were being hurled against this poor remnant of an army, in which companies represented battalions and whose weary veterans had been fighting constantly for two months and a half. "About 2 P.M. reports came in reporting a critical situation north of Menin road, owing to gap in First Brigade line. All Divisional and Corps reserves are moved to block it and drive back a force of twelve hundred Germans who are advancing on it. I send Gough to see Landon and find out what General Fitzclarence has been doing."

Haig was to learn all too soon what Fitzclarence had been doing. Before the messenger could reach him, he had organized a counterattack which had driven the Germans at the point of the bayonet out of the wood that they had recently captured. At nightfall his whole brigade was reduced to four officers and about three hundred men, but he was still determined to recover his lost trenches, and when the commander of the First Division put two additional battalions under his command—some five hundred men in all—he arranged for another attack to take place in the early hours of the morning. While going forward himself to reconnoitre, he was mortally wounded by a rifle bullet. The First Corps and the whole army suffered a loss that they could ill afford.

On November twelfth, the situation seemed from the point of view of the English to be still extremely critical, but the Germans failed to take advantage of it. Haig was aroused at 5 A.M. "by very heavy rifle fire about two miles off" where apparently the Germans were attacking the French, but without much result. He spent the day visiting his divisional and brigade commanders and expecting an attack which never materialized. He recorded it in the evening as "on the whole a quiet day after a very anxious morning".

Haig issued the following message to the troops on November twelfth:

The commander in chief has asked me to convey to the troops under my command his congratulations and thanks for their splendid resistance to the German attack yesterday.

This attack was delivered by some twelve fresh battalions of the German Guard Corps which had been specially brought up to carry out the task in which so many other corps had failed: viz., to crush the British and force a way through to Ypres.

Since its arrival in this neighborhood the First Corps assisted by the Third Cavalry Division, Seventh Divison and troops from the Second Corps has met and defeated the Twenty-third, Twenty-sixth and Twenty-seventh German Reserve Corps, the Fifteenth Active Corps, and finally a strong force from the Guards Corps. It is doubtful if the annals of the British Army contain any finer record than this.

Although it was difficult for the men themselves to realize it, they had in effect on November eleventh won the long first battle of Ypres, though for many days fighting continued. On the twenty-second Haig crossed to England for five days' leave. His wife met him at Victoria. He wrote in his diary, "It seemed as if a hundred years had passed since I parted with Doris at Aldershot."

The five days of this first period of leave were spent very quietly at his sister's house in Prince's Gate. Younger men coming home would naturally plunge into gaiety, but all that Haig wanted was peace. Every evening was spent at home, and the only events of the day were important interviews. On the first morning he spent two hours with Kitchener. On the following day he was received by the King, who was "most complimentary"; and his two little girls arrived from Wales, where they were living with their aunt. On November twenty-fifth he saw the prime minister in the morning, who was also "most complimentary regarding the work of the First Corps and myself." The last morning of his leave was spent at the War Office with the adjutant general, Sclater, and Lord Kitchener. He impressed on the former the lack of officers, and said, "Send out young Oxford and Cambridge men as officers; they understand the crisis in which the British Empire is involved." The last afternoon was spent with the children at the zoo. The next morning he returned to France. Nothing of importance had occurred at the Front during his absence, and the remainder of the year was to prove uneventful.

With the opening of 1915 the melancholy conviction began to force itself upon the minds of those who were responsible for the conduct of the war that the hope of an early decision on the Western Front no longer existed.

Simultaneously there arose among the military and civil authorities on either side two conflicting schools of military strategy. On the one hand there were those who, with whatever forebodings, gravely accepted the grim prospect of a long struggle in the main arena, entailing slaughter and sacrifice beyond anything previously contemplated, and only terminating when one of the protagonists was reduced to accepting whatever terms were dictated.

There were, on the other hand, some who refused to admit to their minds so fearful a conclusion. Wars had not been so mercilessly fought out in the past, why should the present one prove an exception? Genius could find out a way, closed to the purblind vision of military experts, which would take the professional strategists by surprise and prove a sure and easy road to victory. For the next four years these rival schools of thought strove with one another for predominance in the councils of war. The majority of the trained soldiers leaned toward the former theory, but a large number of the more active-minded politicians adopted the latter. They knew enough of the subject to be aware that the main principle in strategy is to turn the opponent's flank. Assuming that this was no longer possible on that line that was held from the North Sea to the Swiss frontier, they argued that it was necessary to go beyond these limits, and by winning a decisive victory in the east render the position of the Central Powers in the west no longer tenable. Lord Fisher had thought it possible to turn the enemy's flank in the west by attacking in the Baltic with a large fleet specially constructed for the purpose, but the design, which was never very seriously undertaken, was abandoned when he left the admiralty in May, 1915.

Against those who advocated such methods, it was contended that the enemy's great advantage lay in their central position and in the comparative shortness and complete security of their lines of communication, which enabled them to transfer troops from one front to another with the maximum of speed and the minimum of risk. If, therefore, the allies sought to deliver their attack through Austria or through Turkey, they were increasing these very advantages which the Central Powers already possessed and increasing their own disadvantages by prolonging their lines of communication.

It was further argued by those who had studied military problems most deeply that no victory in the east could prove decisive in its effect upon the war so long as the principal enemy remained undefeated. That enemy was the German Army entrenched in France and Belgium. So long as it remained there the allies could not be victorious, and so long as it remained there any weakening of the Forces that opposed it might result in the allies' defeat.

The historian should beware of taking sides in controversies that must for ever remain controversial, and of asserting what would have occurred in hypothetical circumstances that never arose. He should be still more careful of attributing praise or censure to those who sincerely held opinions as to the wisest course to pursue in the interests of their country. But it is legitimate for him to remind readers of facts whch throw light upon theories, and of actual experience from which lessons may be drawn. In two centuries the British Army has had repeated warnings by disaster of the danger of indulging in those diversions from the main theatre of war to which the term "side shows" has been applied. This experience was amplified and extended in the last war. While it is perfectly fair and just to argue that this expedition or the other might have succeeded, that indeed it ought to have done so, it is equally fair to reply that, as a matter of fact, it failed. While those who still speak and write of the fruitless slaughter in the west ought to remember that it was in the west that the war was won and that all that tragic slaughter bore its victorious fruit in the end.

The enemy's experiences are also instructive. They also were fighting on more than one front, they also had more than one school of strategy and, owing to their advantage, which has been already mentioned, their adventures in the east were more successful than those of the Allies. When we are told of the enormous advantages that would have accrued if we had knocked out Turkey, if we had forced Austria to make a separate peace, if we had prevented Bulgaria from coming in, we ought to remember that Germany did knock out Serbia, that she did knock out Roumania, that she did prevent Greece from coming in, and that she did dictate terms to Russia, one of the greatest and most powerful of her principal opponents, and yet she did not win the war, and could not win it so long as the French and British armies held their ground and so long as the British Navy sailed the sea.

There could be little doubt which of the two contending theories would recommend itself to the mind of Sir Douglas Haig. He was by nature orthodox, and his profound studies of military history and science had strengthened his belief in the main tenets of military theory laid down by the great writers and practised by the great captains of the past. In his *Cavalry Studies,* published in 1907, he had written: "Napoleon's constant preoccupation, as must be that of every commander in the field, was how to reduce the number of troops employed on matters of secondary importance, in order to increase the numbers available for the decisive battle." And in the same chapter he quoted his master as having written in a report to Robespierre in 1794, "War must be waged on the same principle as a siege: fire must concentrate on a single point. Once a breach is made, the equilibrium is broken, the other defences become valueless and the place is taken. Attacks must not be scattered but concentrated."

When therefore it was suggested to him that Great

Britain's military effort should be directed toward more than one theatre of war, he had no hesitation in forming his opinion of such a proposal. The first that he heard of it was at a conference with the commander in chief on January fourth. "Sir John French read a letter from K. in which the latter hinted that the new army might be used better elsewhere than on the French frontier. A suggestion has been made of co-operating with Italy and Greece. I said that we ought not to divide our military force, but *concentrate on the decisive point* which is on this frontier against the German main army. With more guns and ammunition and more troops the allies were bound in the end to defeat the Germans and break through." To this opinion he steadfastly adhered for the next four years.

Sir John French shared this view, but he had not yet realized all that it implied in loss and sacrifice, in patience and tenacity. On January 20, 1915, having recently returned from a visit to London, he "hazarded the opinion that the new army was not likely to be here before June, by which time, he thought, the war would be over".

Haig entertained no such optimistic illusions.

An old friend, Sir Henry McMahon, who was on his way to the East to take up the position of high commissioner for Egypt, visited him at his headquarters in the Maire's house at Lillers toward the end of December. He was surprised in those sternly military surroundings to hear the voices of children playing in the passages. More than once during his visit one or two of them would burst into the room while the gravest matters were under discussion, and he remembers the smiling serenity with which the first army commander, upon whom such fearful responsibilities rested, would gently shoo these intruders back to their own quarters.

The forthcoming battle of Neuve Chapelle was to be the

first of those long-prepared, carefully co-ordinated offensives which were to prove the features of the war.

In February General John Edmond Gough, while visiting his old battalion of the rifle brigade in the vicinity of the front line, was struck by a stray bullet, and two days later he was dead. It was a loss to Haig, not only of a wise counsellor, but also of a dear friend.

After many conferences had been held by the commander in chief and the corps commanders, Sir William Robertson came to discuss with Haig the date of the offensive. "He told me that the French Parliament was pressing that General Joffre should gain ground and *do something.*" That vague demand for undefined action was to come with increasing regularity from more than one parliament during the next four years, and was to be varied only by criticism of such action as the demand produced. "Sir John has decided that we must do something about the seventh March, and 'it must be an offensive on a big scale'. I replied that owing to the waterlogged state of the ground the tenth March would be the very earliest date for my main attack, and even then we had only the means to carry out a small operation."

Haig's prognostication proved exact. Henceforward, March tenth was the date toward which he worked, and the date on which the attack was delivered. Preparations went on with increasing intensity as the date approached. Every day Haig visited the officers upon whom the principal responsibility would rest, and impressed upon them above everything the importance of making it plain to every subordinate exactly what his own part was to be. Each evening he would enter in his diary the opinion he had formed of the character and capacity of the officers he had interviewed.

Every precaution was taken to prevent leakage of information. On February twenty-eighth, he paid a visit to

General de Maud'huy, commanding the French Tenth Army on his right. "I was very warmly received as he said we were old friends, having fought next to each other on the Aisne and having exchanged many letters, though this was the first time of our meeting. . . . He is a small, active man, about fifty-eight, sandy-coloured hair . . . quite the old type of Frenchman whom one has seen on the stage of the Louis XIV period."

The French general, however, could only offer assistance from his artillery, as he had not sufficient men in his sector to undertake an offensive.

On March second, "I motored to Merville and conferred with Sir Henry Rawlinson at 12.30 A.M. regarding his proposed plan. As to the general scheme, I said that our objective was not merely the capture of Neuve Chapelle. Our existing line was just as satisfactory for us as if we were in Neuve Chapelle. I aimed at getting to the line Illies-Herlies and the line of the La Bassée road to Lille and thus cut off the enemy's troops occupying the front between Neuve Chapelle and La Bassée, and thus, if possible, break the enemy's front."

The final orders for the attack were sent out from Haig's headquarters at nine P.M. on March eighth, and the last two of the heavy guns arrived from England only on the morning of March ninth. At 7.30 A.M. on the tenth, the bombardment began.

In comparison with what was to come in the future the preliminary bombardment before the battle of Neuve Chapelle was insignificant, but nothing like it had been heard before in the history of the world. Simultaneously, as the hands of the clock pointed to the given hour, one hundred and fifty guns rent with a vast roar the silence of the morning. During the thirty-five minutes that followed, three thousand shells fell upon the German trenches, flattening the wire defences, obliterating the parapets and killing or wounding the majority of the defenders. At a prearranged moment, the belt of fire shifted from the enemy's front line to a line farther back, thus cutting off the retreat of the survivors, and, as the line of falling shells moved forward, the infantry advanced to capture what remained of the enemy's battered trenches. By nine o'clock Haig learned that the village of Neuve Chapelle had been captured, but the delay caused by difficulties on the right and left prevented any attempt to continue the advance until the afternoon, and in the interval the Germans had time to recover from the shock that the unexpected bombardment had given them, and had been able to organize and strengthen their new line of defence. Nevertheless, at the end of the day an advance had been made, and all the front-line defences of the enemy had been captured on a front of four thousand yards. Seven hundred and forty-eight prisoners had been taken.

On the following day, Haig ordered the attack to be continued. Weather conditions proved less favourable, for a heavy mist prevented effective observation from the air. Further, the Germans were prepared for battle and not only offered an obstinate resistance, but also delivered vigorous counterattacks which were successfully repulsed, but which obviated the possibility of an advance.

"Sir John French called to congratulate me on the result of yesterday. He said that he was most grateful and that he realized the fine state of the First Army was due to me. He was having an anxious time with the Second Army, and had been obliged to find fault with Smith-Dorrien."

The atmosphere was still more opaque the next morning, and the advance which had been timed for 10.30 was postponed till noon. Meanwhile, the Germans again attacked, in spite of the fog, and, although they were driven back with considerable loss, the British were unable to make any progress, for the sector of the front which faced them had been heavily reinforced. Haig was quick to appreciate the new situation and altered his plans in order to meet it. Abandoning the idea of continuing to hammer on the door that was now firmly barred and bolted, he gave instructions that the line now held should be strengthened with a view to its retention as a defensive position while the next blow should be delivered at some other point so as to take the enemy once more by surprise.

The battle of Neuve Chapelle may be therefore said to have ended on March twelfth. Any further attack was, for the time being, rendered impossible by the shortage of ammunition. The experience gained on this occasion was of great value. The possibility of breaking into the enemy's line was proved, and also the great difficulty of converting an initial "break-in" into a permanent "break-through".

The events of those two days produced a deep impression both on the enemy and on our allies. The German front that faced the British Army was henceforth held in greater strength, and the French discarded any doubts they might have entertained as to the fighting value of the English.

Much activity certainly was going on in the political world during those fateful months of 1915, and Haig was thankful that such activity did not concern an army commander. He was able to take five days' leave at the end of March. There are not many men who, in his position, would not have welcomed the opportunity of visiting London in order to discuss recent events and the future with the powers that were, both at the War Office and in Downing Street. There were rumours already of great changes in the personnel of both military and civilian authorities. At such moments presence on the spot and personal contact may prove invaluable to the fortunes of an individual. It is typical of this great, simple, unselfseeking soldier, that he telegraphed to his wife to meet him at Folkestone, that he spent the whole of those five days alone with her, playing golf during the day and dining together at their lodgings in the evening, that he even respectfully declined a suggestion that he should go to London for an interview with the King, and that he returned to France without having seen a single individual in authority, but having refreshed his soul with five days of deep, untroubled peace.

When he returned to France he found his staff in great indignation over the official report of the battle of Neuve Chapelle, which the commander in chief had caused to be circulated. This report had naturally been drawn up at the headquarters of the First Army under the supervision of General Butler, the chief staff officer. When, however, the report was submitted to general headquarters, instructions were received that for the words "General officer commanding the First Army" at the begining of the report, there should be substituted "Commander in chief"—it thus being made to appear that the whole plan had been worked out by Sir John French, who had, in fact, no hand in its preparation whatever. Haig's comment is characteristic—"The whole thing is so childish that I could hardly have credited the truth of the story had I not seen the paper. The main thing, however, is to beat the Germans *soon* and leave to the British public the task of awarding credit for work done after peace has been made."

A few days later another incident occurred throwing a curious light upon the state of Sir John French's mind at this period. Haig had written a letter to Sir William Robertson stating his proposals for exploding mines and generally harassing the Germans during the next few weeks, and explaining a system of building shelters in the vicinity of the front line in order to deceive the enemy as to the exact position of the troops. He had concluded by suggesting that orders should be given to the Second Army to make similar arrangements. In reply he received a letter from the commander in chief practically telling him to mind his own business, and not to make suggestions with regard to troops other than those under his own command. "I infer", he wrote in his diary, "that something must have upset Sir John's balance of mind. Some think that Lord K. has found him out, as he has gone out of his way to assert his position. However, the only thing that one ought to consider is how best to act so as to end the war."

About the same time General Huguet, the head of the French mission, told Haig that General Foch was anxious to see him "but was desirous not to cause displeasure to Sir John French, who apparently does not like Foch to see anyone of the British force except himself."

Later Foch had luncheon with Haig, who was fully alive to the importance of making acquaintance and sharing experiences with the outstanding personalities of the French Army. The diary gives his first impressions of the future leader of the allies:

General Foch (commanding the group of French armies in Northern France) with his chief of staff (Weygand) and A.D.C. came to lunch at twelve o'clock. After lunch he questioned me closely about my views on the attack at Neuve Chapelle. He had been told by General Joffre to "study the method of attack adopted by the British." Indeed, all French corps commanders had been directed to study what had been done. General Foch is the writer of *Les principes de la Guerre* and is regarded in the French Army as their most capable general. So it was a compliment that he should have come to ask me for information, and showed the French to be now in a very different attitude of mind to that assumed by them at the beginning of the campaign. Hitherto they have looked upon us rather as "amateurs" than as "professional" soldiers.

In talking of our future plans, I urged the necessity for the French to press the enemy about Haisnes so as to prevent him detaching troops to oppose our advance on the north side of the canal. Foch would say nothing more definite than that he would support me with five heavy batteries, and that his main attack would be made at a point farther south. He told me how during peace he and the French staff had studied about the possibilities of fighting in every part of France except Flanders! They never thought a French Army would ever have to fight there.

Foch was not the only one who had been impressed by the Battle of Neuve Chapelle. Lord Esher, who was in France at this time, told Haig that the officers of the French Army whom he had seen "were much impressed with our recent success at Neuve Chapelle. Until then they had said that our troops were all right on the defensive but could not attack. . . . Lord Esher also told me he had met an American during the winter who had just returned from Berlin, where he dined with the Kaiser. The latter said that the 'First Army Corps under Douglas Haig is the best in the world'. This was after our retreat from Belgium, the battle of the Aisne and the battle of Ypres. Esher said the Kaiser emphasized 'D.H. in command'. In my opinion, however, 'the command' greatly depended on the excellent staff which had worked together in peace and had been trained with the troops at Aldershot.

"Anyhow in my view the praise is a compliment to Aldershot methods, and is a valuable one because it is made by one who ought to be a judge for he has had much experience of good and bad army corps, both under his command as well as opposed to him."

It was on April twenty-second that the second Battle of Ypres began, when for the first time the Germans made use of poison gas with far greater effect than they had themselves anticipated or were prepared to follow up. The First Army, however, took no part in this battle beyond sending reinforcements and endeavouring to learn from it such lessons as might prove of assistance in the future.

In the ensuing months, however, Haig's army engaged in a series of severe if not decisive actions. The battle of

Aubers Ridge was a failure, as the Germans had learned from Neuve Chapelle to strengthen their trenches and defend them with machine guns. Also, Haig was hampered by a shortage of ammunition. The next battle, Festubert, lasting for two weeks, was a demonstration that with bombardments continuing day and night the enemy lines could be pierced. The Germans fell back to new defences. Haig was congratulated by the commander in chief and by Joffre, Foch and d'Urbal. He received a visit from Joffre. Shortly afterward Prime Minister Asquith came to headquarters and asked that Haig write to him whenever he could spare the time.

A few days later at a meeting with the commander in chief "Sir John stated that the prime minister had expressed himself as greatly pleased with his visit to the First Army and (for my own information) had drawn comparisons between the First and Second armies greatly to the disparagement of the latter. Sir John attributed this difference to the way in which Smith-Dorrien interfered with his brigadiers and others under him, so that no one knew exactly what was wanted. I said I thought I had an advantage in having had two divisions complete under my command for over two years at Aldershot. We had tried to arrive at a common 'doctrine', and my subordinate commanders realized the importance of discipline, and had maintained it."

But Haig's visitors were not confined to generals and prime ministers. On June eleventh "Ben Tillett, the leader of the dockers and strikers, came to see me. He seems to have been quite converted from his anarchist views, and has his heart now thoroughly impressed with the necessity of getting the labour class to help to end the war. With this in view, he has come out here to see some of his old docker friends who are now soldiers, and is then going to stump the country on his return to England. After going round a few units he came to lunch, he was accompanied by a French socialist, a M. Broule, a truly patriotic Frenchman. Tillett confessed to me how he had been mistaken about the British officer. At first his impressions were derived from the picture papers and society journals. He thought them 'fops and snobs'. He is astonished now to find that 'his friends' have unbounded confidence in their officers, and could not get on without them. His experiences in Germany before the war, where he attended a conference of socialists at Munich, were most interesting, and showed clearly how the German socialist is first of all a German soldier before everything else. Ben Tillett is a small active little man, a good speaker, and seems most determined about the cause he has now taken up. I think it is a very good thing that he has come and visited the troops at the Front. He expressed himself as most grateful for my help."

"I wrote to Mr Asquith as requested by him," Haig wrote in his diary. "I discussed nature of operations and need for *heavy* guns and ample ammunition.

"But even if ample guns and ample ammunition, etc., be provided, progress will be disappointing unless young capable commanders are brought up to the Front. Some of the present captains should be chosen to command battalions, majors brigades, etc."

It was about this time that the Cabinet, growing nervous in view of the stationary situation that seemed to have arisen in France, and of the failure to force the Dardanelles, asked Sir John French and Sir William Robertson to appear before them, and to indicate what they considered would be the best line of retreat. "Poltroons!" was Robertson's indignant comment in a letter to Haig, and he went on to emphasize the importance which he attached to keeping the British Army in touch with the French. The alternative view, which was held by Sir John French, was that the Channel ports were so vital to England's safety that they must at all costs be defended even if it necessitated separating our army from that of our allies. This had been from the beginning of the war the one most disputed point of strategy on the Western Front, and it was to remain so almost until the end. Haig's view was perfectly clear and definite now, as it was to prove in March, 1918.

It is obvious that the occupation of the Channel ports cannot decide the issue of the war, but without them our operations would be greatly hampered. On the other hand, if the enemy inflicts a decisive defeat on the French, the British could not fight on land without allies. In my opinion, therefore, the important thing is for the British Army to remain united with the French. When the German Army was much more efficient than it is now, it failed against the two allies united. If, however, the British were to separate and to take up a position in front of Calais and Boulogne, it would certainly mean defeat in detail, because the enemy could contain us with a comparatively small force, while he massed in great strength and defeated the French.

Robertson wishes to discuss the problem with me and will come to see me Tuesday. Apparently there is no "direction" of the war in London, but British strategy seems to be guided by the most persuasive talker, Winston, for instance! The cause of this is the obliteration of the general staff in London. It must be re-established and allowed to function.

On July ninth Haig left for six days' leave in England. He intended, as on the previous occasion, to spend the time quietly with his wife by the sea. Alan Fletcher, his aide-de-camp, had lent him a house at Westgate, where he spent five out of the six days. But when it was conveyed to him in the most tactful manner that the King would be pleased to see him, he felt that he could not again ignore a request of such a nature, and on July fourteenth he travelled to London, returning the same night. At his interview with His Majesty the war in all its phases was discussed, and the two found themselves in substantial agreement both as regards principles and personalities. Before leaving he received the G.C.B. from the King's hands, who said that nobody had more thoroughly earned it.

In the afternoon he visited Lord Kitchener at the War Office. The interview was extremely friendly. "We spoke about the nature of the operations in Flanders. K. seemed to me very ignorant of what is being done, and how trenches are attacked and how bombarded. He admitted that the nature of the modern lines of defence was quite new to him, and he said he 'felt quite at sea' on the subject. I respected him for being so honest. As regards artillery, he did not know the term 'counterbattery', or how some guns were told off to deal with hostile infantry and some with the hostile guns."

The battle of Loos, in the autumn of 1915, followed much urging by Joffre that the British should make a strong attack on the enemy.

On August seventeenth Haig had luncheon with French and discussed the forthcoming attack. According to the entry made the same day in his diary, he then insisted on the importance of his being provided with sufficient reserves to ensure the success of the operation. At the same interview French warned him "not to talk about the forthcoming operations to Lord Kitchener", who was arriving in France that day on a short visit; "If Lord K. were to know," said French, "he would tell the others in the Cabinet and then all London would know. And the Germans would also get to hear of the proposed attack."

That French should have lacked confidence in Kitchener's discretion is less surprising than that he should have thought it possible to conceal from the secretary of state for war the decision to deliver the most important Anglo-French offensive that had yet taken place. Kitchener was of course perfectly aware of all that was intended, and discussed the prospects with Haig when he visited the First Army two days later.

"After washing his hands, Lord K. came into my writing room upstairs saying he had been anxious to have a few minutes' talk with me. The Russians, he said, had been severely handled, and it was *doubtful how much longer their army could withstand the German blows.* Up to the present he had favoured a policy of active defence in France until such time as all our forces were ready to strike. The situation which had arisen in Russia had caused him to modify these views. He now felt that the allies must act vigorously in order to take some of the pressure off Russia if possible. He had heard, when with the French, that Sir J. French did not mean to co-operate to the utmost of his power when the French attacked in September. He (Lord K.) had noticed that the French were anxiously watching the British on their left! And he *'had decided that we must act with all our energy, and do our utmost to help the French, even though, by so doing, we suffered very heavy losses indeed'.*

"I replied that my army was all ready to attack. All we wanted was ammunition. He said we would get all he had."

After several postponements the date of the attack was fixed for September fifteenth, and a few days later it was further postponed until September twenty-fifth. The British were to use poison gas for the first time. The continual postponements, which were the fate of most offensives during the war, were highly undesirable, as, when once an attack had been decided upon, every day that it was postponed increased the chances of the enemy coming to hear of it. Haig wrote in his diary on this occasion, "This extra delay may well jeopardize the success of what I am undertaking, because at present we know that the enemy's troops have no proper protection against gas, only small respirators. They may hear of our getting up the gas cylinders and issue effective gas helmets. On the other hand it would be foolish for a portion of the allies to attack until the whole are ready for a combined effort."

On the twelfth Foch paid Haig a visit, the real object of which, in the latter's opinion, "was to find out whether we British really meant to fight or not". Haig endeavoured to convince him on that point and assured him that "Joffre's orders were the same to me as those of Marshal French". He also took this opportunity of impressing upon Foch the importance of having the reserves close up to the battle line and asked him to speak to French on the subject, for already he was feeling uneasiness owing to French's reluctance to put sufficient reserves at his disposal, and to place them where they would be readily available.

On the eighteenth there was a meeting at G.H.Q. to discuss the forthcoming offensive when Haig discussed this all-important question of reserves with the commander in chief. On the following day "written instructions at last received from G.H.Q. regarding the attack. The reserves are not to reach the area south of Lillers till twenty-fourth. This is too late! So I send Butler with a letter to see the C.G.S. on the subject, and repeat what I said at the commander in chief's conference yesterday."

Apart from the question of the reserves the main source of Haig's anxiety was connected with the decision to make use of poison gas. An army's first experiment in real warfare with a weapon that they have never employed before must always be attended by considerable doubt and uncertainty, which were increased upon this occasion by the fact that the weapon in question could only be made use of if a sufficiently strong wind were blowing from the right direction. Haig had suggested that the date of the attack should be made to some extent dependent upon weather conditions, and should take place either on the twenty-fourth, the twenty-fifth or the twenty-sixth, as it was probable that on one at least of the three days the wind would be favourable. But he had been overruled, and it was definitely decided that, whether gas could be used or not, the twenty-fifth was to be the day. The diary entry of that day follows:

September twenty-fifth, 1915. Battle of Loos. An anxious night wondering all the time what the wind would be in the morning. The greatest battle in the world's history begins today. Some eight hundred thousand French and British troops will actually attack today.

At 2 A.M. General Butler came to my bedroom and reported Mr Gold (meteorological expert) was waiting for a telegram from the War Office before making a forecast. Wind had fallen.

At 3 A.M. I saw Mr Gold. Wind in places had fallen to one mile per hour. He could not say anything definitely beyond that "the wind would probably be stronger just after sunrise (5.30) than later in the day". The Indian Corps required two and a half hours notice, as they had a mine to explode. I therefore fixed zero for 5.30 A.M., which would mean the main attack going in 6.30 A.M.

I went out at 5 A.M. Almost a calm. Alan Fletcher lit a cigarette and the smoke drifted in puffs toward the N.E. Staff officers of corps were ordered to stand by in case it were necessary to counterorder attack. At one time, owing to the calm, I feared the gas might simply hang about *our* trenches. However, at 5.15 A.M. I said, "Carry on." I went to the top of our wooden lookout tower. The wind came gently from S.W. and by 5.40 had increased slightly. The leaves of the poplar trees gently rustled. This seemed satisfactory. But what a risk I had run of gas blowing back upon our own dense masses of troops.

When he had given those orders, and with those two words "carry on" had shouldered the vast responsibility of launching for the first time in British history a gas attack on an extensive front with a faint and variable wind behind it, there was nothing left for Haig to do but to await, with such patience as he could command, the reports that would dribble in from the gas-masked infantry who were climbing out of their trenches in the grey dawn to follow the yellow clouds of poison that the breeze bore all too slowly toward the enemy.

The First Army at this time consisted of four Corps—the I, the III, the IV and the Indian Corps.

The first stages of the attack were remarkably successful. The Fourth Corps advancing at 6.30, forty minutes after the release of the gas, some of them dribbling a football in front of them, others inspired by the sound of the bagpipes, either found the enemy's trenches deserted when they reached them, or else had little difficulty in overcoming all opposition. When they reached the village of Loos the enemy were taken completely by surprise and either hid in the cellars or took to flight.

Only on the extreme left of the Fourth Corps' front were serious difficulties encountered. A capricious breeze blew some of their own gas back into the British trenches before the attack began and caused a large number of casualties. There was also some loss of direction, and the opposition put up by the enemy was far more obstinate here than anywhere else, with the result that the advance, which did eventually take place, was considerably delayed.

The First Corps, attacking simultaneously with the Fourth, were also unfortunate with their gas, and they also were less successful with their left wing, the Second Division, than elsewhere. Nevertheless, they accomplished a great deal, and in the centre especially their advance was extremely rapid despite the serious obstacles that opposed it.

We have seen how Haig had insisted upon the importance of having the reserves close up and easily available, and how he had wished that they should be put under his command. He was, in fact, in charge of the battle. It was about 7 A.M. when the first news reached him of the successful advance of his two corps. He immediately despatched a messenger to French "urging the necessity for having Haking's corps ready to advance at once in pursuit". At 8.45 an officer arrived from the commander in chief with his congratulations. "I sent him back at once to tell Sir John that the reserve brigades of the First and Fourth Corps had already reached the German trenches, and to beg him to place Haking's corps under my orders. *Reserves must be pushed on at once.*"

But still no action was taken to grant this urgent request, and about 11.30 French himself arrived at Haig's headquarters, and only then said that he would put two of Haking's three divisions under Haig's orders. The two that were selected were the Twenty-first and Twenty-fourth, which had only recently arrived in France and had had no experience of warfare. That which French retained under his own command was the Guards Division. It was not until 2 P.M. that Haig heard definitely from Haking and was able to give him orders. He then directed him to advance immediately "between Hulluch and Cité St Auguste and occupy the high ground between Pont à Vendin and Harnes, with the crossings over the canal to the east and south of that line".

Further delay unfortunately took place before these orders were transmitted from corps headquarters to the brigades concerned, with the result that after a long march, and without a meal, both the Twenty-first and the Twenty-fourth Divisions were overtaken by darkness before they reached the battlefield, and were unable to take any part in the fighting that day.

The results of the following day were less satisfactory. In the night the Germans, who had brought up their reinforcements, counterattacked in force and succeeded in reoccupying some of the positions they had lost. The performance of the Twenty-first and Twenty-fourth Divisions, coming under fire for the first time after a long night march and losing early in the day one or two of their senior officers, including a brigadier general, was disappointing. The earlier reports received at army headquarters on the previous day had emphasized the successes and minimized the casualties.

When French came to visit Haig on the morning of the twenty-seventh he was shown "how long it had taken for the reserves to come up, even with the greatest energy on the part of everyone concerned". It is not recorded that he made any comment. Haig himself was clear in his own mind that the lack of success was "solely on account of the initial mistake of the commander in chief in refusing to move up the reserve divisions close to the rear of the attacking troops before the commencement of the operations".

On the twenty-eighth he decided to press the attack no farther, but to consolidate the positions that had already been gained. It was arranged that the Twenty-first and Twenty-fourth Divisions should be withdrawn for further training. Haig felt that a great opportunity had been lost and that it was entirely due to French's refusal to follow the advice, which his own knowledge of military science ought to have supported. The positions in rear of the German front line which would have fallen easily before a determined attack a few days before were now strongly defended. "Unfortunately", he wrote, "the enemy has had time to construct defences at Pont à Vendin. It was quite undefended last Saturday and the enemy had no troops in his second line. It is thus certain, that even with *one* division in reserve and close up, as I had requested, we could have walked right through his second line! And all our present preparations would have been unnecessary. When the commander in chief remains blind to the lessons of war in this important matter (handling of reserves) we hardly deserve to win."

The bitterness with which he wrote is not surprising. "Sir John French at his interview with me today" (September twenty-eighth) ". . . seemed tired of the war, and said that in his opinion we ought to take the first opportunity of concluding peace, otherwise England would be ruined. I could not agree but said we cannot make peace till the German military power is beaten."

On the twenty-ninth he wrote to Kitchener:

Personal and Private

Hinges,
Wed., Sept. 29, 1915.

MY DEAR LORD KITCHENER,

You will doubtless recollect how earnestly I pressed you to ensure an adequate reserve being close in rear of my attacking divisions, and under my orders. It may interest you to know what happened. No reserve was placed under me. My attack, as has been reported, was a complete success. The enemy had no troops in his second line which some of my plucky fellows reached and entered without opposition. Prisoners state that the enemy was so hard put to it for troops to stem our advance that the officers' servants, fatigue men, etc. in Lens were pushed forward to hold their second line to the east of Loos and Hill 70.

The two reserve divisions (under commander in chief's orders) were directed to join me as soon as the success of the First Army was known at G.H.Q. They came on as quick as they could, poor fellows, but only crossed our old trench line with their heads at 6 P.M. We had captured Loos twelve hours previously, and reserves should have been at hand *then.* This, you will remember, I requested should be arranged by G.H.Q. and Robertson quite concurred in my views and wished to put the reserve divisions under me but was not allowed.

The final result is that the enemy has been allowed time in which to bring up troops and to strengthen his second line, and *probably* to construct a third line in the direction in which we are heading, viz. Pont à Vendin.

I have now been given some fresh divisions, and am busy planning an attack to break the enemy's second line. But the element of surprise has gone, and our task will be a difficult one.

I think it right that you should know how the lessons which have been learned in the war at such cost have been neglected. We *were* in a position to make this the turning point in the war, and I still hope we may do so, but naturally I feel annoyed at the lost opportunity.

We were all very pleased to receive your kind telegram, and I am,

Yours very truly,

D. HAIG.

The Battle of Loos was over by the end of the month and the result of it was tantalizingly inconclusive. On the one hand it could be pointed out that after the sacrifice of more than forty thousand British casualties the allies were no nearer victory than they had been before. On the other hand it could be argued that over eight thousand yards of the German front line had been captured, that British infantry had in some places advanced to a distance of two miles, and that strong points which had been fortified at leisure with all the skill and ingenuity of the most accomplished German engineers had fallen before them. This surely proved that the front was not impregnable and that given good luck (a better wind, for instance, for the gas), and good management (having the reserves, for instance, in the right place at the right time), it would be possible to smash the line and secure a crushing and decisive victory.

It has been seen, and it has been regretted, that since the beginning of the war relations between French and Haig had not been based upon that spirit of complete mutual confidence which should exist between commander in chief and subordinate, and which had existed between them in the South African War with such happy and glorious results. The question of the reserves at Loos brought matters to a head. It was a matter of common knowledge. The whole army in France was discussing it and the discussion spread to the civilians at home.

On October ninth Lord Haldane arrived for luncheon and afterward asked Haig to give him his views on the question of the reserves. "He said that feelings were so strong on the subject in England that he had come to France to help in arriving at the truth. I gave him all the facts. The main criticism to my mind is that the reserves were not at hand when wanted. The causes for this seem to me to be:

(1) Neither the commander in chief nor his staff fully realized at the beginning (in spite of my letters and remarks) the necessity for reserves being close up before the action began.

(2) The two divisions were billeted in depth a long distance from where they would be wanted, and no attempt was made to concentrate them before the battle began.

(3) When the course of the fight showed that reserves were wanted at once to exploit the victory, the two divisions were hurried forward without full consideration for their food etc., with the result that the troops arrived worn out at the point of attack and unfit for battle.

(4) But the Twenty-first and Twenty-fourth Divisions, having only recently arrived in France, with staffs and commanders inexperienced in war, should not have been employed for this work. It was courting disaster to employ them at once in fighting of this nature. There were other divisions available, as shown by the fact that they arrived three days later upon the battlefield, namely the Twenty-eighth Division, the Twelfth Division and the Guards Division.

"I also felt it my duty to tell Lord Haldane that the arrangements for the supreme command during the battle were not satisfactory. Sir John French was at Philomel (near Lillers) twenty-five miles nearly from his C.G.S. who was at St Omer with G.H.Q. Many of us felt that if these conditions continued, it would be difficult ever to win.

Lord Haldane said he was very glad to have had this talk with me, and seemed much impressed with the serious opinion which I had expressed to him."

A week later Haig had an important interview with Robertson, who had recently returned from London, where he had been requested in the highest quarters to give his frank opinion with regard to the competence of the commander in chief. Both officers were in difficult positions. The problem of divided and opposing loyalties must puzzle the brain of the most subtle of moralists. Robertson was French's chief of staff, the post which Haig had filled in South Africa, and both were bound to him by all the obligations of faithful duty which a soldier feels for his superior officer. But they were something more than mere subordinates. They occupied high positions of great responsibility, and when in an hour of danger the government of their country demanded their advice as military experts on a military matter—the competence of an officer—they would surely have been guilty of a grave dereliction of duty had they allowed any considerations to prevent them from speaking the truth.

Robertson had hesitated to make a definite pronouncement when he was in London as he wished first to find out whether his opinion was shared by Haig. He had therefore come to consult him.

"I told him at once that up to date I had been most loyal to French and did my best to stop all criticism of him or his methods. Now at last, in view of what had happened in the recent battle over the reserves, and in view of the seriousness of the general military situation, I had come to the conclusion that it was not fair to the Empire to retain French in command on this, the main battle front. Moreover, none of my officers commanding corps had a high opinion of Sir John's military ability or military views; *in fact, they had no confidence in him.* Robertson quite agreed, and left me saying he knew how to act. . . . He also told me that the members of the Cabinet, who up to the present had been opposed to removing French, had come round to the other opinion."

Meanwhile French sent home his own account of the Battle of Loos and on November the second his despatch appeared in the *Times*. This document contained two statements to which Haig felt it his duty to take exception. Writing of September the twenty-fifth the field marshal stated, "At 9.30 A.M. I placed the Twenty-first and Twenty-fourth divisions at the disposal of the G.O.C. First Army who at once ordered the G.O.C. Eleventh Corps to move them up in support of the attacking troops." And further on it was stated that "at 6 P.M. the Guards Division arrived at Noeux-les-Mines, and on the morning of the twenty-sixth I placed them at the disposal of the G.O.C. First Army".

Haig immediately wrote to G.H.Q. pointing out that neither statement was correct. He did not get in touch with the commander of the Twenty-first and Twenty-fourth divisions until 2.30 P.M. on the twenty-fifth, and he did not receive the message informing him that the Guards Division was under his command until 4.15 P.M. on the following day. Copies of telegrams and orders had of course been kept, which Haig enclosed with his message to G.H.Q. and which substantiated his statement beyond the possibility of argument. He therefore requested that these mistakes in the despatch might be corrected.

The reply from G.H.Q. was to the effect that "the statements in question were substantially correct and called for no amendment". Haig felt obliged to return to the charge, pointing out that the despatch conveyed the impression "that at 9.30 A.M. on the twenty-fifth of September I was able to use the Twenty-first and Twenty-fourth divisions in support of the attacking troops, and similarly that I could make use of the Guards Division on the *morning* of the twenty-sixth—this was not the case and I beg to request that this fact may be placed on record."

Here the correspondence seems to end. More important matters connected with the future rather than the past were engrossing the attention of those concerned in it. Kitchener was visiting the Near East in order to report on the position in the Dardanelles and at Salonica. Many believed and some hoped that he would not return to the War Office. Haig had a soldier's distaste for politics and had struggled, hitherto successfully, against becoming involved in them. But as his position increased in importance and his prestige developed, his opinion was naturally sought by those who were anxious for guidance and he could not withhold it. His old friend, Lord Esher, who exercised more influence behind the scenes than anyone, visited him in November and discussed the situation. Haig felt strongly the lack of an organized direction of war policy. The Imperial General Staff which Haldane and he had built up had practically ceased to function. He believed that new life could be put into it by transferring Robertson from France to London. He knew that all the eloquence of all the politicians in England could not shift Robertson one inch. If Kitchener had to go, which now seemed probable, let him be made viceroy of India. Haig was strongly opposed to the proposal to make Kitchener commander in chief in the Near East, "because wherever he is, by his masterful action he will give that sphere of the operations an undue prominence in the strategical picture". Lord Esher undertook to support Haig's views in London.

He no doubt did so with considerable effect, for when Haig himself went on leave a few days later he found that Robertson's appointment had been practically settled. He discussed the matter with the prime minister with whom he had luncheon on November the twenty-third. "The prime minister", he wrote in his diary, "agreed and added that

General Robertson had been of great assistance to him. The matters we discussed were of such vital interest to the Empire that I never alluded to my own affairs and the differences which I had had with Sir John French over the despatch he published the second of November."

The incident had now no longer any save historical interest, for, during Kitchener's absence in the East, Mr Asquith himself had taken charge of the War Office, and while there he had come to an important decision. He had been a good friend to French so long as he felt that he could trust him, but with characteristic integrity the moment his commander in chief lost his confidence he decided to replace him. "Asquith", according to his biographers, "seldom laid stress on his own part in any transaction, but he repeated more than once that the substitution of Haig for French was entirely his own act, uninfluenced by any outside pressure."

It was Robertson who first told Haig of the decision to remove French on November the twenty-fifth. Haig left the same day for Wales to visit his family who were staying with Lady Haig's sister, Miss Vivian, near Bangor. When he returned he had several interviews with Kitchener at the War Office, and at his request drew up a lengthy memorandum on the defence of Egypt. In all these conversations it was assumed that he was to become commander in chief, but he returned to France on December the fourth without any official notification of his appointment. Before he left, Kitchener impressed upon him the importance of keeping on good terms with the French, and said that Joffre should be looked on as the commander in chief in France.

The first definite information that reached him with regard to his promotion came, curiously enough, from his old friend Mr Leopold de Rothschild, who was a regular correspondent. On December the seventh he wrote from London that "all had been satisfactorily arranged".

The Prime Minister wrote on the following day:

Secret. Dec. 8, 1915.

MY DEAR SIR DOUGLAS,

Sir J. French has placed in my hands his resignation of the office of commander in chief of the forces in France.

Subject to the King's approval I have the pleasure of proposing to you that you should be his successor.

I am satisfied that this is the best choice that could be made in the interest of the army and the country.

I ought to add, in the strictest confidence, that it is probable that Sir W. Robertson may be summoned home to take up a position here, and that the difficult question may therefore have to be faced of replacing him as chief of the staff in France.

I should be glad to know what would be your views in that event.

For the moment all these changes ought to be kept private.

Believe me,
Yours very sincerely,
(Sd.) H. H. ASQUITH.

"I wrote at once accepting the appointment," is Haig's only comment. Several days passed before he received any official notification, but he concluded from the telegrams of congratulation that reached him on December the sixteenth that an announcement had been made, and the following morning he read it in a day-old newspaper.

He saw French once only before taking over the command on December the nineteenth. The interview was cold and formal, nothing was mentioned save matters of military routine. So they parted.

CHAPTER VII

Commander in Chief

On Sunday, December 19, 1915, Haig wrote in his diary—"Fine, clear, frosty morning. At twelve noon I assumed the chief command of the British Expeditionary Force in France and Flanders." He had under his command three armies, which were shortly to be increased to five, with four corps in each. He had always believed in victory, but he had never been a lighthearted optimist, nor dismissed the possibility of defeat. He knew that upon his conduct now depended the future of the Empire that he had served all his life. And in this period of supreme trial, which was to prove longer than all expectation, he was supported from first to last by his deep religious belief.

The faith in which he had been brought up, and which had hitherto played no great part in a full and fortunate existence, now entered into the very fibre of his being and remained with him to the end. The twentieth century is generally considered an age of agnosticism, nor are soldiers usually accounted the most religious of men, yet piety appears to have been an outstanding characteristic of the most successful commanders on the Western Front. A little later, when the French were considering the appointment of a new commander in chief, Lord Bertie wrote to Haig from Paris, "Foch is objected to because he has a Jesuit brother, Pétain because he was brought up by the Dominicans, and Castelnau still more because he goes to Mass."

Though naturally reticent, Haig did not hesitate, on occasion, either to write or to speak of these solemn matters. He had visited General Gough while the fighting round Loos was still in progress, and had found him "rather downhearted for him", owing to the failure of a certain division to carry out his orders. "I reminded Gough", he writes, "that we shall win 'Not by might, nor by power, but by *my spirit,* saith the Lord of hosts'."

Henceforward Haig rarely missed attendance at divine service on Sunday, and seldom failed to note in his diary the text of the sermon, of which he frequently wrote down a brief account.

There are possibly no two races that experience greater difficulty in understanding one another than the English and the French. No few miles of salt water in the world have exercised so estranging an influence as the Straits of Dover. There is no natural antipathy between the races, nor did all the centuries of warfare ever breed a spirit of hatred; there is only a complete failure of mutual comprehension. They approach every problem from a different standpoint, and if they arrive at the same conclusion, they reach it by different roads. And perhaps the key to the enigma lies in the fact that the one quality they have in common is a deep-seated arrogance, which is too confident to breed boasting, but which at the bottom of the hearts of the inhabitants of both these countries assures them that they are superior to any other people on the earth. Hence they will make no effort to understand foreigners from whom they can have nothing to learn, and the Englishman can never be persuaded that there is not something slightly comic about a Frenchman, and the Frenchman remains convinced that the average Englishman is a fool.

In the military sphere, these difficulties, far from being

diminished, are increased. The British officer is certainly not broader-minded than his fellow countrymen, and so strong are the traditions of the service that he does experience a real difficulty in believing that a pot-bellied little individual wearing, perhaps, pince-nez, obviously caring nothing for the cut of his uniform, indifferent to athletics and uninterested in sport, can be a fine soldier and a leader of men. Equally to the French the importance that the English attach to smartness of appearance, to proficiency in horsemanship and even in games, to precision of drill, to scrupulous cleanliness of uniform and equipment seem strange idiosyncrasies which have little or nothing to do with military efficiency.

Haig was a man of his race and of his class. He had spent brief sojourns in France and had acquired some fluency in the French language, but he did not easily make friends, even among his own compatriots, and he never succeeded, as Henry Wilson did, in even approaching intimate relations with a Frenchman. Had his character been cast in a more cosmopolitan mould, had he been more hail-fellow-well-met with all and sundry, many difficulties which arose might have been avoided; but in that case he would not have been Douglas Haig, and many difficulties which were avoided might have arisen.

As has been seen, he had appreciated long before the war the difficulties that were to be expected in dealing with an ally, and that would be increased if the war were being carried on in that ally's territory. The fact that the ally, owing to his superior numbers, was the senior partner in the alliance did not render the position any easier. Haig's instructions, which he received soon after taking over the supreme command, differed slightly from those of his predecessor in this respect. French had been told "to coincide most sympathetically with the plans and wishes of our ally". Haig was informed that "the closest co-operation between the French and British as a united army must be the governing policy". French had been assured that "You will in no case come in any sense under the orders of any allied general"—but in Haig's instructions the assurance had been qualified: "You will in no case come under the orders of any allied general further than the necessary co-operation with our allies above referred to."

Haig's first interview with Joffre, after assuming the command, took place at Chantilly on December the twenty-third, when they had an informal discussion of the situation. "General Joffre", he wrote, "was quite hopeful, said his armies would have unlimited ammunition in the spring, and he expected to drive the enemy back by April. I had intended to spend only half an hour, because he lunched at 11 A.M. I found it was 11.30 when I rose to go. The old man was evidently very much pleased with my visit, and came and saw me into my car at the entrance to the garden. He shook me by the hand most warmly twice, and held it so long that I thought I was never to be allowed to go. Altogether it was a very satisfactory interview."

In the following week, on the twenty-ninth, a more important meeting took place at Chantilly. The president of the Republic was there together with Monsieur Briand, the prime minister and general Galliéni, the minister for war, "the latter in plain clothes, I suppose to match the civilian ministers, and looking like an old rag-and-bone man, gaunt and thin."

The meeting went off well. The military leaders were in complete accord and reported themselves satisfied with the situation of their armies. One of the French generals complained of the inefficacy of the French gas masks, and Haig offered to supply them with ten thousand English masks a day while they were experimenting with a new model. The discussion was followed by a most cordial luncheon. Haig found Briand "a most charming man and most alert. He said that if the present good feeling had existed between us from the commencement the situation would now be very different. But it was too late.

"Time went on and, while I was talking to some of the generals, I noticed a little discussion going on amongst the ministers in a corner, and suddenly M. Poincaré advanced to me in the most charming way and said that he had much pleasure in promoting me in the Legion of Honour to the grade of 'Grand Cordon', and that from henceforth I must wear my 'plaque' on the *left* side.

"Then the ministers departed. The soldiers then had a little discussion with General Joffre. I found General de Langle de Carey an exceptionally gentlemanly man, and a fine soldier. He certainly has 'la flamme'. Foch is a 'méridional' and a great talker. He was much chaffed about his book, *Principes de la Guerre*."

General Huguet, who had hitherto been head of the French mission at British G.H.Q., was replaced at the end of the year by Colonel des Vallières who took over his new position on January the first. Haig sent for him the same morning. "I told him that when I am at my headquarters I see all my head staff officers at 9.30 A.M. daily, and I hoped he would attend also. He was much pleased. I am quite impressed with him. So quiet and silent for a Frenchman—and such a retiring gentlemanly man. Yet he has seen much and read much. He was professor of infantry tactics at the French staff college before the war, and recently commanded an infantry brigade in the attack in September in Champagne.

"I showed him the instructions which I had received from the secretary of state for war containing the orders of the government to me. I pointed out that I am *not under* General Joffre's orders, but that would make no difference, as my intention was to do my utmost to carry out General Joffre's wishes on strategical matters, as if they were orders! I explained my views as to the tactics which should be adopted in the future, with a view to defeating the enemy. He agreed, and seemed much pleased with my being so frank and straightforward in my dealings with him."

Haig felt justified in reporting to Kitchener, to whom he wrote the same day, wishing him a happy New Year, that "As directed by you, I have done my best to start on friendly terms with the French. I think I have made a good beginning."

Nor was it only to the secretary of state for war that he wrote so cheerfully of his first experience of co-operation with the French. Referring to the interview at Chantilly, he wrote to Mr Leopold de Rothschild, "I thought that the meeting was good for the generals as well as for the government. Generals after a certain time of life, especially French, are apt to be narrow-minded and disinclined to take advantage of modern scientific discoveries. The civilian minister can do good by pressing the possibility of some modern discovery. I found all at Chantilly most friendly, and I feel sure that our relations with the French G.H.Q. will run quite smoothly."

This quotation from a confidential letter to an old friend displays a breadth of mind which many ignorant writers have failed to find in Haig's mental equipment. It is doubtful whether anything analogous could be discovered in the private correspondence of contemporary politicians, or whether they ever appreciated that they had something to learn from soldiers as this soldier appreciated that he had something to learn from them.

For the other great problem, which presented itself to the commander in chief and which had not existed for the army commander, was connected with the maintenance of friendly and confidential relations between himself and the representatives of the civil power. Here again no immediate difficulties were to be anticipated. Despite his natural suspicion of politicians, Haig had already learned to respect Mr Asquith—a sentiment which was to be increased by further knowledge. At the War Office he had two soldiers to deal with, and under a new arrangement, which coincided with Robertson's promotion, the importance of the position of secretary of state had been diminished in favour of that of the C.I.G.S. In that office Robertson was to prove an invaluable link between the commander in chief and the Cabinet.

It would be difficult to exaggerate the importance of the position that Robertson filled, and it is typical of the spirit of paradox that pervades English public life, that such a man should have been called upon to fill it. Here, if ever, there seemed to be an opportunity for the born diplomatist, for the man who had seen something both of military affairs and of the interior of politics, who had mixed in both worlds and could interpret one to the other, and who from long experience had grown tolerant of stupidity and quick to interpret misunderstandings. The man who was selected for this office was one who had risen from the ranks and who knew nothing save what the British Army had been able to teach him. The success with which Sir Willaim Robertson performed this high function is a proof of his remarkable qualities. Clarity of vision and honesty of purpose made up for the lack of worldly knowledge and of diplomatic training. It was not the men but the system that was at fault.

And the defects of the system began early to manifest themselves. The British Constitution, which had been developed during centuries of isolation from world conflict, was admirably adapted for periods of peace, but woefully deficient for warfare on a vast scale. From the beginning until the end of the war the difficulty of the prime minister was that he had to choose between a slow, simple and costly strategy, bluntly stated by laconic soldiers, and half a dozen different brilliant schemes of swift and devastating effect urged upon him with burning eloquence and absolute sincerity by advocates who possessed every quality except prolonged military training and a lifetime spent in the study of strategic problems.

Robertson soon realized the difficulties of his position. "There is dreadful need of superior control of the war," he wrote to Haig; "I am doing all right on the war committee, but it is difficult to keep one's temper. At the last meeting Balfour weighed in with a proposal that as the Western Front is so strong we should transfer all possible troops to co-operate with Russia on the Eastern Front! Words failed me, and I lost my temper."

Soldiers and politicians had the same objective. All wanted equally to win the war. But their training had been so different, their minds worked along such different grooves that the language they spoke was hardly the same, and the difficulty that they found in understanding one another was comparable only to the difficulty experienced by men of different races. It is illustrated by the incident just recounted. To Balfour's fine intellect and broad intelligence there could appear no harm in throwing airily onto the table a suggestion which seemed to merit a moment's consideration. If it had been torn in pieces he would not have raised an eyebrow in objection, and would have smilingly agreed that there was nothing in it. But Robertson took no intellectual pleasure in the discussion of abstract propositions. His mind was direct, his views were settled and his time was fully occupied. To him the discussion in Cabinet of a futile proposition seemed as wicked as it would to a clergyman to raise a debate on the possibility of immortality in Convocation, or to a city magnate if a director at a board meeting were to question the desirability of accumulating wealth.

Haig experienced the same difficulty as Robertson, but the entries in his diary prove beyond question that whenever he came face to face with one of the black-coated, suspected tribe of politicians, he took the man on his merits and allowed no previous prejudice to influence his view.

It was in this month, January, 1916, that Haig first made the acquaintance of Lloyd George, whom he had of course frequently met already. The inability of these two men to understand one another or to work harmoniously together is a melancholy fact which has to be recorded. That it was not due to any narrow prejudice on Haig's part against either politicians or men who were outside the public school tradition is proved by the entry in his diary after the first evening spent with Lloyd George and Bonar Law, who arrived at his headquarters together. "Mr Bonar Law strikes me as being a straightforward, honourable man. . . . Lloyd George seems to be astute and cunning with much energy and push; but I should think shifty and unreliable. He was most anxious to be agreeable and pleasant, and was quite delighted at my having arranged for his two sons to stay and see him. They seem quite nice boys."

Lloyd George's first impression of Haig, on the other hand, was favourable. He informed Lord Riddell after his visit to the new G.H.Q. that "things are much more businesslike than in French's time. There is a new spirit. Haig seems very keen on his job and has a fine staff."

He also wrote a letter of thanks. "I want to thank you so much for the great courtesy which you showed to me during the interesting visit which I paid to your headquarters. I was specially touched by the kindness shown to my two boys.

"The visit, if you will permit me to say so, left on my mind a great impression of things being *gripped* in that sphere of operations; and whether we win through or whether we fail, I have a feeling that everything which the assiduity, the care, and the trained thought of a great soldier can accomplish, is being done."

The terms of the letter breathe something more than mere civility, and it is equally to be regretted that Lloyd George's first opinion of Haig should have altered and that Haig's first opinion of Lloyd George should have remained.

Joffre's first request to Haig was that he should relieve a portion of the French Tenth Army by extending the right of the British First Army, which Haig readily consented to do.

The allies' plan of campaign was to stage a simultaneous offensive on all fronts in the summer. Joffre was anxious that in preparation for this, as it was hoped, decisive operation the British Army should "wear down" the German resistance by a series of local, but powerful, attacks. Haig was ready to play his part in the general offensive, but feared that the so called "wearing-down" operations (*batailles d'usure*) might do more harm than good. It would be impossible to explain to the world what their real purpose was, and failing such explanation it would appear that they had accomplished nothing, and the battles that took place would be reckoned as failures, if not as defeats.

He was also doubtful as to the wisdom of Joffre's selection of the spot where the main blow should be delivered. Joffre had decided that this should be astride the river Somme, that is to say, about the centre of the German line. Haig would have preferred to attack near the seacoast, that is to say, on the German right, in the hope of turning the flank of the enemy.

As usual, however, there existed governing circumstances which prevented the British commander in chief from exercising a free choice. In the first place there was his obligation to co-operate so far as possible with the wishes of the French. In the second place it was generally stated at this time, and it was not denied by the French, that their man power was almost exhausted and that they would be able to take part in only one more offensive on a grand scale. In the third place there was the already threatening collapse of Russia. Daily the allies dreaded to learn that the Germans were transferring large bodies of troops to the east with a view to destroying one of their three greatest adversaries and forcing her to a separate peace. Should this intelligence at any moment reach them, the allies had to be prepared to strike at once.

On January 19, 1916, Joffre visited Haig. "He was most open, told me of the *shortage of men* in France and of the highly unsatisfactory state of munitions. I got the impression that Joffre felt that the French Army could not do much more hard fighting."

The interview was extremely friendly and was followed by the investiture of Haig and other generals with the Legion of Honour.

Then we went to Château Philomel (near Lillers) where the Second Brigade with a detachment of guns and R.E. was drawn up. General Joffre, after inspecting the troops, presented decorations. I received the "Grand Cordon" and Sir H. Rawlinson and H. Wilson "Grand Officier" of the Legion of Honour, also ten N.C.Os and men the "Croix de Guerre." The general shouted out "au nom du président de la République", etc., etc., and then placed the ribbon of the Order round my neck, fixed the plaque to my left breast, and then, before I quite realized what was going to happen, kissed me on both cheeks! I could hardly refrain from laughing. Then Rawlinson's turn came, but he only got the plaque as a grand officier, and it was put on his right side. He was duly kissed, and the long Henry Wilson had to bend down for a little fat "generalissimo" to perform this part of the ceremony! There were numerous cameras directed on them, so I expect an interesting picture will shortly appear in the picture papers. General Joffre congratulated me, and said what a great honour he felt it was to have been commissioned to give me the "Grand Cordon".

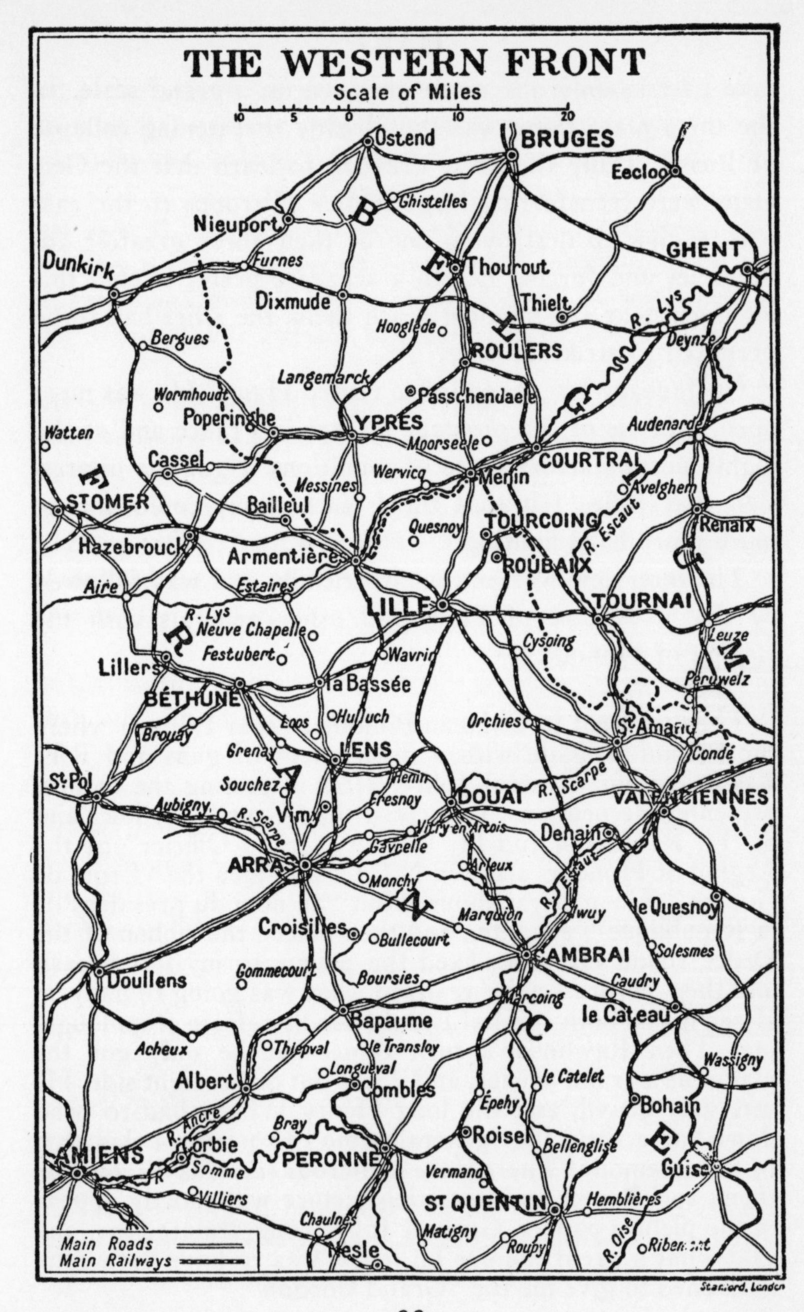
THE WESTERN FRONT
Scale of Miles
10 5 0 10 20
Ostend
BRUGES
Eecloo
Ghistelles
Nieuport
Dunkirk
Furnes
Thourout
GHENT
Dixmude
Thielt
R. Lys
Hooglede
Deynze
Bergues
ROULERS
Langemarck
Passchendaele
Wormhoudt
Poperinghe
YPRES
Watten
Audenarde
Moorseele
Cassel
COURTRAI
Wervicq
Menin
Messines
Avelghem
STOMER
Bailleul
TOURCOING
R. Escaut
Renaix
Quesnoy
Hazebrouck
Armentières
ROUBAIX
Aire
Estaires
LILLE
TOURNAI
R. Lys
Neuve Chapelle
Leuze
Cysoing
Festubert
Wavrin
Lillers
Peruwelz
la Bassée
BÉTHUNE
Loos
Hulluch
Orchies
Bruay
St Amand
Grenay
LENS
Condé
St Pol
Souchez
Henin
R. Scarpe
Aubigny
Fresnoy
DOUAI
VALENCIENNES
R. Scarpe
Vimy
Vitry en Artois
Denain
Gavrelle
ARRAS
Arleux
R. Escaut
Monchy
Marquion
Iwuy
le Quesnoy
Croisilles
Bullecourt
CAMBRAI
Solesmes
Gommecourt
Doullens
Boursies
Caudry
Marcoing
le Cateau
Bapaume
Acheux
Thiepval
le Transloy
Wassigny
Longueval
le Catelet
Albert
Combles
Epehy
Bohain
R. Ancre
Bray
Roisel
Corbie
AMIENS
PERONNE
Bellenglise
Somme
Guise
Vermand
Villiers
ST QUENTIN
Hemblières
Chaulnes
Matigny
Roupy
R. Oise
Nesle
Main Roads
Main Railways
B E L G I U M
F R A N C E
Stanford, London

On February the twenty-first came the concentrated endeavour of German military thought, German technical ingenuity, German courage, devotion, discipline and efficiency against that section of the French front which will be for ever memorable under the name of Verdun. It was the second great effort of Germany to win the war. It was the supreme test of French heroism and French endurance, a test from which France emerged scarred and battered, but triumphant.

As in March, 1918, when the great offensive was directed against the English, the French hesitated to come to their assistance, believing that the first attack might be a feint, and that a more serious advance was meditated elsewhere, so now British Headquarters at first suspected that another and a more formidable attack might be intended on their own front. But once Haig was convinced of the seriousness of the situation he was not slow to act.

Less than a fortnight before at Chantilly, when Joffre had asked him whether he accepted, *in principle,* the proposal that the British should relieve the Tenth Army, he had replied in the affirmative. Joffre had then asked him how soon he could carry it out, to which Haig had replied "next winter". The old man laughed, and Haig went on to demonstrate how the relief could not be carried out sooner. But now all was changed. In face of the grim realities of warfare what had seemed impossible becomes routine, and the unthinkable turns into a matter of fact.

There were delays, there were hesitations, there were uncertainties, but on February the twenty-seventh Haig was able to write in his diary "I telephoned to General Joffre that I had arranged to relieve all his tenth army and that I would come to Chantilly tomorrow to shake him by the hand, and to place myself and troops at his disposition."

It was on the first of March that the Fourth Army came officially into existence, and Sir Henry Rawlinson was ap-

THE COMMANDER IN CHIEF, TAKEN IN FRANCE BY 2ND LIEUT. ERNEST BROOKS

pointed to command it. At the beginning of the war Haig had not felt complete confidence in Rawlinson, who was an intimate friend of Henry Wilson and shared some of his characteristics. He was a brilliant and ready talker, full of ambition and suspected to be not incapable of intrigue. These were all qualities calculated to arouse Haig's distrust, but the more he saw of Rawlinson in the course of the war, the more rapidly did that distrust diminish until it came to be replaced by complete confidence. It is no small tribute to Haig's character and personality that of all those who served under him as army commanders during three years, there was not one with whom he ever quarreled or upon whom he ever ceased to rely. The confidence, as all true confidence must be, was mutual. A year before, when Rawlinson had incurred Sir John French's displeasure, Haig had stood up for him, and Rawlinson commenting on the incident in his diary had written, "It was very good of him and I am certain that I have a staunch ally in his strong character and personality. . . . I feel quite sure that I shall get justice at D.H's hands."

In the early days of March the relief of the French Tenth Army was completed, the British Third Army extending their left northward to join hands with the right of the First Army which extended to the south. The new Fourth Army came in on the right of the Third Army and the section of the front held by British troops was now continuous from the banks of the Yser to those of the Somme.

During the four months that followed the launching of the great German attack on Verdun it was the duty of the commander in chief of the British Army to watch carefully the progress of that terrific struggle, to prepare to throw the whole weight of his four armies into the battle when the right moment should arrive, and to keep ever present to his mind the dangerous possibility that he might be compelled by the desperate plight of his ally to take the offensive before his preparations were complete.

Month after month the British and French prepared for the Somme, that longest of battles (July 1 to November 18, 1916), which, though it did not end the war, was to save Verdun and discredit the Germans' ideas of their invincibility. The plans that were made and abandoned, the conferences and controversies, the interference of politicians—all the changing currents in and behind the front lines during that spring and early summer make an almost interminable military history. It is possible here to touch only the high points of the record.

On April the first general headquarters were transferred to Château Beaurepaire, a commodious and comfortable house two and a half miles southeast of Montreuil, which was to remain the home of Haig and his immediate staff for the rest of the war.

On the afternoon of April the seventh Joffre arrived to discuss plans. "Before tea," wrote Haig in his diary, "I discussed alone with him the proposed operations. There were, I thought, three main points to settle:

"The objective;

"The dividing line between our two forces;

"The timing of our attacks.

"I explained my views but Joffre did not seem capable of seeing beyond the left of the French Army (which the French propose should be at Maricourt), or indeed of realizing the effect of the shape of the ground on the operations proposed. He said that I must attack northward to take Montauban Ridge, while the French troops attacked eastward from Maricourt. I at once pointed to the heights away to the northeast of Maricourt, and showed that his proposed movement was impossible until the aforesaid heights were either in our possession or closely attacked from the west.

"The old man saw, I think, that he was talking about details which he did not really understand, whereas I had been studying this particular problem since last January, and both knew the map and had reconnoitred the ground. The conclusion I arrived at was that Joffre was talking about a tactical operation which he did not understand, and that it was a waste of my time to continue with him. So I took him off to tea. I gather that he signs everything which is put in front of him now and is really past his work, if, indeed, he ever knew anything practical about tactics as distinct from strategy. Joffre was an engineer."

The following week Haig crossed to England in order to acquaint the government with his intentions and obtain authority to proceed with them. In his first interview with Lord Kitchener and Sir William Robertson he "asked them definitely, did H.M. Government approve of my combining with the French in a general offensive during the summer? They both agreed that all the Cabinet had come to the conclusion that the war could only be ended by fighting, and several were most anxious for a definite victory over German arms, viz., the secretary for foreign affairs (Grey) and the chancellor of the exchequer (McKenna)."

On the following day he attended a meeting of a Cabinet committee where the question of conscription, which was then violently agitating the political atmosphere and threatening the dissolution of the government, was under discussion. From a military point of view the problem seemed so simple and the solution so obvious that Haig, who could not appreciate the parliamentary difficulties, found it hard to understand why there should be any hesitation in arriving at a decision. "We adjourned", he wrote, "at 1.40, no definite decision having been come to. I felt sad that the inner Cabinet of this great country should be so wanting in decision and public spirit."

During this same visit he informed the authorities of his

desire to make use of the recently invented tanks during the forthcoming battle.

Of Clemenceau, who came to see Haig, the diary says:

"He is evidently well informed of what is going on in most of the theatres of war. His object in coming to see me was to get me to exercise a restraining hand on General Joffre, and prevent any offensive on a large scale from being made until all is ready, and we are at our maximum strength. We cannot expect that Russia will be able to do much toward the defeat of Germany, so we must rely on ourselves (British and French).... He is seventy-five years old, he told me, but is wonderfully active, and spent two hours in the front trenches today. I found him most interesting, and we parted quite friends, for as the proverb says, 'Friends are discovered, not made.' I suggested that he should see Joffre. But he said the latter would not see him, as he (C) had criticized him (J) in the press."

The opening days of the month of June were marked by the Battle of Jutland and the death of Lord Kitchener. Intelligence of the latter event was conveyed to Haig on his way to England. "On reaching Dover, Military Landing Officer showed me telegram from police stating it was reported that Lord Kitchener on H.M.S. Hampshire had been drowned. Ship struck a mine and sank. Sea very rough."

The North Sea had completed the task which Lord Kitchener's colleagues had been afraid to undertake. Kitchener had been effectually got rid of, and Asquith was about to take the fateful decision of appointing Lloyd George to take his place.

Briand came to visit British G.H.Q. "Monsieur Briand and I", writes Haig, "took a little walk before dinner. He is certainly a very charming but a cunning, quick-minded man. He is full of compliments for the British Army and of confidence in me. He is well pleased with the result of the secret session of the Chambre, and says he will have no more real trouble for some time to come. We had a very cheery dinner. Briand thoroughly French and full of jokes and stories."

On the following day Briand made a tour of inspection and on his return expressed his delight and surprise at all he had seen. "He told me he had no idea of the tremendous organization of the British Army. I told him it was not for me to publish our doings in the newspapers either in France or in England."

After several postponements the end of June found everything in readiness for the attack which was to launch the battle of the Somme. On the night of the thirtieth Haig concludes his diary for the month with these words, "The weather report is favourable for tomorrow. With God's help, I feel hopeful. The men are in splendid spirits, several have said that they have never before been so instructed and informed of the nature of the operations before them. The wire has never been so well cut, nor the artillery preparation so thorough. I have seen personally all the corps commanders and one and all are full of confidence."

CHAPTER VIII

The Battle of the Somme

FROM BRITISH GUNS alone over 1,600,000 shells were hurled into the German lines in the seven days' bombardment preceding the infantry attack on July 1, 1916. The French bombardment had been equally heavy. What the enemy had suffered surpassed, by his own admission, all previous experience or imagination. In many places it had proved impossible to bring up any supplies for three days and the troops had not only eaten their iron ration, preserved for the last emergency, but had subsequently been without food for many hours. They knew that the great attack was coming and they prayed that it might come soon. The barrage at last lifted, and along sixteen miles of front the British infantry leaped from their trenches and surged forward to the assault, their fixed bayonets gleaming in the early sunshine of a perfect summer morning.

Haig sat by the telephone, waiting for news. The first that arrived, at about 8 A.M., was satisfactory. The British infantry were reported everywhere to have crossed the enemy's front trenches. But gradually information began to be received of troops being held up at various points and some of the earlier more favourable reports began to be contradicted.

It had been confidently anticipated that after the terrific bombardment not only would the German front line be utterly obliterated, but also that the troops, who should be occupying it, would be too demoralized to fight. The extent to which the Germans had recently improved and perfected their system of underground defences was not yet known to the allies. Haig had suggested that advance trenches for the purpose of the assault should be dug within two hundred yards of the enemy's front line. Divisional commanders, however, had protested that the digging of such trenches would afford warning to the enemy and after some discussion the decision was left to the corps commanders who, for the most part, did not adopt the suggestion. There is no doubt that, if the distance between the two front lines had been shorter, thereby enabling the attackers to reach their objectives before the defenders had had time to emerge from their dugouts and man the parapets, the results of the day's fighting might have been very different, and would not have justified the remark of an American general, who said that the battle of the Somme was lost by three minutes.

On the following day there took place an unfortunate interview with Joffre which, since many inaccurate versions of it have reached the public, had best be described in Haig's own words.

By request I received Generals Joffre and Foch about 3 P.M. today. The object of the visit was to "discuss future arrangements." Joffre began by pointing out the importance of our getting Thiepval Hill. To this I said that in view of the progress made on my right near Montauban, and the demoralized nature of the enemy's troops in that area, I was considering the desirability of pressing my attack on Longueval. I was therefore anxious to know whether in that event the French would attack Guillemont. At this, General Joffre exploded in a fit of rage. *He* could not "approve of it". He *"ordered* me to attack Thiepval and Pozières". "If I attacked Longueval I would be beaten," etc., etc. I waited calmly till he had finished. His breast heaved and his face flushed. The truth is the poor man cannot argue, nor can he easily read a map. But today I had a raised model of the ground before us. There were also present at the meeting Generals Kiggell and Foch and Renouard (from G.Q.G.) and Foch's chief staff officer (Weygand). Only Joffre, Foch and I spoke. When Joffre got out of breath I quietly explained what my position is relatively to him as the "generalissimo". *I am solely responsible to the British Government for the action of the British Army;* and I had approved the plan, and must modify it to suit the changing situation as the fight progresses. I was most polite. Joffre saw that he had made a mistake and next tried to cajole me. He said that this was the "English battle" and "France expected great things from me". I thanked him, but said I had only one object, viz. to beat Germany. France and England march together, and it would give me equal pleasure to see the French troops exploiting victory as my own. After this there was a more friendly discussion between Foch and me. Joffre and I then went out into the garden where Joffre presented General Kiggell with the "Grand Officier" of the Legion of Honour, and Davidson with the next rank of the order and kissed them each twice, a resounding smack on each cheek. I soothed old Joffre down, and he seemed ashamed of his outburst and I sent him and Foch off to Amiens. All present at the interview felt ashamed of Joffre. This is evidently the way he behaved before Gillinsky, the Russian general, who was the first to tell me of Joffre's impatience. Still Joffre has his merits. I admire the old man's pluck under difficulties, and am very fond of him. However, I have gained an advantage through keeping calm. My views have been accepted by the French staff and Davidson is to go to lunch with Foch tomorrow at Dury to discuss how they (the French) can co-operate in our operation, that is the capture of Longueval.

The unusually authoritative tone that Joffre assumed on this occasion may have been due to the fact that in the attack of July the first the French troops, operating on the right of the British, had been far more successful in obtaining their objectives. This was to be attributed partly to their adoption of the method of advance by small parties and quick rushes, partly to the concentration of all their preliminary bombardment onto the enemy's front line, and partly to the Germans' conviction that after the punishment the French had received at Verdun they were not likely to advance at all.

The battle was to continue, with varying results, through four months and eighteen days. At times victory seemed in sight. After the British success in the middle of July, congratulations flowed in to Rawlinson and to Haig. But, as so often happens in warfare, the exploitation of the victory left something to be desired. Cavalry had been brought up and it did seem at one moment that they might be used with effect and that the resumption of open warfare was at hand. But the opportunity, if it existed, was lost. The enemy were able to bring up their reinforcements, counterattacks were delivered and the long battle went on.

About this time the importance of the press was forcibly obtruded upon Haig's notice by a letter he received from Sir Reginald Brade, the permanent under-secretary to the War Office. He was informed that Mr Lloyd George was most anxious that "some special attention" should be paid to Lord Northcliffe, who was intending shortly to visit the Australian troops at the invitation of Mr Hughes, the Australian prime minister.

It would have seemed strange to Wellington in the Peninsula, strange to Raglan in the Crimea, strange even to Kitchener in the Soudan or to Roberts in South Africa, if they had received a request, which from the secretary of state for war amounts to an instruction, to show special attention to the owner of a newspaper. But times had changed and the power of the press, which had been developing rapidly, had at this moment reached its apogee, a point which it had never approached before and has hardly maintained since. In time of war the influence of newspapers increases together with, but out of proportion to, their circulation. Anxious men and women are a prey to every rumour. News is their daily sustenance. Those whose business it is to present the news, to draw conclusions from the facts and to mould opinion in conformity with those conclusions, exercise at such periods an influence over the minds of their fellow subjects which it would be difficult to overestimate. Even in the Crimean War the *Times,* with its minute circulation according to modern standards, had largely contributed toward the downfall of Lord Aberdeen's administration. But in 1916 the owner of the *Times* spoke through its columns to an enormously increased circulation and was able to express the same opinions in a louder voice with larger headlines to the million readers of the *Daily Mail.* A score of minor publications conveyed reflections of identic views through many different channels in many parts of the country to countless sections of the community.

Lord Northcliffe was undoubtedly the most powerful newspaper owner that has yet existed in this, or perhaps in any country, and during the war he was at the height of his power. He arrived at Haig's headquarters on July the twenty-first. Haig as usual allowed no previous opinions to prevent him from forming a fair judgment. The entry in his diary is as follows: "Lord Northcliffe arrived today and stayed the night. I was favourably impressed with his desire to do his best to help win the war. He was most anxious not to make a mistake in anything he advocated in his newspapers, and for this he was desirous of seeing what was taking place. I am therefore letting him see *everything* and talk to anyone he pleases."

Frank and open-minded as ever, Haig had succeeded in making a friend, for the time being, of one who could prove a dangerous enemy.

It was during these days of constant fighting that Haig learned to appreciate the splendid qualities of the Australian troops that were serving under him. Although the fighting and the shell fire were far more severe than anything they had experienced at Gallipoli, and although they found the German a very much more formidable foe than the Turk, their high courage and their high spirits remained indomitable.

Attack, counterattack—ground gained, lost, regained and lost again—a long-drawn-out and bitter tale of effort, suffering, failure and glory. It is not the duty of the commander in chief's biographer to describe in detail each or any of these continual actions which in the scale of world warfare become almost insignificant, but which, judged by the standards of the past, would have made each autumn day in 1916 as memorable in the annals of the countries concerned as the anniversaries of Agincourt, of Rossbach or of Valmy.

"The powers that be are beginning to get a little uneasy in regard to the situation," wrote Robertson at the end of July. "The casualties are mounting up and they are wondering whether we are likely to get a proper return for them."

The powers that were are not to be blamed for their anxiety. Had each of the ministers concerned been a dictator he could have afforded to trust his generals and disregard public opinion. But, as it was, each minister depended for his continuance in office on the support of the elected representatives of the people, and was therefore in duty bound to lend an ear to rumours of discontent. That such rumours were carefully fomented and spread by those who desired a change in the administration may well have happened, but no minister in a democratic community can be blamed for listening to and being influenced by the voice of the people.

Haig replied categorically to such questions as the Cabinet asked, such criticisms as they adumbrated. He pointed out that the effect of the fighting had already been to relieve the pressure upon Verdun; and it was, after all, the pressure upon Verdun and nothing else that had caused the attack to be delivered at that place and at that time. He added that the remarkable success achieved by the Russian offensive—the last Russian success in the war—would have been checked easily if the enemy had been free to transfer troops from the Western to the Eastern Front. Further, not only had tremendous losses been inflicted on the enemy, but also it had been proved that the best German troops in the most carefully prepared and most strongly defended positions were not invincible, and that the new British Army, composed of civilian volunteers, was capable of meeting on equal terms and of vanquishing any soldiers in the world.

The explanation was considered sufficient. On August the eighth the war committee of the Cabinet agreed unanimously that "the C.I.G.S. should send a message to General Sir D. Haig assuring him that he might count on full support from home".

The King paid another visit to France during this month of August and on his return to London wrote Haig the following letter in his own hand:

Buckingham Palace,
Aug. 16, 1916.

MY DEAR HAIG,

I have arrived home and wish to lose no time in letting you know how greatly I have enjoyed my visit to your splendid army. It is especially pleasing to me to find that the absolute confidence I have in you, is shared throughout your command.

The spirit of loyalty which unites every part of the army must give it an additional strength in your hands; I heard from all sides what a happy army it is.

I was deeply interested in everything I saw and only wish that my stay could have been longer. I will not repeat the views expressed in my general order of yesterday.

I thank you sincerely for your kind hospitality, and also

for placing at my disposal Major Thompson, who was not only a charming companion, but the greatest help to me in arranging our daily programs, the details of which must have given him much work and trouble. In the eight days I motored 687 miles.

Hoping that all may go well

Believe me

very sincerely yours,

GEORGE, R.I.

Lloyd George paid G.H.Q. a fleeting visit about this time and his relations with the commander in chief were most amicable. He assured him that he had "no intention of meddling and that his sole object was to help".

Relations between Haig and Foch steadily improved as their acquaintance grew. They had not taken to each other immediately, Foch being as intensely French as Haig was intensely Lowland Scottish, but Haig throughout the war realized the vital importance of maintaining friendly relations with French generals and spared no effort to achieve his purpose.

Through Haig's headquarters flowed a steady stream of French generals and English notabilities, both politicians and journalists, each of whom he received with an open mind and summed up in a shrewd comment.

St Loe Strachey of the *Spectator* he found "rather a talker but an honest man with the courage of his opinions". In Gwynne of the *Morning Post* he commended a healthy distrust of politicians but detected a tendency to exaggerate the power and importance of journalists. Spender of the *Westminster Gazette* seemed "an honest patriot" and Geoffrey Dawson of the *Times* was "an intelligent and honest fellow".

Edwin Montagu, who had succeeded Lloyd George as minister of munitions, impressed him as "a capable and agreeable man, who seemed to understand his job though he has only recently taken over. He is full of determination to help the army as much as he possibly can."

Barthou, of tragic memory, struck him as "a pleasant little man. . . . His only son was killed early in the war. We had a long talk and I gather that he is prepared to carry on until Germany is beaten in order to have a permanent peace."

It would be absurd in face of tributes such as these to maintain that Haig harboured any ineradicable distrust of politicians, but unfortunately the only one in whom it seemed impossible for him to repose confidence was the secretary of state for war. He had no reason at present to suppose that he himself was regarded with disfavour. On August the twenty-ninth Robertson wrote to him reporting a conversation with Lloyd George in which the latter "repeated what he has said many times lately, that he thinks you are playing absolutely the right game, and doing your job in absolutely the right way. You can attach any importance you choose to his opinion, but it will be satisfactory to you to know that he at any rate thinks you are doing quite the right thing." This was after the battle of the Somme had been in progress for a month.

If confirmation of Robertson's testimony were needed, we have it in Lloyd George's own handwriting. Three weeks later, the battle still continuing, he wrote as follows:

September 21, 1916.

MY DEAR GENERAL,

I found a considerable accumulation of work on my return from France or I should have written to you before to say how much I enjoyed my visit to your command and how agreeable were the impressions I carried away as regards both the preparations for what was then the new offensive to come and the spirit of the commanders and the troops. I am more than glad to feel that all the thought and work, which go to make the success of an attack under modern conditions, have given you and your staff just cause for satisfaction.

I can say, on behalf of my colleagues in the Cabinet as well as for myself, that the heartening news of the last few days has confirmed our anticipations and hopes that the tide had now definitely turned in our favour.

I congratulate you most warmly on the skill with which your plans were laid, and on the imperturbable bravery of your troops. Such a combination augurs well for further successes, though I realize the difficulties that have to be faced and overcome.

The story of the tanks has interested me greatly, and has quite captured the attention of the public.

With best wishes,
Yours sincerely,
D. LLOYD GEORGE.

I hope you will let me come over to visit the scenes of your fresh triumphs.

Such praise and appreciation come strangely from one who has since written of "the horrible and futile carnage of the Somme", and has maintained that he was opposed to it from the first. Oddly enough even at the time the words were uttered they failed to convince the man to whom they were addressed of their author's sincerity. Both Asquith and Lloyd George had recently been staying at G.H.Q., and in a letter to his wife Haig had conveyed the several impressions they had made upon him.

"Lloyd George has been with me during the past two days so I have been able to notice the differences in the two men and to realize how much superior in many ways Mr Asquith is to L.G. I have got on with the latter very well indeed and he is anxious to help in every way he can. But he seems to me to be so flighty—makes plans and is always changing them and his mind. Most unpunctual (except when coming to meet me I must confess). But he was one and one-half hours late at lunch with General Foch, and

M. Thomas told me that was his usual habit when visiting Verdun and the French. On the other hand Mr Asquith has such a clear and evenly balanced mind.

"His visit too was on business lines. L.G's has been a huge 'joy ride'. Breakfasts with newspaper men and posings for the cinema shows pleased him more than anything else. No doubt with the ulterior object of catching votes! From what I have written you will gather that I have no great opinion of L.G. *as a man* or *leader*."

This letter was written on the thirteenth of September and a few days later he obtained striking proof that the instinctive distrust with which Lloyd George had inspired him was not unjustified. On the seventeenth of September Foch came to visit Haig and after a brief conversation on the military situation "asked me to leave the others and go into the garden. He then spoke to me of Mr Lloyd George's recent visit to his (Foch's) H.Q. Lunch was at twelve noon and L. G. said he would bring two or three people with him. He actually arrived at 1.45 and brought eight people! Afterward L. G., using Lord Reading as interpreter, had a private talk with Foch. He began by saying that he was a British minister and as such he considered that he had a right to be told the truth. He wished to know why the British, who had gained no more ground than the French, if as much, had suffered such heavy casualties. Foch replied that the French infantry had learned their lesson in 1914, and were now careful in their advances. He often wished that they were not so well instructed. He would then have advanced much farther and more quickly. In reply to questions about our artillery, Foch said that, in his opinion, the British had done wonders. L. G. also asked his opinion as to the ability of the British generals. Foch said 'L. G. was sufficiently patriotic not to criticize the British commander in chief', but he did not speak with confidence of the other British generals as a whole. Foch's reply was that he had had no means of forming an opinion.

"Unless I had been told of this conversation personally by General Foch, I would not have believed that a British minister could have been so ungentlemanly as to go to a foreigner and put such questions regarding his own subordinates."

Foch's statement that the secretary of state for war had not actually criticized the commander in chief is, however, contradicted in the account which Foch himself gave of the same conversation to Henry Wilson and which the latter recorded in his diary. There we read that "Lloyd George said" to Foch "he gave Haig all the guns and ammunition and men he could use and nothing happened. Foch said that Lloyd George was *très monté* against Haig, and he did not think Haig's seat was very secure."

On the fifteenth of September there took place the most important advance that had occurred during the fighting on the Somme. Courcelette and Martinpuich were both captured, the former by the Canadians, the latter by the Scots. On this day for the first time in history the tanks were seen upon the field of battle. Haig, who was ever ready to welcome new inventions, had encouraged their construction and was eager to make use of them. It may be readily admitted that if the use of the tanks had been delayed until a thousand or more of them could have been thrown into the field simultaneously, if it had been possible during that necessarily lengthy interval to perfect the machinery, train the crews, instruct the infantry how to co-operate and at the same time maintain the secrecy of the invention, the effect when it was finally produced would have been tremendous. But it is very easy to be wise after the event, and to show what should have been done in the light of subsequent history. Had a man known that the war must continue until November the eleventh, 1918, every decision would have been influenced by that knowledge.

Throughout the month of October the battle fitfully continued, and the enemy was granted but little breathing space. On November the thirteenth was launched the last attack which brought the battle of the Somme to a close. It was more successful than any that had hitherto been delivered. The Fifth Army attacked astride the river Ancre and swept all before them. But by the eighteenth the weather brought all to a standstill, and the longest battle that had been fought in the world's history was over.

There are still those who argue that the battle of the Somme should never have been fought and that the gains were not commensurate with the sacrifice. There exists no yardstick for the measurement of such events, there are no returns to prove whether life has been sold at its market value. There are some who from their manner of reasoning would appear to believe that no battle is worth fighting unless it produces an immediately decisive result, which is as foolish as it would be to argue that in a prize fight no blow is worth delivering save the one that knocks the opponent out. In point of fact the final blow may be one of the feeblest, and even the finest judge of the noble art watching the ring most closely would hesitate to lay down definitely which of the blows delivered in the contest contributed most to the result.

As to whether it were wise or foolish to give battle on the Somme on July 1, 1916, there can surely be only one opinion. To have refused to fight then and there would have meant the abandonment of Verdun to its fate and the breakdown of co-operation with the French. When Falkenhayn struck at Verdun he believed that he was striking at the heart of France, and that if he could win Verdun the beating of that heart would cease. Who shall say that he was wrong? All military writers are agreed that the battle of the Somme saved Verdun, and if no further justification were forthcoming that alone would suffice.

But the Somme did more than this. The British Army that advanced so confidently on the first of July was a citizen army, only half trained to war. The survivors in mid November were veterans who could have discussed the military profession as equals with their ancestors who had passed through all the South African, the Crimean or the Peninsular campaigns. As the final test of a new weapon must be the battlefield, so also is the battlefield the only furnace wherein are forged the armies of victory. It was the survivors of the Somme who two years later formed the backbone of the force that smashed the Hindenburg line and drove the invaders off the soil of France.

The German Army, on the other hand, came into battle not with the courage of ignorance, but with the confidence of knowledge. The world has never seen a more highly trained and perfectly disciplined machine. From birth every German had been taught to think himself a soldier, he had been fed from childhood on the glorious traditions of Sadowa and Sedan, he had been trained from youth in the exercise of arms, and the military supremacy of Germany had been with him the first article of faith.

On the Somme they were not taken by surprise; they had had full time to prepare the fortifications behind which they awaited the coming onslaught, and the elaboration, ingenuity and intricacy of those earthworks marked a new epoch in trench warfare. Even Germany could produce no finer soldiers than the men who manned them. Yet after a bombardment such as they had never imagined they found themselves driven at the point of the bayonet out of positions they had believed impregnable. Fighting fiercely, disputing every inch of the ground, inflicting fearful punishment upon the foe, they were none the less compelled to relinquish the trenches they had sworn they would hold to the last. Falkenhayn had given orders that "not a foot's breadth on the ground must be abandoned". Von Bülow had laid down that "only over our dead bodies may the enemy advance". And for the German soldier the result of the Somme was not the loss of a few lines of trenches nor the bitterness of temporary defeat; it was the end of a great tradition, it was the bankruptcy of a religious faith. Two instances were brought to Haig's notice of German officers who, being prisoners, had attempted to commit suicide—a fact of profound significance.

German writers have frankly admitted the psychological effect produced. The historian of the Twenty-seven (Württemberg) Division writes, "In the Somme fighting there was a spirit of heroism which was never again found in the division, however conspicuous its fighting power remained until the end of the war."

Captain von Hentig of the general staff tells us that "the Somme was the muddy grave of the German field army and of the faith in the infallibility of German leadership. . . . The most precious thing lost on the Somme was the good relationship between the leaders and the led."

Another German writer asserts that "the tragedy of the Somme battle was that the best soldiers, the stoutest-hearted men were lost; their numbers were replaceable, their spiritual worth never could be."

But the most conclusive of all evidence is the testimony of General Ludendorff in his book, *My War Memories.* As the result of the Somme fighting he admits that "we were completely exhausted on the Western Front. . . . If the war lasted our defeat seemed inevitable. . . . I cannot see as I look back how the German G.H.Q. could have mastered the situation if the allies had continued their blows as they did in 1916."

When certain British politicians, alarmed by the number of the casualties, rallied to the cry of "No more Sommes", they little knew that their latest slogan was also the muttered and heartfelt prayer of the whole of the German

Army, from the men in the trenches to the commander in chief.

These then were the results of the first great battle fought under the supreme command of Haig: Verdun was saved, the maintenance of Anglo-French co-operation was assured, the British were taught to fight, and the heart of the German Army was broken.

CHAPTER IX

New Leaders, New Methods

THE BEGINNING of 1917 found new leaders, political and military, striving to solve the stalemate of war for the allies. In England Lloyd George had succeeded Asquith as prime minister. The French had deposed Joffre, appointing General Nivelle as commander in chief on the Western Front, and General Lyautey had come from Morocco to be minister of war. Haig's support at home was sufficient to keep him in command of the British armies in France and Belgium, though the opposition seemed at times strong enough under Lloyd George's leadership to make his tenure doubtful.

Henceforward two facts were to exercise an unhappy influence over the conduct of the war. The prime minister of England had, from now on, no confidence in his own commander in chief, and he disbelieved in the main strategic principle upon which the governments of France and England had decided and to which, in spite of him, they were to adhere. Whether in any circumstances a prime minister can be justified in retaining during the crisis of a great war a commander in chief whom he considers unfit for the position, and whether a prime minister should not resign rather than be a party to the sacrifice of human life owing to the pursuance of plans which he firmly believes to be disastrous, are questions which may engage the attention of students of political morality. But it must be remembered, in Mr Lloyd George's defence, that he undoubtedly would have got rid of his commander in chief if he could, and that he spared no effort from the beginning of his premiership until the end to divert the energies of the allies into different channels. The excuses which he has subsequently put forward for not dismissing Haig are two. The first is that, although he was a bad general, the whole British Empire could not produce a better. Such an admission of imperial bankruptcy can hardly be taken seriously, and will therefore be accepted by Haig's admirers as a handsome tribute. The second excuse, and the more convincing, is that, although he wanted to get rid of Haig, his Cabinet colleagues, the press and public opinion, prevented him from doing so. He himself has never lacked courage, and if the storm was one that he dared not face we may be sure that it would have proved something more than a squall. The truth is that, for some curious reason which he cannot explain, the people of Great Britain, who are not always lacking in sagacity, had greater faith in the stupid soldier than in the clever politician.

Much of the deplorable bitterness which pervades the pages of Lloyd George's *War Memories* may be attributed to the fact that, although the war was won within the period of his premiership, the strategy which he advocated was never adopted, and the commander in chief whom he distrusted was never displaced. He must therefore be at pains to show that it might have been much more easily won by other means and under other leaders, and that the vast edifice of the German Empire might have been dashed to the ground without the fearful sacrifices that were demanded from the allies.

Haig called on Nivelle at Chantilly, January first, and on the way back he visited at Clermont General Franchet d'Esperey, who had succeeded Foch in command of the northern group of French armies. For Foch was under a cloud these days and, the reputation of ill health having been given as an excuse, he had been relegated to a position of comparative inactivity at Senlis. Of Franchet d'Esperey, by whose side he had fought on the Aisne in September, 1914, Haig wrote, "He is a clear-headed, determined little man, and hitherto I have got on very well with him."

At a meeting in London on January fifteenth, Lloyd George compared the British Army unfavourably to the French, criticizing the tactics on the Somme and assuring Haig that the country would not stand a repetition of it. Haig listened patiently and then defended to the best of his ability the British Army on the charges made against it, reminding the prime minister that the Somme battle had been undertaken and continued in order to relieve the pressure on the French at Verdun.

When Nivelle came to a meeting of the British War Committee his plans for the next great attack, first proposed for February and then delayed until early April, were supported by Lloyd George in spite of Haig's view that the British should not agree to all the details of what the French commander demanded. Robertson subsequently wrote to Haig:

"Until Nivelle arrived in London the prime minister in particular and the Cabinet in general were frightfully anxious that you should not go off until you were fully ready and all the allies ready too. More than once he has expressed alarm lest you should go off prematurely. Nivelle's appearance has caused an entire change and on several occasions since you attended the conference the prime minister and Lord Curzon have emphasized the importance of your going off as soon as possible. . . .

"I cannot follow what the prime minister has now got in his mind, but he seems to have an idea that you and Nivelle are going to do something very effective in the course of three weeks, although he has always hitherto told me that he doubted if we would ever be able to do anything useful on the Western Front."

The flow of distinguished visitors to Haig's headquarters continued. "Mr John Masefield came to lunch. He is a poet, but I am told that he has written the best account of the landing at Gallipoli." (Poets, the descendants of Homer, who also wrote accounts of fighting near Gallipoli, will smile a little sadly at the conjunctive "but".) "Now he wishes to write about the deeds of our men in the battle of the Somme. To this I readily gave permission and said I would gladly put him in the way of those most concerned with the various actions, so that he could get firsthand information."

On another occasion, "Mr Bernard Shaw (the author and playwright) came to lunch. An interesting man of original views. A great talker! On sitting down to lunch I at once discovered he was a vegetarian. As if by magic, on my ordering it, two poached eggs appeared, also some spinach and macaroni, so he did not fare badly."

Mr Belloc is described as "an English M.P., but very French in appearance. A most interesting and well-informed man."

It was not, however, only English journalists and men of letters whom he felt it his duty to receive; representatives of the French press were also often admitted, and in this connection an incident occurred which, although insignificant in itself, provided Haig with an intimation of the extent of the animosity with which he was regarded in certain quarters, and of the nature of the tactics which would be resorted to in order to secure his undoing. Anything that journalists desired to report of what he had said to them would in the natural course of events be submitted for his approval before receiving publication. On this occasion, however, owing to an oversight on the part of a subordinate, a report of an interview appeared in certain French newspapers without his knowledge or approval. The article, in fact, contained no sentiment with which he disagreed, but the somewhat over self-confident language in which it was couched would have come more naturally from the mouth of a Gascon than from that of a Scotsman. He was represented as having prophesied that the war would end in the year 1917, but in any case there must be no peace without victory, and also as having boasted of all that Great Britain was doing for the cause.

His own first irritation on reading a translation of the interview which appeared in the *Times* is recorded in his diary: "London papers to-day published an alleged interview between myself and some French journalists. The *Times* gave a translation of the statement, and also published a leading article approving my statements in highest terms. As a matter of fact, I gave no 'interviews', but from time to time I have received eminent French journalists who have visited our front. On these occasions I merely talked platitudes and stated my confidence in a victorious termination of the war. By some mistake a summary of one of these talks has slipped past the censor. I am much annoyed, as I hold that it is quite wrong for the commander in chief's views to be published in the press at all. The government at home should give out all such reports."

But three days later, "Telegram from Lord Derby regarding the 'interview' which I am supposed to have given some French correspondents. A question is now being asked in the House of Commons on Monday and he wants to know what should be said. I sent a wire stating that I had seen correspondents privately before they left the British area, that the various reports in the papers are their general recollections of a conversation between five persons and were in no case quotations. The reports were passed by the censor as they contained nothing of any use to the enemy, and without my knowledge. Lytton, who went to Paris to find out the feeling there, returned and said that the papers and the public were delighted with what was published and have never been so friendly toward the British as they are now. They cannot understand why so much fuss is being made in England over it."

But the fuss in England continued, assiduously fostered by a small section of the press and a few members of Parliament. In the House of Commons Philip Snowden, with characteristic intemperance of language, referred to the commander in chief's "blazing indiscretion" which, he said, "had shaken the confidence of many people in his judgment and common sense."

Haig sent Neville Lytton, who was then in charge of the press censorship at G.H.Q., to explain the whole matter to the secretary of state. He was directed to attend a meeting of the War Cabinet and on his return gave the following account of what had taken place:

"He told me that Lloyd George and Lord Curzon were most hostile and cross-examined him as if he were trying to tell what was untrue! Mr Balfour, on the other hand, supported me very warmly, and put the case in its true light. L.G. seemed to resent my bulking large in the public eye at all. He wishes to shine alone. As for Curzon, it seems that he still has a grudge against the soldier and would like to reintroduce a new system with a military member as at Simla. However, Mr Bonar Law's statement in the House of Commons was well received, and the question is considered ended. The attacks seem to have been made by discredited socialists and 'peace at any price' people. What concerns me is the desire of certain people, including the prime minister, to make capital out of a trivial incident and to misrepresent the actual nature of the so-called interview in order to rouse public opinion against me, and then to order my recall."

Haig wrote in his diary on February the seventh:

We willingly play a second role to the French—that is we are to make a holding attack to draw in the enemy's reserves so as to make the task of the French easier. We shall at any rate have heavy losses, with the possibility of no showy successes, whereas the French are to make the decisive attack with every prospect of gaining the fruits of victory. I think it is for the general good that we play this role in support of the French, but let the future critics realize that we have adopted it with our eyes open as to the probable consequences.

Haig's main fear was lest Nivelle's impetuosity should cause the attack to be delivered before adequate preparations had been made, and these preparations were being continually delayed owing to the breakdown of the French railways. He was, however, much reassured by an interview which he had with Nivelle on February the sixteenth. The French general arrived at G.H.Q. in the afternoon together with Colonel d'Alençon, of whom Haig remarks that "he seems to have great influence with Nivelle, but unfortunately is very anti-British in feeling". He goes on to record:

After tea Nivelle and I had a long talk. He said he preferred to talk with me alone rather than with staff officers present. Briefly, our discussion was most satisfactory. He was most frank. We discussed the railway situation. I explained our difficulties; how we are given only seventy trains a day when we require two hundred to carry our minimum of material for the coming offensive.

He at once sent a stiff wire to the French government recommending that the Nord Railway Company be placed on a sound footing at once. As regards the date of attack, he fully realized that we are dependent on the railway, but he agreed with me that no attack should start until all our requirements had been provided. From the information which he had of the Chemin de Fer du Nord, he thought that we should not be delayed more than ten days beyond

HAIG OF BEMERSYDE

Photopress photograph

the original dates agreed upon. I said I would do my utmost to meet these views, but that my preparations depended on the amount delivered by the railways.

I was much pleased with the results of our meeting, as I had feared that Nivelle wished to attack in any case, whether the British were ready or not. He seems now to be in complete agreement with me.

A few days later Lyautey paid Haig a visit. "General Lyautey (minister of war) arrived in Fourth Army area this morning from Paris. He visited the battle front, lunched with Gough at headquarters Fifth Army, saw some schools, etc., and eventually motored to his train at Brimeaux station about two miles from here, and arrived about 7 P.M. for a talk with me before dinner. We also had a long talk after dinner. He spoke most frankly and said he felt quite at home with me and my staff, whereas he distrusted 'the politicians'. When he mounted the tribune to address the chambre des députés he pinched himself to make sure that it was really he who had to talk! He hated the whole thing so. At the War Cabinet meetings in Paris he sat next M. Poincaré (the President of the Republic). M. Ribot (finance) was on the right of the latter, while on the other side of the table was M. Briand (the premier) with Admiral Lacaze on his right and M. Albert Thomas (in charge of munitions) on his left. 'It usually happens that Briand and M. Poincaré get into lengthy discussions and weaken in the matter of taking decisive action.' Then Lyautey 'looks across to Thomas, and breaks into the discussion'. Thomas at once supports him and the matter is settled! Lyautey finds 'his greatest support in this little revolutionary socialist. He is the most patriotic of all the Cabinet and is determined to spare no effort in order to beat the Germans.

". . . I found Lyautey most sound in his views and straightforward in his actions. He and Nivelle seem so far to be a great improvement on their predecessors."

It was in this happy mood of refreshed confidence in his French colleagues that on the twenty-sixth of February Haig set forth for Calais to take part in a conference which was to become the subject of historic controversy. After a talk on transportation problems the meeting was turned into a general discussion of military plans. Haig wrote in his diary:

I . . . explained that I was doing my utmost to comply with the strategical requirements of Nivelle's plan, but in the matter of tactics I alone could decide. That is to say, Nivelle having stated that his plan required the British to break the enemy's front north of the Somme and march on Cambrai, I decided where and how I would dispose my troops for that purpose. Lloyd George at once said, "he did not understand about strategy and tactics, he would like it clearly stated what the respective responsibilities were." It was then about 6.45 P.M. He therefore asked the French to draw up their proposals for a *system of command* before dinner, so that he, Robertson and I could discuss it after dinner, and a subsequent conference with the French government would then be held tomorrow morning to decide finally. This was agreed to.

Robertson and I walked about till time to dress for dinner. L.G. said he was ill and did not come to dinner. At table I sat opposite Briand, with Lyautey on my right and Nivelle on my left. We had quite a cheery talk. After dinner I went to Robertson's room and found him most excited over a typed paper which L.G. had given him containing the French proposals. These were briefly to organize a British chief of general staff and staff at Beauvais (French G.Q.G.) with what they called a "quartermaster general". This C.G.S. is to report to the war committee at home. The commander in chief would apparently only administer the discipline and look after reinforcements.

Robertson and I then went in to L.G's room. The latter now told us that the "War Cabinet had decided last week that since this was likely to be the last effort of the French, and they had the larger numbers engaged, in fact it was their battle", the British Army would be placed under the French commander in chief's orders.

He then asked me my views. I said that in my opinion it would be madness to place the British forces under the French, and that I did not believe our troops would fight under French leadership. At the beginning of the war there was much dissatisfaction in the army with G.H.Q. because there was an idea that British interests were being sacrificed to those of the French. He agreed that the French demands were excessive, but insisted on Robertson and myself considering "a scheme for giving effect to the War Cabinet's decision".

I went with Robertson to his room. He seemed thoroughly upset with the attitude of our prime minister. Colonel Hankey (secretary war committee) further added to our dissatisfaction by saying that "L.G. had not received full authority from the War Cabinet" for acting as he was doing.

General Kiggell took part in our discussion, and we agreed we would rather be tried by court-martial than betray the army by agreeing to its being placed under the French. Robertson agreed that we must resign rather than be partners in this transaction.

And so we went to bed, thoroughly disgusted with our government and the politicians.

The next morning, before the conference assembled, General Lyautey sent his personal staff officer to beg Haig to go to his room as he had something very important to tell him.

I found Nivelle with him. They both spoke of the "insult offered to me and the British Army by the paper which Briand had had produced". They assured me that they had not seen the document until quite recently. Indeed, as regards Lyautey, he had not seen or heard of it until he entered the train at Paris to come to Calais today. I understand that the paper was drawn up in Paris with Lloyd George's approval, and of course that of Briand.

Thinking over the proposals of the French, and the

decision of our government, I thought it best to put my conclusions shortly in writing to the C.I.G.S. This I did . . . before breakfast (8.15 A.M.) and gave it to Robertson requesting him to put it before L.G. and that I would not go to see him unless sent for.

SECRET
Calais,
February 27, 1917.

To THE C.I.G.S.

I have in the short time available considered the decision of the War Cabinet (of which Mr Lloyd George informed us last night) viz., to place the British Army in France under the orders of the French commander in chief, and the proposals of the French to give effect to that decision.

In my opinion there are only two alternatives, viz.:

1. To leave matters as they are now, or

2. To place the British Army in France entirely under the French commander in chief.

The decision to adopt the second of these proposals must involve the disappearance of the British commander in chief and G.H.Q. What further changes would be necessary must depend on the French commander in chief and the French government under whom he acts.

So drastic a change in our system at a moment when active operations on a large scale have already commenced seems to me to be fraught with the gravest danger.

D. HAIG, F.M.
Commanding British Armies in France.

At an interview with Lloyd George I objected to this and insisted on having added that I have "a free hand to choose the means and methods of utilizing the British troops in that sector of operations allotted by the French commander in chief in the original plan". This was concurred in by Nivelle. A document was then drawn up embodying these points. As it stands, the way in which I have worked with the French is not changed. I have always acted on General Joffre's "general instructions" as if they had been orders, but retained absolute freedom of action as to how I carried them out. This power must however remain to me.

In Nivelle's present proposals I am relieved of responsibility both for the plan of the battle now being prepared, as well as for the details of execution of the plan. . . .

The two documents were then signed by all of us, and a copy taken by each government. I am to receive a copy of the "procès verbal" of the proceedings.

More important than the agreement concluded at Calais, or the events that sprang from it, was the manner in which the whole business had been conducted. The sequel will show that, so far as the actual fighting was concerned, Nivelle's new position produced no consequence of great importance, and that, although relations between him and Haig were never so frank and friendly again, no untoward event occurred which a better understanding between them could have avoided.

Lyautey apologized to Haig for the insult offered to him and to the British Army. He spoke the language which soldiers all over the world would understand. What were the actual words in which on the same occasion Nivelle disclaimed any but recent knowledge of the document produced by Briand we do not know, but it has now been proved that the document itself had actually been drafted at Nivelle's own headquarters a week before.

Unity of command is a phrase that in many people's minds has come to produce the effect of a talisman. Not only do they believe that it was unity of command which was responsible for winning the war in 1918, but also they are convinced that had it been resorted to at any earlier period the result produced would have been the same, and that the lack of it was responsible for all our troubles.

In this connection there are certain facts which should be clearly realized. The first is that from the very beginning of the war, so far as the strategy of the Western Front was concerned, unity of command virtually existed. Only once, when French threatened to withdraw his army south of the

Seine, was such unity seriously threatened. That threat was removed by the action of Kitchener. Had French hesitated to respond to Joffre's appeal to turn and fight on the Marne, it would have been again imperilled. But he did not hesitate, and on the Marne and on the Aisne, at Loos and before Ypres, and throughout 1916, every action in which the British Army was engaged was fought with the full approval of the French commander in chief, who even during that period was referred to in common parlance as the generalissimo.

There was an important difference between the arrangement in which Haig cheerfully acquiesced in 1918 and that which was forced upon him in 1917. In 1918 there were two armies, the French and the British. Pétain continued to command the one and Haig the other. Over both of them, as supreme generalissimo, was Foch. He had no more to do with the French Army than with the British. Pétain's position as commander in chief of the French Army was no less subordinate than that of Haig. They both continued to function as independent commanders in chief. But the situation which Nivelle had envisaged was entirely different. He was to remain commander in chief of the French Army and the British Army was to become merely a part of his force, its former commander in chief being reduced to the position of an army or a corps commander, taking orders from him in the same way as would any other subordinate.

Nivelle lost no time in making plain to Haig the meaning which he attached to the convention of Calais and the spirit in which he intended to interpret it. On the same day that he returned to his headquarters he addressed to the British commander in chief a letter couched in more peremptory terms than the latter was accustomed to employ when writing to his subordinate army commanders. Nivelle, for instance, ordered Haig to furnish him not only with copies of his instructions to his army commanders, but also to let him know what steps the army commanders had taken to carry out their instructions. Haig, on the other hand, had never been in the habit of asking his army commanders to let him see the instructions which they sent to their subordinates in charge of corps or divisions, let alone the actions which such subordinates had taken to comply with their instructions. He further required Haig to place Henry Wilson at the head of the British mission at French headquarters and gave orders for the redistribution of British troops.

"Briefly," wrote Haig, "it is a type of letter which no gentleman could have drafted, and it also is one which certainly no commander in chief of this great British Army should receive without protest.

"By the Calais agreement I only come under his orders after the battle commences and then only for operations in the sector assigned to me already. I intend to send a copy of the letter with my reply to the war committee with a request to be told whether it is their wishes that the commander in chief in command of this British Army should be subjected to such treatment by a junior *foreign* commander.

"It is too sad at this critical time to have to fight with one's allies and the home government in addition to the enemy in the field."

Robertson wrote of Lloyd George to Haig on February the twenty-eighth, "His story at the War Cabinet this morning gave quite a wrong impression. He accused the French of putting forward a monstrous proposal, and yet you and I know that he was at the bottom of it."

The Cabinet passed a resolution to the effect that the commander in chief should be informed that the only object of the Calais convention had been to secure "a clearly defined unity of control" and that "it was in no sense an aspersion on the ability and qualifications of Sir Douglas Haig in whom the War Cabinet continue to entertain full confidence". Lord Derby forwarded the above to Haig with a private covering letter assuring him of stronger support and of warmer regard than the somewhat colourless text of the resolution conveyed.

It appears that the secretary of state for war was almost as much in the dark as the chief of the Imperial General Staff with regard to the prime minister's intentions at the Calais conference. Lord Derby wrote to Haig on March the third,

"If I had known there was to be any proposal to put you and our army under the full control of the French, I should most vigorously have protested. . . .

"The proposal of the French was a preposterous one. As to who was the real originator I should not like to say. I know that both Robertson and you think that its source was England, but, from what I have heard, I am not quite certain that it was not the politicians (*not* the soldiers) of France who were the primary instigators. I quite believe that neither Lyautey nor Nivelle knew of it until just before the meeting, and I also believe their assurances given, I think, to Robertson and you that they neither originated it nor desired it.

"Of course the proposal was an impossible one, and could not have been accepted by anybody. I am not sure, however, that I like the new proposal much better. It all turns on the interpretation given to the word 'conform'. If that word means the carrying out 'by agreement' the general plans agreed upon, altering them as circumstances may require, well and good, because I am certain that your one wish has been loyally to carry out the wishes of the Cabinet in this matter, and that, even if not in complete agreement, you would subordinate your views to Nivelle's, so long as they did not jeopardize your force, or any part of it.

"But if 'conform' to orders means to obey orders given, then it seems to me that the necessity for agreement goes by

SIR WILLIAM ORPEN'S PORTRAIT OF HAIG, PAINTED AT G.H.Q., IN MAY, 1917

Imperial War Museum photograph. Copyright Reserved

the board, and that you and the British Army come directly under French control, with the power to move our troops how and where they like."

Nivelle's letter of February the twenty-seventh proved that Derby's fears with regard to the working of the convention were justified, and that Haig's hopes of a satisfactory understanding were vain. Nivelle's case has never been stated. His apologist has not yet appeared. To the student of Haig's career Nivelle presents a problem. Until the date of the Calais conference he appears to have been a loyal, reliable and accommodating colleague; but from that date onward he became vain, peevish, intractable and dictatorial.

"All would be so easy if I only had to deal with Germans," wrote Haig in his diary.

While counsel was being darkened and action delayed, the enemy had not been idle. During these days the German Army was successfully accomplishing that strategic retreat to previously prepared positions which shortened their lines, and enormously strengthened their defence. This series of withdrawals began with the evacuation of the Bapaume salient on February the twenty-third, and concluded with the main retirement to the so-called Hindenburg line on March the sixteenth. The actual front upon which Nivelle designed to deliver his main attack was not affected, save in so far as the strengthening and shortening of the line naturally rendered it easier for the enemy to transfer reinforcements to a threatened sector.

A further conference was held in London on March the twelfth. Before the meeting Haig called on the secretary of state. He thought Lord Derby looked "more pulled down with worry over the Calais conference than even Robertson did last night. He condoled with me, said government had treated me disgracefully. I assured him that although I realized that fact, I felt no ill will against

THE NIVELLE OFFENSIVE

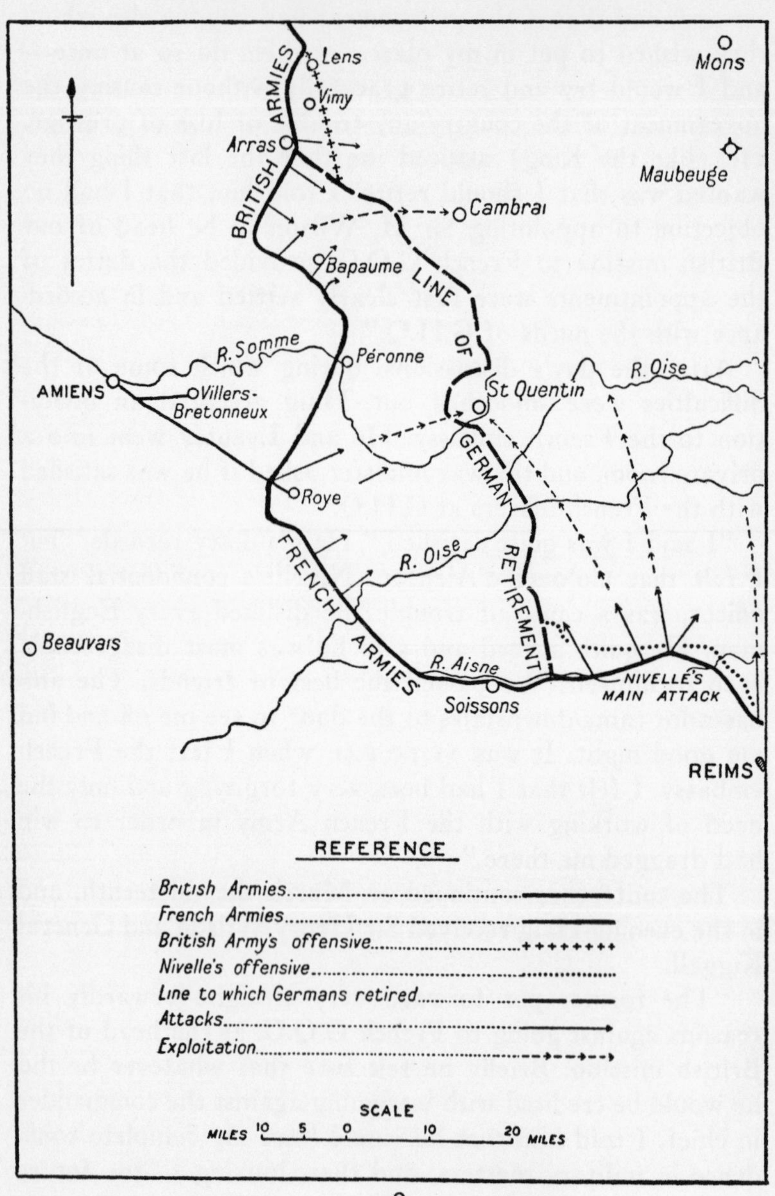

any of them. That I wanted nothing more in the way of reward, and that if the government had anyone else whom they wished to put in my place, let them do so at once—and I would try and retire gracefully without causing the government of the country any trouble or loss of prestige. He (like the King) assured me that the last thing they wanted was that I should retire. I told him that I had no objection to appointing Sir H. Wilson to be head of our British mission to French G.Q.G. provided the duties of the appointments were first clearly settled and in accordance with the needs of G.H.Q."

After the day's discussions, during which some of the difficulties were smoothed out, Haig accepted an invitation to the French embassy. He and Lyautey went into a private room, and the war minister asked if he was satisfied with the French officers at G.H.Q.

"I said I was quite satisfied," Haig's diary records, "but I felt that Colonel d'Alençon, Nivelle's confidential staff officer, was a cause of trouble; he disliked every Englishman. He quite agreed and said he was most disagreeable even to himself. We parted the best of friends. The ambassador came downstairs to the door to see me off and bid me good night. It was 11.15 P.M. when I left the French embassy. I felt that I had been very forgiving and only the need of working with the French Army in order to win had dragged me there."

The conference continued on March the thirteenth, and in the evening Haig received Sir Henry Wilson and General Kiggell.

"The former put forward very straight-forwardly his reasons against going to French G.Q.G. as the head of the British mission. Briefly he felt sure that whatever he did he would be credited with intriguing against the commander in chief. I told him that he would have my complete confidence in military matters, and that, looking to the future and the possibility that Nivelle's plans might not meet with a full measure of success, it seemed most desirable to have a senior British officer and one who is trusted by the French at Nivelle's headquarters. So we decided that he should go to Beauvais."

The agreement eventually arrived at between the two governments, and signed by the two commanders in chief, was far from being entirely satisfactory to Haig, but he was prepared to make almost any concession in order to secure an amicable settlement. Before signing the document, however, he wrote above his signature:

"I agree with the above on the understanding that, while I am fully determined to carry out the Calais agreement in spirit and letter, the British Army and its commander in chief will be regarded by General Nivelle as allies and not as subordinates, except during the particular operations which he explained at the Calais conference. Further, while I also accept the agreement respecting the functions of the British mission at French headquarters it should be understood that these functions may be subject to modifications as experience shows to be necessary."

The London conference did something to retrieve the errors of the Calais conference, but nothing more. Haig was slow to take offence and quick to forgive. So far as Nivelle was concerned he was unwilling to believe that a fellow soldier could have been guilty of double dealing. That he should have presumed too much upon the authority that he believed the Calais convention had given him was regrettable but not unpardonable; that he had had nothing to do with the ambush into which Haig and Robertson had been led at Calais Haig continued and preferred to believe.

On March the fifteenth Nivelle wrote to Haig:

I have read the postscript that you thought you ought to add to the agreement of March 13, 1917. I have no observation to make on it since it only registers a state of affairs which already existed. I don't think, as a matter of fact, that I have adopted an attitude toward the British Army or their commander in chief which could give ground for fear that I considered them as subordinates and not as allies. It would have proved a narrow conception of our loyal collaboration and would have been a sign of ill breeding.

And it will be the same, do believe me, at all times and even during the particular operations to which you refer.

May I add that I sincerely hope that I shall not have to be present at similar meetings, and that it is a genuine satisfaction to my conscience to assert that neither the French government nor I myself was in any way responsible for the last two meetings. The first was in fact summoned by the English government and three telegrams and a very pressing letter were required to persuade us to attend the conference in London, which was caused by the memorandum which you sent home.

I shall be very happy to meet you as soon as possible whether you will do me the pleasure of coming here or whether you will suggest a meeting anywhere else.

How far Nivelle was sincere in his protestations is extremely questionable, but sincerity was so much a part of Haig's nature that he was slow to suspect a lack of it in others and he did not hesitate to reply in the frankest and most cordial terms:

Your kind letter of 15th inst. reached me last night. Many thanks for writing. I heartily reciprocate your wish that there should be no more conferences of the Calais type, and I feel confident that "unity of *effort*" will be assured with absolute certainty if you and I are allowed to settle our own affairs together without interference from London or Paris. In any case I can honestly say that I have only one objective in view and that is to "beat the German armies". To attain that end it is of vital importance that the relations existing, not only between you and me, but between every fraction of our forces, should be of the most friendly character. I have always striven to ensure this, and, as I stated at Calais, the relations between all ranks of our armies seem *now* to be more genuinely united than at any previous time in the war. Hence my fervent desire that nothing should be done which might in any way tend to change these mutual good feelings.

I do hope and believe that the shadow which the Calais conference seemed at one time to have cast across our path has disappeared, and, as far as I personally am concerned, you can rely on my wholehearted support, and my earnest desire to fall in with your plans to the utmost of my power.

It is not impossible that Nivelle's increase of civility was due to the fact that he no longer felt his own position was secure. Briand had been from the first his main supporter, but on March the seventeenth Briand's government fell. Ribot became prime minister, and Painlevé succeeded Lyautey as minister of war.

CHAPTER X

Nivelle's Failure and the Aftermath

THE SPRING of 1917 saw great events in the history of the world. Almost simultaneously the Russian Empire crumbled into revolution and the peace-loving republic of the United States under a pacifist president decided to take part for the first time in a European War. Both these facts profoundly affected the strategic situation in the west. Two divergent schools of thought sprang into being. There were those who argued that, having now the vast wealth and man power of the United States behind them, the allies would be wise to rest upon the defensive until the weight of all that wealth could make itself felt and until that man power could be transferred to the scene of battle. Others, who believed—as it turned out, rightly—that Russia could not carry on a revolution and a war at the same time, realized that the armies of Germany defending the broad spaces of her eastern frontier might soon be free to reinforce the west, and that it was therefore more than ever incumbent upon the allies to strike soon and to strike hard.

Nivelle had boasted too long and too loudly of how he would destroy the German Army in forty-eight hours. He had deliberately scorned secretive methods and courted publicity. He knew, as well as another, how nearly the French Army had approached the limits of endurance, and he believed that it was wise for the men themselves to be made aware that only one more great battle divided them from victory and peace. The coming offensive was therefore proclaimed from the housetops and it became common knowledge in the trenches on both sides of the front. So well were the Germans informed of the attack that was coming and so many were the delays before it came that they had ample time to make their preparations in order to ensure that it should fail. They transferred to that section of the front which Nivelle intended to attack, the whole of their First Army from the area of the Somme. It thus happened that when the attack was delivered in April, instead of in February as Joffre had planned, there were sixty-six German divisions where there had been twenty-one two months before, and on the exact front of the attack there were forty-three divisions where there had previously been ten.

This knowledge was not in the possession of the French commander in chief, but he must have realized that the methods of publicity he had pursued, and the delays he had permitted, made it probable that the enemy should have got wind of his plans, in which case they would certainly have taken steps to defeat them. If such considerations did not give him pause, the fact that he had lost the confidence not only of the government in Paris but also of his own generals in the field might have deterred the most obstinate of men; but it had no effect upon Nivelle. Of the commanders of the three great groups of armies, Pétain, Micheler, Franchet d'Esperey, there was not one who believed that the generalissimo could accomplish what he had undertaken. Messimy, a deputy and a former minister for war, but also a professional soldier and recently in command of a brigade, drew up a solemn indictment of the high command and submitted it to ministers. The result was the calling of a special conference at Compiègne which was attended by ministers, generals and the President of the Republic. There, having heard the gravest doubts expressed by every general present, except the commander in chief, the government decided, largely under the influence of the President, to proceed with the original plan.

On the morning of April the ninth, the postponed attack was finally launched by the British, after prolonged bombardments. The early objectives were gained and four Canadian divisions and the Sixth Corps distinguished themselves. On the thirteenth Haig received a message from Nivelle to the effect that the French army group commanders were anxious to postpone operations for another day, a proposition to which he would not consent unless Haig concurred in it. Haig agreed reluctantly. It is curious to note how when plans were being made two or three months in advance it was usually the French who demanded an earlier date and usually Haig who, taking into account all the preparations that would be required, found it necessary to insist upon a longer delay; but when it actually came to delivering the blow Haig was always punctual to the day and the hour, whereas the French almost invariably insisted on a postponement.

At last, on April the sixteenth, the long proclaimed and oft postponed attack of the French Army was delivered. While in many places considerable success attended the operations of this first day, it was made plain by evening that the high hopes entertained by Nivelle had been illusory and that his proud boasts would never be fulfilled.

"It is a pity that Nivelle was so very optimistic as regards breaking the enemy's line," Haig observed in his diary.

He rightly feared that the result would be a great reinforcement for that school of thought which believed in marking time until the Americans could take the field. On the eighteenth of April he wrote, "I must say at once that it would be the height of folly for the French to stop now, just when the Germans have committed the serious fault of retiring, meaning to avoid a battle, but have been forced to fight against their will. The enemy should be pressed everywhere without delay by all the allies. If offensive operations are stopped in France, the enemy will be given time to recover from the blows he received on the Somme, at Verdun, Arras and now on the Aisne. He will also be able to transfer troops to other theatres which will call for countermeasures on our part. This will mean increased demand on our shipping and help the German in his submarine campaign. He would also have troops available for a threat against England."

To the chief of the Imperial General Staff, on April nineteenth, Haig wrote:

> In my opinion the decision to cease offensive operations now, until Russia and America are in a position to join in, (probably not until next spring) would be most unwise.
>
> The struggle is following a normal course. Great results are never achieved in war until the enemy's resisting power has been broken, and against a powerful and determined enemy, operating with great numbers on wide fronts, this is a matter of time and hard fighting. . . . Delay in forcing the issue would increase the danger to our shipping from submarines, and might result in the allies being unable to exert their full strength next year.
>
> I consider that the prospects of success this year are distinctly good if we do not relax our efforts, and that it would be unwise, unsound and probably, in the long run, more costly in men and money to cease offensive operations at an early date.

Although the allies made gains in the ensuing days the advance was not what the French government or public had been led to expect. The powers in Paris began to make plans for removing Nivelle. Conferences of Haig with

Painlevé and Ribot are reported in the British commander's diary. Ribot asked his opinion of Pétain.

"I of course could not discuss this. I said I knew him very slightly and had not had an opportunity of judging his military qualities."

Two months earlier the French government, with the enthusiastic support of the British prime minister, had been seeking to compel the British commander in chief to become a mere automaton under the inspired guidance of his more gifted French colleague. Now the French minister of war, Painlevé, was almost on his knees to that same British commander in chief to furnish him with material that might help him to get rid of that same French colleague.

And in every respect events had vindicated the opinions of Haig, justified his doubts and proved his prescience. He had believed in the methods of the Somme, continuous attacks and limited objectives. So far as he had put those methods into operation he had been conspicuously successful. More, in fact, had been and was still being accomplished in the fighting before Arras than could be claimed for any similar period in the battle of the Somme. If these attacks had been delivered earlier in the year, as Haig and Joffre had intended, before the German withdrawal had been effected, it is impossible to say how much more important the results would have been. There are many historians, French and English, who believe that they might have proved decisive.

But Haig had loyally accepted the decision of his government and had loyally served the foreign general who had been placed over his head. Now that general had lost his glamour in the eyes of politicians and his own government were hoping that Haig's testimony would assist them in effecting a change. Some men might have been tempted to pay out an old score, and might have yielded to or resisted the temptation, but to Haig the temptation simply did not occur. There is not a line in his private diary or in his intimate correspondence to suggest that the sudden reversal of positions ever struck him, or that he enjoyed the poetic justice of the situation. He had only one thought. If Nivelle remained, the French would continue to attack; if he were removed they would stop. Therefore he was in favour of Nivelle remaining. The past was forgotten. Personal considerations did not exist. His one concern was to win the war. There was no room for thoughts of petty malice or of mean revenge in that high and honourable mind.

For months the British commander had been thinking of a campaign in the north, with the object of turning the Germans' right flank and barring them permanently from the Channel ports. This had become an urgent need since the Germans began their unrestricted submarine warfare on February the seventeenth, and a food shortage in the British Isles was threatened.

"I think the time has nearly come for me to take up our 'alternative plan' in earnest," Haig wrote to Robertson late in April, "and to this end we should ask the French to relieve some of our divisions on our right while we relieve their divisions on the Belgian coast. But pressure on the German Army must not be relaxed in the meantime. This seems to me of first importance for the success of our plan."

General Pétain, now that Nivelle's plans had failed, was appointed assistant to the French minister of war early in May, and not long afterward succeeded Nivelle as commander in chief. Meanwhile, on May the fourth, a military conference took place at Pétain's office. Nivelle was present as well as Haig, Robertson, Maurice and Kiggell. Agreement was reached both as to continuing the present offensive so far as possible and also as to the forthcoming attack in the north. It was agreed that the British were to deliver the main attack and the French were to assist, both by taking over part of the British line and by attacking on their own front. It was further decided that the greatest secrecy should be observed and that even the respective governments should only be acquainted with the main principles, but with no details in regard to the date or the place of any attack.

After luncheon with Ribot Haig walked with Lloyd George in the Champs Elysées before attending the conference at the Quai d'Orsay. "Mr Lloyd George made two excellent speeches in which he stated that he had no pretensions to be a strategist, that he left that to his military advisers; that I, as commander in chief of the British forces in France, had full power to attack where and when I thought best. He (L.G.) did not wish to know the plan, or where or when any attack would take place. Briefly, he wished the French government to treat their commanders on the same lines. His speeches were quite excellent."

After the conference Haig returned to his headquarters in a far happier frame of mind. Not only had the French undertaken to support him, but he felt also that he had for the first time the confidence of his own prime minister. How easily his generous nature forgave personal injury is proved by a letter that he wrote to his wife on the following day:

"I was very pleased with the way Lloyd George tackled the military problem at the conference in Paris yesterday. In fact, I have quite forgiven him his misdeeds up to date in return for the very generous words he said yesterday about the British forces in France, and the way in which he went for the French government and insisted on *vigorous action*. He did well."

Shortly before Nivelle was superseded Haig was surprised to receive the following letter from Henry Wilson:

DEAR FIELD MARSHAL,

I am sorry to trouble you with a personal matter at a

time like this but I feel I would not be carrying out my compact with you—made in the middle of March in London —if I did not tell you quite frankly what I was thinking of.

It seems to me that since April the twenty-fourth when you had your last interview with General Nivelle at Amiens I have for some reason, which I cannot even guess at, lost your confidence. I say this in no spirit of complaint or of criticism but simply because it appears to me to be so, and I say it because from that day to this although the French high command has been passing through, and is still passing through, a serious and a dangerous crisis you have never asked for my opinion nor called on me for assistance in any shape. Again I am not complaining but it seems to me that if I have not got your entire and absolute confidence and if I get the feeling that my opinion on the present French military situation and the prospects of the future are of no value to you, then the sooner I go back to England the better.

I can only add that you have had no more loyal subordinate than I have been since I came on your staff and I am more grieved than I can say to think that I have lost your confidence.

Very sincerely yours,

HENRY WILSON.

Haig's reply was brief.

MY DEAR HENRY,

Don't be a B.F.! I expect to see you here to-night. I would have asked you to come before but did not wish to bring you away from what seemed to me the most important work viz.: to get my requests for relief of troops, etc. accepted by our allies.

Yours

D. H.

About this time Haig lost his director general of transportation, Eric Geddes, during whose sojourn in France order had been restored out of chaos and the problem had been solved which at one period had threatened to produce serious consequences.

On May the eighteenth Haig held a conference with Pétain at Amiens.

"I then asked him straight, 'Did the French intend to play their full part as promised at the Paris conference?' 'Could I rely on his wholehearted co-operation?' He was most outspoken and gave me full assurance that the French Army would fight and would support the British in every possible way."

Haig's plan of attack north of the river Lys was carefully explained with maps to Pétain, who neither then nor at any future date expressed to Haig an unfavourable opinion with regard to it. In conversation with Henry Wilson, according to a letter from the latter, he doubted whether the distant objectives of Zeebrugge and Ostend would ever be attained, but no such misgivings were conveyed in the two letters which he addressed to Haig during this month.

Before final agreement was reached on the details of the coming attack, distressing intelligence was brought to Haig's headquarters by General Debeney, who arrived there on June the second with a letter from Pétain authorizing him to lay the whole situation of the French Army before Haig and to conceal nothing. How much was communicated in the interview that followed is uncertain. Debeney may have hesitated, for reasons easily understood, to speak of mutinies, or Haig may have hesitated to entrust such information even to the pages of his diary. All he records is that Debeney stated that the French soldiers were dissatisfied because leave had been so long suspended, that leave must be reopened at once, and that this would prevent Pétain from fulfilling his promise to attack on June the tenth.

Haig accepted the inevitable philosophically and continued his preparations for the first phase of his campaign. This was to take the form of an attack upon the Messines ridge to be undertaken by the Second Army under Plumer. On the twenty-second and twenty-third of May Haig had visited their headquarters and had been most favourably impressed both by Plumer and by Harington, his chief of staff.

At ten minutes past three on June the seventh, as the dawn was breaking, the air was shaken by the crash of such an explosion as the work of man had never before produced on the face of the earth. Two years of patient, dangerous labour underground, five miles of tunnelled galleries, nineteen separate mines charged with nearly a million pounds of high explosive had contributed to the preparation of that awful moment. And simultaneously every gun along that sector of the British front, over two thousand five hundred, opened fire upon the enemy's position. Behind that barrage, deafened by that thunder, the infantry advanced to the attack.

The confidence of Plumer and the other officers of the Second Army had not been misplaced. The battle of Messines was the most perfectly planned and successfully conducted operation in the whole war. All through that morning tidings of victory flowed in to Haig's temporary headquarters in the train. This time there was no exception, no hold up, no setback, no counterattack recovering ground previously occupied.

In the afternoon Haig visited Plumer to congratulate him. "The old man", he wrote, "deserves the highest praise, for he has patiently defended the Ypres salient for two and a half years, and he well knows that pressure has been brought to bear on me to remove him from the command of the Second Army. I left him about 5 P.M. Before I came away he had received news of the capture of the Oostaverne line", his final objective.

"The capture of the Messines-Wytschaete ridge is without doubt a great feat. An officer prisoner, taken at Messines, said that the German command never imagined we would attack Wytschaete on account of its strength. The 'Jägers', he said, 'had been posted there to hold it at all costs'. He said the place was 'impregnable'. Great was his astonishment when he saw batches of prisoners of these very Jägers being marched into the cage where he was. 'Then', he said, 'the ridge is lost and we can never retake it now'."

The same evening, "I met General Pétain in his train at Cassel station. He had seen the King of the Belgians this morning, and was on his way back to Compiègne. Our interview was most satisfactory. General Rucquoy was also present, as representing the King of the Belgians. Pétain brought a document embodying the points already agreed upon between us by correspondence regarding the forthcoming operations in Flanders. This document or 'protocol' was read aloud by me and was finally signed by the three of us. It placed the French six divisions entirely under my orders, appointed General Anthoine to command them, and left all points remaining in doubt to be decided by me. Altogether I found Pétain most anxious to help in every way and thoroughly businesslike.

"Pétain and I then had a private talk. He told me that two French divisions had refused to go and relieve two divisions in the front line, because the men had not had leave. Some were tried and were shot. The French government supported Pétain. They also refused to allow the leading French socialists to go to Stockholm for a conference with German socialists. The situation in the French Army was serious at one moment, but it is now more satisfactory. But the bad state of discipline causes Pétain grave concern.

"General Allenby came to dinner to say good-bye before leaving to take up the Egyptian command." He was succeeded by General Byng in command of the Third Army.

The first phase of the northern campaign having now been accomplished with brilliant success, all Haig's energies were directed toward preparing for the second.

On June the twentieth, at a meeting of the war policy committee, a statement was made which was to affect profoundly the future conduct of the war and was to prove the determining factor in the control of Haig's policy during the next six months. Haig does not record it in the general record of the day's events but adds it as a special note, headed "Secret".

"A most serious and startling situation was disclosed today. At today's conference Admiral Jellicoe, as First Sea Lord, stated that owing to the great shortage of shipping due to German submarines it would be impossible for Great Britain to continue the war in 1918. This was a bombshell for the Cabinet and all present. A full enquiry is to be made as to the real facts on which this opinion of the naval authorities is based. No one present shared Jellicoe's view, and all seemed satisfied that the food reserves in Great Britain are adequate. Jellicoe's words were: 'There is no good discussing plans for next spring—we cannot go on.' . . ."

Subsequently Haig told an intimate friend that Admiral Jellicoe had reinforced this opinion in private conversation. He had told Haig that "if the army can't get the Belgian coast ports the navy can't hold the Channel and the war is lost". It was with this knowledge in his mind, based on the opinion of so distinguished a sailor, that Haig persisted for so long in his fierce, obstinate struggle for the Belgian coast.

Apart from the danger of losing command of the Channel, which would indeed have meant the end of the war—and Haig could not have been justified in disregarding Jellicoe's solemn warning—the next gravest menace in his and in Robertson's opinion was the transference of a large number of troops to Italy which, as Lloyd George believed, would defeat Austria and thus knock away one of the props under Germany.

The danger of arguing by analogy is proverbial. If Austria, Turkey and Bulgaria had really been the props upon which the German Empire was resting, it would have been wise policy to knock them away, but a moment's reflection will show that they were nothing of the kind. They were rather—to pursue the architectural metaphor—ornamental pillars decorating the façade of a very solid building, and while their disappearance would have impaired its dignity it would hardly have caused its collapse.

On June the twenty-first there was a further meeting of the War Cabinet which Haig attended. "Lloyd George made a long oration, minimizing the successes gained and exaggerating the strength of the enemy," records the Haig diary. "His object was to induce Robertson and myself to agree to an expedition being sent to support the Italians. It was a regular lawyer's effort to make black appear white! He referred with a sneer to my optimistic views. I told him that war could not be won by arithmetic and that the British Army being in touch with the enemy was able to realize how much the latter's morale has decreased. L.G. stated also that he had grave misgivings as to the correctness of the advice given by the military advisers of the government. 'Robertson', he said, 'had changed his opinions.'

"The prime minister so insisted on sending an expedition to Italy that I thought he had already promised support to the Italians. Finally, he requested Robertson and myself to think carefully over the views he had expressed, and then to submit a further report by Monday."

Lloyd George was perhaps, from his own point of view, unwise to ask Haig and Robertson to submit further reports. Both could express themselves on paper far more efficiently than in the council chamber, and on this particular matter they had both thought so deeply and so long that they produced statements which were difficult to answer. Even Lloyd George, with genuine doubt still in his heart, was compelled to bow to them.

Before Haig returned to France on the twenty-seventh, he declined Lord Derby's offer to recommend him for a peerage. He wrote:

"I realize that in honouring me, their commander, you are in a way honouring the whole army. Still I feel that it is best for me to remain as I am, for the personal reasons . . ."

On the same visit to London he had a reconciliation with Lord French.

"He was very pleased to see me, and said that the order to give up his command in France came as a great blow to him and that he was so upset that he knew he thought and said and did things then which he now was ashamed of. He felt now that it was the best thing for the country that he had given up his command, because he was then in bad health and not fit to carry out the terrific duties which at that time rested upon him. I shook him by the hand and congratulated him on speaking out like a man. I invited him to France, and we parted the best of friends. I was with him for about half an hour."

At the beginning of the month the King came to spend a few days in the war area and inhabited a house at Cassel where Haig had been accustomed to stay. Haig visited His Majesty on the evening of his arrival in order to see that all had been done to render him comfortable, and after a short interview was about to take his leave when to his great surprise the King presented him with the insignia of a Knight of the Thistle. He was genuinely and frankly delighted with this, the highest honour that a Scotsman can receive, and his pleasure was increased by the obvious satisfaction that the King had in handing it to him, and by the knowledge that the Duke of Buccleuch had declined to accept it until it had been bestowed upon the "greatest living Scotsman".

It was not until the evening of July the twenty-first, five days after the preliminary bombardment had begun, that the commander in chief received a letter definitely conveying Cabinet approval of the campaign, but even then it was expressed in such language as carried with it no accompaniment of confidence. On the twenty-ninth he wrote this in his diary: "I replied to a kind letter from Lord Derby in which he assured me of his friendship and support, and hoped that I would shift any additional worry onto his own and Robertson's shoulders. I told him I have not any doubt about him or Robertson supporting me. No worries on that score. What does cause me anxiety is that the government do not give some *practical signs* that *they* have confidence in my plan! Something more than words is wanted. They should show they mean business by making an effort to concentrate all available resources at this, the decisive spot; at this, the decisive moment of the war; eighteen-pounders should be got from somewhere, and drafts provided in abundance, etc. Instead of this, reserves which we can ill spare are being sent to Italy."

Those who talked glibly about the desirability of unity of command, as between the allies, failed to realize the far more pressing and urgent need of unity of mind and purpose among the responsible authorities of Great Britain. A platoon commander who before an attack allowed his non-commissioned officers to suspect that they had lost his confidence would rightly be condemned as unfit for his position. Nor can a prime minister be held guiltless, who on the eve of a great battle allows the impression to prevail that he distrusts the strategy of the whole campaign and doubts the capacity of his commander in chief.

CHAPTER XI

The Battle of Passchendaele

BEFORE WE ENTER upon the grim story of the long battle which was now to be so fiercely fought upon the plains of Flanders, it may be well to recapitulate the causes which rendered it imperative for the British Army to fight then and to fight there.

First comes the fact, which was not known at the time in England and which is still insufficiently appreciated, that the French Army, which had so heroically held the enemy at bay for three years, could no longer be relied upon. Haig, who had inherited the deep discretion of his race, and who was also bound by obligations of honour to his French colleague, forbore both in official dispatches and in private correspondence from referring to a secret that was fraught with such fearful danger. Had knowledge of it leaked out to the Germans, who heard nothing of it but the vaguest rumours, they would have been swift to take advantage of an opportunity which might actually have proved disastrous to the allied cause.

Haig, who had a lofty disregard for his own reputation during his lifetime, relying with quiet confidence on the verdict of history, seldom alluded, even when the danger was past, to this, one of the principal motives which at the time controlled his conduct. In a letter, however, which he wrote to General Charteris on March the fifth, 1927, there occurs the following passage, "As to Winston's book, he asked me if he could publish a wire I sent him thanking him for good work done in matter of munitions. He mentioned that he had criticized me over the Passchendaele operations.

"I replied I did not care what criticisms he made as long as he clearly stated the facts, as far as it was possible to know them. He said he intended to do so, and thanked me for giving him the permission he asked. . . . It is impossible for Winston to know how the possibility of the French Army breaking up in 1917 *compelled me to go on attacking.* It was impossible to change sooner from the Ypres front to Cambrai without Pétain coming to press me not to leave the Germans alone for a week, on account of the *awful* state of the French troops! You even did not know the facts, as Pétain told them to me in confidence."

Charteris was his chief intelligence officer at the time, yet even to Charteris Haig had not felt justified in repeating all that Pétain had told him.

The second reason, which, if it had stood alone would in itself have been hardly less compelling, was the stark, unqualified affirmation of Admiral Jellicoe that unless the Belgian ports were captured the war could not go on. "It is no use making plans for 1918" had been his actual words. Others may have been more optimistic, but none spoke with greater authority. Jellicoe's opinion was reinforced by Admiral Bacon, commanding the Dover patrol, who had written a paper in June in which he stated that Dunkirk would have to be abandoned as a main port unless Zeebrugge and Ostend could be taken before the winter. These statements meant nothing less than that Great Britain was faced by defeat abject, humiliating and immediate, and that, in the opinion of those best qualified to judge, such defeat could be averted only by a successful advance in Flanders.

Moreover, the plan which circumstances must have compelled him to adopt was one which he had long been contemplating with favour. Long before the submarine menace had materialized and while the French Army was still in the plenitude of its strength and efficiency, Haig had believed that the best place to attack was in Flanders, and had only been prevented by other circumstances from attacking there earlier.

It was not the fault of the British commander in chief that the attack in Flanders was postponed until August, 1917. The whole year's timetable had been thrown out from the beginning by Nivelle. A few weeks, or, as will appear, even a few days, might have made an immense difference to the ultimate achievement.

The Russian situation provided another powerful argument in favour of assuming the offensive without delay. Information as to conditions on that front was scanty, but that Russia would remain a combatant was still possible. Even though the fighting value of her troops was reduced by indiscipline, the mere fact that she retained so many German divisions on her frontier rendered her continued presence in the field invaluable to the allies. While her decision was yet uncertain nothing could be better calculated to affect it favourably than a successful advance in the west, which would raise hope of early victory.

If, on the other hand, hope of keeping Russia in the war had to be abandoned, then there was still stronger cause for striking in the west without delay, before Germany could transfer her troops from one frontier to the other.

Haig hoped as a first stage to secure the Passchendaele-Staden ridge. In the second stage, in which the Fourth Army and naval forces were to take part, he aimed at winning the line Thourout-Cockerlaere. On the morning of the thirty-first of July he was awakened at 4.15 by the sound of heavy firing. The ground on which his train stood was shaking on account of the terrific bombardment. On

BATTLE OF PASSCHENDAELE
AUGUST - NOVEMBER, 1917

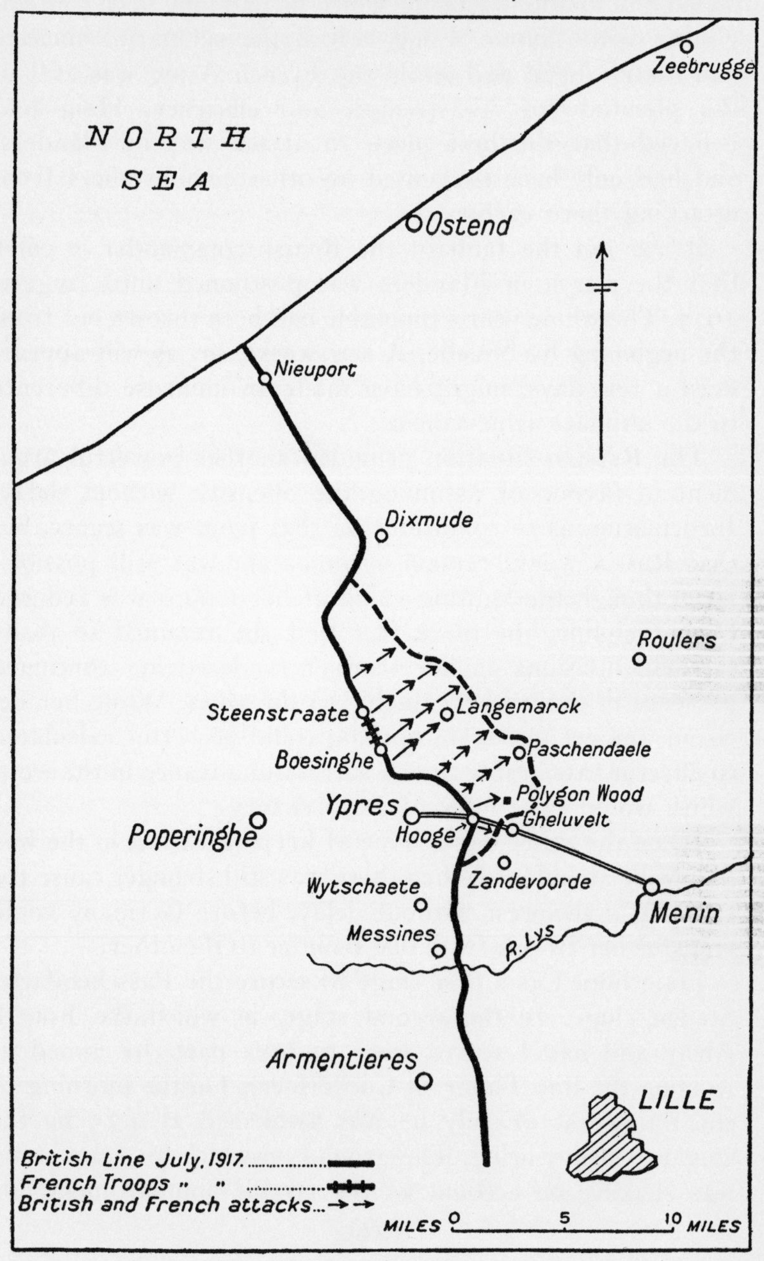

the whole the day was satisfactory. Large numbers of prisoners were taken, and British casualties were comparatively light. The French divisions on the left had been conspicuously successful, a fact to which Haig attached great importance, hoping that the report would improve the morale of the French Army as a whole.

"As regards future operations," the diary says, "I told Gough to continue to carry out the original plan; to consolidate ground gained and to improve his position, as he may deem necessary, for facilitating the next advance; the next advance will be made as soon as possible, *but only after adequate bombardment and after dominating the hostile artillery.*"

During the melancholy fortnight that followed, with a continuous downpour of rain, there was all too little work to occupy the time of the commander in chief. But he did not waste time. He visited his army commanders, he discussed with them the situation, he studied the lessons to be derived from the most recent fighting, and he inspected hospitals.

A very slight improvement having taken place in the weather, advantage was taken of it to renew the advance on the sixteenth.

The attack was successful along most of the front: only the right of the Fifth Army was not able to gain, on the Ypres ridge south of Hooge, all that was intended.

"Sir William Robertson arrived from England at 3 P.M.," Haig recorded. "I had a talk with him till 4.30 P.M. The prime minister sent me a friendly message by him, with an expression of confidence in me. This was, I gather, due to his having said at the recent London conference (with reference to my present operations) that 'he thought we had put our money on the wrong horse. We ought instead to have reinforced the Italians'.

"In reply, I told Robertson to thank the prime minister

for his message, but what I want is *tangible* support. *Men, guns, aeroplanes.* It is ridiculous to talk about supporting me 'wholeheartedly' when men, guns, rails, etc. are going in quantities to Egypt for the Palestine expedition; guns to the Italians, to Mesopotamia and to Russia. Robertson agreed, and said he was entirely opposed to any Italian venture."

The new weapon which came into prominence during this day's fighting was the small ferro-concrete nest of machine guns, which came to be described as a "pillbox", and with which General Sixte von Arnim had studded his lines of defence. Continuous rain prevented any renewal of the battle on a wide scale during August, although some local attacks took place and were accompanied with varying success.

Although the Passchendaele-Staden ridge had not yet been reached, the question whether to put into execution the original plan of a naval demonstration and a landing by the Fourth Army on the coast near Ostend was anxiously discussed by Haig, Admiral Bacon and General Rawlinson. This move was postponed indefinitely for strategic reasons.

On the twenty-second an attack was delivered by the Second Corps, on the right of the Fifth Army, along the Menin road, where small progress was made at the cost of heavy casualties. The fighting continued for the two following days, every inch of the ground was fiercely disputed.

The last days of August were worthy of the beginning of that fearful month. High winds, heavy rain and winter cold depressed the spirits and increased the discomfort of the troops. Haig devoted some of these days to the inspection of the Canadian forces, which had steadily increased in numbers and efficiency.

At Les Quatre Vents I was met by General Burstall, commanding the Second Canadian Division, and George

Black with the horses. A ride of about ten minutes across country brought us to where the Fourth Canadian Brigade (Rennie) was drawn up. General Currie, commanding Canadian corps, met me here. He has sprung a tendon in his leg (calf) playing badminton, and is very lame. Currie is a very big, tall, heavy man. He must have been in great pain, but he stuck it all day. Big legs are necessary to support such a large frame as General Currie has.

After inspecting the brigade, the troops marched past me, re-formed and gave three cheers. They asked me if I had any objection to the latter: "they wished to do it, and cheering does us good", so of course I agreed, though it would have seemed out of place in our old regular army to cheer except on the King's birthday. . . .

The experience and training of the past year have done wonders for the Canadians. Their morale is now very high, and though they have been opposed by the flower of the German Army (Guards, etc.) they feel that they can beat the Germans every time. I was greatly pleased with the smart turnout, and the earnest determined look of all ranks. The officers and all ranks were, I think, honestly glad to see me, because several C.O's thanked me for my visit, and said how much trouble their men had taken to turn out smart for my inspection.

These two Canadian divisions have "knocked out" seven German divisions, viz.: the Seventh, Two Hundred Twentieth, Fourth Guard, First Guard Reserve (these are four of the very best divisions in the German Army), Eleventh Reserve, Thirty-sixth Reserve (these are not so good) and Eighth Division (also very good). This fact in itself is an indication of the enemy's loss of morale. That these two Canadian divisions are now in such a fine state is due to having ample reserves to replace casualties, i.e. the result of a sound organization.

Two days later it was the turn of the Australians. "At 10.30 A.M. I inspected the Second Australian Division under Major General Smythe. The division was drawn up in column of brigades about half a mile west of Campagne (on the St Omer-Aire road). After my inspection, one battalian per brigade marched past by platoons. The men looked in fine health and marched past very well. The sight of the whole division on parade was a splendid spectacle. Brigades were commanded by Smith, Paton and Wisdom."

The Australians have never looked better since they came to France than they did this morning. I was greatly pleased with their bearing and evident desire of each one to do his very best to show up well at my inspection. These divisions have been out of the line for three months and have benefited from the training which they have undergone. The rain kept off very well, and I got back to Blendecques by motor in time for lunch.

In the early days of September Haig received a telegram from Robertson asking him to go to London in connection with a demand recently received from Foch, who was now chief of the staff in Paris, for a hundred heavy guns to be transferred to Italy from the French contingent then serving with the British Army. In the note which Foch drew up formulating this demand he suggested that the British might be able to continue the battle in Flanders without the assistance of these guns, "a battle", he wrote, "which is indispensable in order to tie down the enemy to prevent the sending over of German reinforcements to Italy". In view of the statement that has been made that Foch was opposed to the Flanders offensive, it is worth noting that he considered it "indispensable" to the right conduct of the war.

Haig crossed to England on September the third and together with General Davidson attended a military conference at the War Office next morning, when Robertson and Foch were present.

"Foch asked for guns to go to Italy because the *political* effect of a success there would be greater, in his opinion, than one in Flanders. He asserted that the French guns would be doing nothing for a month in Flanders. This, of course, I told him, was not the case. French guns on Anthoine's front have a wide sector, and are employed covering our left and supporting the Belgians at the present moment by counterbattering hostile guns. He, however, still continued to argue on the same lines. I returned for lunch to Eastcott and at 3 P.M. I attended the War Cabinet at 10 Downing Street. . . . I explained that at the present time the decisive point was in Flanders and it was most unsound policy to withdraw a single gun from this sector. I produced maps showing where the French guns were situated and how they were employed."

The prime minister was very anxious that some guns should be sent. Bonar Law was, as usual, very weak. Carson and General Smuts were opposed to any guns going. Lord R. Cecil for Foreign Office "dissociated" himself from everything the prime minister proposed.

Finally it was agreed that the matter should be placed in my hands. After explaining that it was the wish of the Cabinet that the guns should be sent if I could possibly spare them, Lloyd George spoke to me alone and said that it was very desirable to help the Italians at this juncture, because the French were trying to supplant us in their affections. We must not give the French the power of saying that *they wanted* to send one hundred guns, but the British would not let them go. I said that I would review the whole gun situation on the battle front and if we could possibly liberate fifty guns it would be done. He said he was very grateful.

At 4 P.M. General Foch arrived, and went through the same performance as this morning, viz. argued that the guns were really doing nothing on our front in Flanders. The proposal of holding a conference with me and Pétain was discussed, and after I had seen Foch we agreed to meet at Amiens on Friday at twelve noon; meantime I am to wire to France and direct Kiggell to discuss the gun situation with Birch and Anthoine with a view to liberating fifty French guns for Italy.

Haig decided to meet the French demand on condition that Pétain would undertake to replace the guns in time for the attack. Pétain consented to do this and the conference therefore passed off very successfully.

Commenting on it afterward, Haig wrote:

"Foch seemed on arrival at Amiens to have all his hackles up, but my few friendly words quickly calmed him, and we were all on the best of terms. His experiences in London should have done him good. He had gone there behind the back of Pétain and myself to get the British War Cabinet to sanction one hundred French guns being withdrawn from *my* command. The War Cabinet then handed the question to me to arrange with Pétain. This we have done satisfactorily for all. I found Pétain today straightforward and clear in his views, and most businesslike. And, as he said himself today, 'the marshal and I never argue and haggle over such matters'."

Haig had gone out of his way in this matter to meet the wishes of the prime minister, although there was division of opinion in the War Cabinet. Lloyd George sent him a telegram—"my colleagues and I are much gratified at the manner in which you have met them in regard to Italy. Please accept our best thanks for the promptitude with which you have carried out our wishes in a matter which was of great importance to the interallied policy."

Several politicians visited Haig's headquarters during the month. Winston Churchill, who had recently become minister of munitions, arrived there on the thirteenth. He had one or two lengthy conversations with the chief of staff and the artillery adviser with regard both to department matters and to larger issues. Haig's comment was, "I have no doubt that Winston means to do his utmost to provide the army with all it requires."

J. H. Thomas he found "a broad-minded patriot, most anxious to help and fully alive to what the gentry of England have done in the war"; and Austen Chamberlain was "a most charming and capable fellow", while Robert Cecil was "an honest, levelheaded fellow". But his highest praise was reserved for Mr Asquith, who stayed for two nights with him in the middle of the month. "I felt", he wrote, "that the old gentleman was head and shoulders above any other politician who had visited my headquarters in brains and all-round knowledge. It was quite a pleasure to have the old man in the house—so amusing and kindly in his ways."

There had been a slight improvement in the weather during the first fortnight of September, and on the twentieth the attack was launched at 5.40 A.M. The result, despite the condition of the ground which inflicted great hardship on the troops, was eminently successful, and Haig fixed September the twenty-sixth as the date of the next attack. That evening the Germans delivered no less than eleven counterattacks in the hope of dislodging the British from the positions they had gained in the morning. Again practically all objectives were gained in what came to be known as the battle of Polygon Wood.

On the eve of the battle the prime minister and Sir William Robertson arrived at headquarters. At dinner the prime minister seemed "in the best of spirits and most friendly. Very much down upon the Italians;* there is now no intention of sending a British force there!"

The next morning, "At 9.30 A.M. I had a meeting in my room with the prime minister, General Robertson and Colonel Hankey, who made notes. I was asked to submit my views as to the role of the British forces in the event of the Russians dropping out of the war—and the Italians and French doing (as they are doing now) very little. I am to give a considered opinion. My opinion without having gone

*The reason for Lloyd George's irritation was that General Cadorna, having extracted one hundred guns from the French and British, had telegraphed to say that he had abandoned the offensive for which they were intended.

into details, is that we should go on striking as hard as possible with the object of clearing the Belgian coast. We should be prepared to make and win the campaign.

"As regards sending a division to Egypt, I stated that the sound policy for the allies is to occupy a defensive attitude *everywhere* except on the Western Front which has been accepted as the decisive front by the British government. . . .

"The prime minister visited Poperinghe this afternoon, and saw some German prisoners recently arrived in the cages. He seems to have been much encouraged by what he saw. A shell fell near his car (one hundred yards off) as he was passing along the 'switch road' near Poperinghe. This also pleased him."

Mr Lloyd George has since expressed surprise at the spirit of quiet confidence which he found prevailing at G.H.Q. during this visit. However bad the position had been, a spirit of confidence would presumably have been preferable to one of nervous anxiety or panic. But indeed there was little cause for dejection. That war is a ghastly business and that a war waged against so powerful and valiant an enemy as Germany can only be won at the price of fearful sacrifice, hideous suffering and wholesale slaughter, were facts that had been present to the minds of all, and often before the eyes of many of the officers at G.H.Q. during the last three years. They were not ignorant of the conditions in which men were fighting. Six young officers of brigade-major rank were deputed to visit regularly the front line and to report to the general staff on the state of the ground as well as on other matters. In addition, the general officer commanding royal artillery, the engineer in chief and the quarter master general had each a liaison officer whose duty it was to keep his chief informed of the effect of the weather upon the operations of their various branches. They in turn informed the commander in chief. The legend of the staff officer who wept when he saw the mud at Passchendaele is either apocryphal or does little credit to the nerves of the man who could not bear to see conditions concerning which he had already received full information.

So much has been written of the mud at Passchendaele that it might almost be believed that mud had never appeared before in the history of war. But mud is an old acquaintance of the soldier and, although it has frequently hindered, it has seldom frustrated the successful conduct of military operations. Mud did not stop the advance of Napoleon in Poland nor that of Grant in Virginia. It was present in varying quantities throughout the war on the Western Front, but it did not stop Rawlinson on the Somme, nor Allenby at Arras, nor even Plumer at Messines, when, in fact, it was worse than it afterward proved at Passchendaele.

It was not until October, that is to say in the final stages of the battle, that it presented a serious problem. "The low-lying, clayey soil, torn by shells and sodden by rain, turned to a succession of vast muddy pools. The valleys of the choked and overflowing streams were speedily transformed into long stretches of bog, impassable except by a few well-defined tracks, which became marks for the enemy's artillery. To leave these tracks was to risk death by drowning, and in the course of the subsequent fighting on several occasions both men and pack animals were lost in this way." These were not the words of an imaginative war correspondent, but the words which Haig himself used in his official dispatch describing the battle.

If there had existed any doubt in Haig's own mind with regard to the successes that were being achieved, it might have been removed by the chorus of approval and the stream of congratulations that reached him not only from London, but from all parts of the Empire. The King telegraphed on the third of October, "The continued success of my gallant troops in Flanders gives me the highest satisfaction and reflects great credit both upon your leadership and the efficiency, endurance and courage of all ranks concerned." Queen Alexandra telegraphed on the same day, and on the following one General Pershing, the American commander in chief, sent a message: "Permit me to extend sincerest congratulations to you and your magnificent army upon the recent important gains in front of Ypres. They give a striking answer to weak-kneed peace propaganda."

On October the sixteenth, further and less successful attacks having been made, Haig was not a little surprised to receive the following telegram from the prime minister:

"The War Cabinet desire to congratulate you and the troops under your command upon the achievements of the British armies in Flanders in the great battle which has been raging since the thirty-first of July. Starting from positions in which every advantage rested with the enemy and hampered and delayed from time to time by most unfavourable weather, you and your men have nevertheless continuously driven the enemy back with such skill, courage and pertinacity, as have commanded the grateful admiration of the peoples of the British Empire and filled the enemy with alarm. I am personally glad to be the means of transmitting this message to you and to your gallant troops, and desire to take this opportunity of renewing my assurance of confidence in your leadership and in the devotion of those whom you command."

Haig copied the message into his diary, and added the comment, "This is the first message of congratulation on any operations from the War Cabinet which has reached me since the war began."

The difficulty that Haig and Lloyd George experienced in working harmoniously together at this period was due to a profound divergence of faith. The fact that they differed temperamentally was of slight importance. Lloyd

George was possessed of charms which, when exercised, could easily overcome Haig's initial distrust, and in any case Haig was more interested in principles than in personalities. But the fact was that Lloyd George no longer believed that the German Army could be beaten. His opinion was shared by many. It had already been voiced by Lord Lansdowne. Foch was prepared to accept it as a hypothesis. Pétain was less optimistic than Foch. Even Robertson had his moments of doubt.

Strong in that faith which others were losing, Haig steadfastly maintained his way, and it will be seen by how few that faith was shared and how solitary that way became. Until the very eve of victory, which still lay twelve months ahead, those doubts persisted in the minds of others and made them difficult colleagues, because they genuinely distrusted the soundness of his views.

Meanwhile, on the morning of October the fourth another limited advance had been made, principally by the Second Army. Once again the attack was heralded by the heavens opening. After a few fine days the weather broke on the night of the third and rain fell in torrents. This persistent ill fortune was, however, on this occasion somewhat compensated for by the fact that the British attack preceded by exactly ten minutes an attack which the Germans themselves were about to deliver. The result was that our barrage fell upon the enemy's infantry at the very moment when they were forming up for the assault, and inflicted fearful casualties upon them. That day all objectives were captured and success was complete.

The combatants by this time were well aware of the demoralization of the German troops. During the Australian attack many had come out of the pillboxes to surrender. We now know that the German high command were also aware of it. In the diary of Crown Prince Rupprecht, whose group of armies was opposing the British, and in the history written by his chief of staff, General von Kuhl, there are many entries which show that certain divisions could not be trusted to counterattack, that others required a six days' rest, that reinforcements from the Russian front were upsetting discipline, and that on account of the great delay in the transport of new divisions no fresh troops were available to relieve those in the Passchendaele sector. Ludendorff, when asked to have a relieving attack made elsewhere, said he could not do so "until the British attacks began to fail in energy and in following close on each other". So orders were issued for giving ground slowly before the British attacks. Rupprecht comments on the twelfth of October, "Change of weather. Rain, I am glad to say, our best ally".

The long deferred attack of the French was launched successfully at Malmaison on October the twenty-third. On the twelfth the British attack had continued and again on the twenty-second, and all objectives had been gained despite the fact that owing to the mud rifles became unusable and clean ones had to be sent up to the men in the front line.

The last phase of the battle opened on October the twenty-sixth, when comparatively little was achieved, and a conference took place two days later.

"At twelve noon I had a conference in my house at Cassel. Generals Plumer, Gough, with their staff officers were present—also with me were Kiggell, Davidson, Birch and Charteris. We discussed the situation on each of the army fronts and fixed the depth to be aimed at in the two next advances, and points of junction of the two armies, etc. It was agreed that the date already fixed for the next attack should hold, but that the date of the second attack should be settled at a conference subsequent to our attack on the thirtieth. Incidentally Gough stated that it was not the mud which prevented the Fourteenth Corps' attack progressing the last day, but the enemy's defences which were very strong and had not been sufficiently bombarded."

On October the thirtieth Passchendaele village was surrounded, and on November the 6th it was finally captured. The last attack was made on November the tenth, when at considerable cost the British position on the ridge was more firmly established. And so the long battle reached its unspectacular end.

The last phase of the battle was the least successful and the most costly. Whether Haig was right or wrong in continuing the offensive after the fourth, or after the twelfth of October, may remain forever a subject of controversy. It is true that the principal reasons for initiating the battle had disappeared or were disappearing: the navy was mastering the U-boat danger, in spite of the Germans holding the Flanders coast; the morale of the French Army was improving, although it had not yet made the Malmaison attack. On the other hand, the Germans were badly shaken, more so than ever before. Ludendorff dared not yet begin to move large reinforcements from Russia. The first since the beginning of July arrived in September, five divisions came that month and four in October. More might soon come—ten came in November; ten more in December. It was a case of now or waiting until the spring—by which time thirty more German divisions had arrived. Had Haig left off at the end of September, he would no doubt have been blamed, as Ludendorff was later for not continuing the March-April offensive when in sight of Amiens and Hazebrouck. While he would doubtless have been acquitted of pigheaded obstinacy, infirmity of purpose would have proved a graver charge.

To the cold gaze of the historian this battle of Passchendaele differs only in degree from those that had gone before and were to follow after. It was longer than most, the conditions were more unfavourable, the sufferings were greater, the results were less demonstrable. Yet all battles in this war were long, and were fought in cruel conditions inflicting fearful sufferings with slight substantial gains until the very end.

The final territorial objectives were not reached, but the tactical position of the British troops was considerably improved. If nothing else had been accomplished this alone would not have justified the heavy losses. But the objectives had not been only territorial. Nothing less than the salvation of the French Army and the protection of the British coast had been the gauges of this great battle. While it was being fought Pétain had splendidly accomplished his stern task of restoring discipline; and the men who fought with Anthoine under Haig had set a noble example which their compatriots were already burning to emulate.

During these same months the power of invention and spirit of heroism, which have never failed the British Navy, had found out the ways and means of mastering their dread adversaries under the water. The dire menace of starvation was no longer present.

While these great changes in the situation were occurring the German Army and their general staff had been hourly engaged. Owing to the continued British offensive they had been given no respite in which to heal their wounds or to produce new plans.

Captured letters and diaries of the enemy and German novels that have been written since the war prove how the despair which was creeping into the heart of the general was already taking possession of the rank and file. This was the second autumn that they had had to face these continually repeated attacks, which seemed to be preceded on each occasion by an increasingly terrific bombardment and to be delivered with growing ferocity and determination. Behind the attackers now loomed a whole new continent of reinforcements. Reading these letters, diaries and novels, it is impossible to doubt that, just as the battle of the Somme had broken the mainspring of the old German regular army, so the autumn offensive of 1917 undermined the resisting power of the German nation.

This war was a war of peoples, not of dynasties nor of religious faiths, not of statesmen nor of generals. It is in this particular respect that it differed from the wars of the past, and many writers have failed to understand it because they have not grasped this fact. Because it was a war of peoples there could be no victory until one side was beaten. A battle may be won by clever strategy, but more than strategy is needed to defeat a nation. Napoleon learned this lesson to his bitter cost in the snows of Russia and under the sun of Spain. There is no braver people than the Germans; no race, by long tradition, more inured to war. Until they were defeated the war could not be won. They could not be defeated in the Dardanelles, nor in Macedonia, nor in the Julian Alps, but only where the flower of their great army was fighting, on the plains of Flanders and in the fields of France. To defeat them demanded every drop of blood that the allies shed, every pang of suffering that they endured. It may well be that the world would have been happier if no war had been fought. But fought it was—and we believe that the failure of the allies would have been a world disaster. Therefore the supreme consolation is ours to know that all the sacrifices which we made to bring us victory, including the sacrifice of Passchendaele, were not made in vain.

CHAPTER XII

The Battle of Cambrai

THE YEAR 1917, which had opened with high hopes in the hearts of the allies, was drawing to its close in an atmosphere of despondency. Belief in the new political leaders was beginning to falter, and the restless brain of the British prime minister was determined to discover some method of restoring it.

At the beginning of October he asked the commander in chief to furnish him with a written statement of his opinion as to the line which future policy should follow in the event, which grew daily more probable, of Russia disappearing from the scene. The memorandum which Haig submitted on the subject was dated the eighth of October. It began by stating a fact that could not be disputed but was often forgotten. Germany and her allies relied upon one thing only for a favourable issue, namely the invincibility of the German Army. If that were to fail, hope would fail with it, and there would be nothing left to keep the enemy in the field. The first question, therefore, to answer was whether or no it was possible to shake that faith either by defeating that army or by so handling it as to bring it "manifestly to the point of breaking down". If the answer to that question was in the affirmative, there could be no doubt as to which was the right policy to pursue.

But even if the answer were in the negative, was there any better alternative open to the allies? He then repeated the familiar argument against the withdrawal of troops from the Western Front, insisting upon the greater facility enjoyed by the Central Powers in the matter of the transfer of troops from one area to another, on the danger that would be incurred by weakening our resistance in the west, and on the deplorable effect on public opinion which would be produced by a cessation of offensive operations, the discouragement it would cause in America, just preparing to take the field, and the fresh heart it would put into the German Army and civilian population.

He concluded by expressing his confidence "that the British armies in France, assisted by the French and American armies, will be quite capable of carrying through a sustained and successful offensive next year under certain conditions". The conditions which he insisted upon were proper reinforcements, both in men and munitions, and refusal to take over more of the French line. "One more indispensable condition of decisive success on the Western Front", he added, "is that the War Cabinet should have a firm faith in its possibility and resolve finally and unreservedly to concentrate our resources on seeking it, and to do so at once."

Referring to the East, he expressed the opinion that "the leading men in the East have a truer conception of what is at stake in this war than they are sometimes credited with. In my belief they realize that it is primarily a struggle between the Anglo-Saxon and the German races and ideals, and that the victor will be the predominant power in the Mahomedan world. They will wait to ascertain which side is likely to be victorious before committing themselves openly, and they have quite sufficient intelligence to understand that the issue will be decided in the theatre where the main German forces are and must be employed. If this were not so the comparative absence of excitement over the Turkish advance to the Suez Canal, our withdrawal from the Dardanelles, and our misfortunes last year in Mesopotamia would seem very difficult to account for."

He was prepared even for another year of unsuccessful warfare rather than accept an unsatisfactory peace.

"It would be better for the future of our race", he wrote, "to fail in next year's offensive than to accept the enemy's terms now when after more than three years of splendid effort we have brought the German resistance so near to breaking point.

"But I see no reason to apprehend failure. . . . In the present state of the German armies and of ours I am confident that if the course I have recommended be adopted wholeheartedly we shall gain far more than a limited success in the field next year."

The expression of these views, which were to be abundantly justified in less than twelve months, has been elegantly described in Mr Lloyd George's *War Memoirs* as "optimistic slosh", but Robertson thought differently. "Your memorandum", he wrote, "is splendid, and I hope greatly that you will credit me with saying the right thing in my memorandum which luckily went in before yours arrived. . . . I gather from Lord R. Cecil that perhaps you are a little disappointed with me in the way I have stood up for correct principle, but you must let me do my job in my own way. I have never yet given in on *important* matters and never shall. In any case whatever happens you and I must stand solidly together. I know we are both trying to do so."

The prime minister, as has already been indicated, was not pleased to find his two principal military advisers in complete agreement. Yet if they were to remain his advisers he could not totally ignore their advice. He therefore had recourse to a remarkable expedient. He caused the whole military situation to be laid before two other distinguished generals, then occupying positions at home, and asked them to give their opinion upon the conduct and the views of his commander in chief and his chief of the Imperial General Staff. And the officers whom he selected for this duty were Lord French and Sir Henry Wilson.

Never before, perhaps, has a commander in chief, who has been superseded on account of failure, been invited by his government to criticize his successor. If it had been proposed at the same time that the actions of the Cabinet during the last twelve months should be enquired into and reported upon by a committee consisting of Mr Asquith and Mr McKenna, it is doubtful whether the prime minister would have welcomed the suggestion. Yet the analogy is exact.

Robertson immediately sent an emissary to consult Haig as to whether he should resign. He himself felt disposed to do so, but Haig's reply was that he should remain at his post until his advice had been rejected. Haig did not approve of officers resigning in wartime. His theory was very simple. So long as the government required a man's services he should render them to the best of his ability. It was for the government to say when they were no longer required. To this theory, under great provocation, he steadfastly adhered.

It has been seen that a reconciliation had taken place between Haig and French, but the temptation to castigate the man who had been preferred above him was too much for human nature; and French was very human. Five sixths of the report which he produced was devoted to adverse criticism of Haig and Robertson. The remainder was a feebly expressed opinion in favour of remaining on the defensive in France, but he would not countenance the dispatch of troops to one of the other theatres of war, the scheme upon which the prime minister had set his heart.

It has been seen that while Henry Wilson was with Nivelle relations between him and Haig had been satisfactory. After Nivelle's fall Pétain had requested that Wilson should be withdrawn and, as he had previously failed to make a success of commanding a corps, Haig was unable to find him employment in France. "Find me something to do soon", he had begged Haig with disarming sincerity, "or I shall get into mischief." He now held the Eastern command in England and was busily ingratiating himself with the prime minister, who appreciated his vivid conversation and lively humour.

Wilson knew as well as French did what it was that Lloyd George wished them to recommend, and it is to the credit of both that they refused to recommend it. French said that it was now too late to adopt the police of "knocking away the props". Wilson, on the other hand, said it was too early. The only point on which they could concur, with the knowledge that it would be well received by the prime minister, was the setting up of some interallied body to take over supreme control of the war. With this recommendation, therefore, Lloyd George was compelled for the time being to content himself, and he lost no time in putting it into effect.

The government's decision in favour of taking over a larger proportion of the line caused Haig much trouble and anxiety during the month of October and throughout the winter. On the eighteenth he had a meeting with Pétain at Amiens, where the matter was discussed.

General Pétain stated that he had been ordered by his war committee to see me regarding taking over a portion of the French front. He told me that M. Painlevé and General Foch had recently visited London, where they had discussed the question with Lloyd George. General Wilson had also taken part in the discussion and had examined reports on the state of the French Army, with the result that *"he* recommended that the British should take over some of the French line".

Pétain's main arguments were that since Russia might go out of the war entirely, we ought to make our defensive arrangements accordingly. He considered the Germans might bring forty-five extra divisions to this front. He had no reserves. His losses were forty thousand a month—the French divisions were being reduced in number to one hundred, each to consist of only six thousand infantry.

He asked me to relieve his Sixth Army, i.e. to extend my right to a point southwest of St Gobain—six divisions front. The date of relief to be settled by me. He was anxious that I should agree to the principle of taking over more line.

General Pétain's arguments seemed to me to be quite unsound. There were two main points. *First,* the possibility of the enemy bringing forty-five extra divisions to this front; *second,* how to counter any increase of strength here. As regards the first, we had worked out thirty-two as the maximum number of divisions, but German divisions are all now of poor quality and not fit to take the offensive. Secondly, the best way to oppose the enemy's increase of strength on this front is to take the offensive. Moreover, instead of employing some of our divisions to take over line from the French, the most effective help would be for us to use them in an attack. Thus they would probably knock out twelve enemy divisions as against only holding an equal number on a defensive front. However, although I did not accept the principle of taking over more line, I said I would do my best to meet his wishes and would transfer the divisions now in the coast sector with their reserves, totalling four divisions, to carry out the relief. If the French government desire the whole Sixth Army to be relieved, and the British government concur, it is impossible for me to take over the extra line, and also retain sufficient men to carry on an effective offensive next spring.

In the letter which Haig subsequently addressed to Pétain he reiterated his opinion that to increase his share of the line as suggested would mean the abandonment of the offensive both in that autumn and also in the following spring. He was therefore reluctantly unable to increase the offer which he had made to take over a four division front. He wrote at the same time a dispatch to the C.I.G.S. stating the attitude he had adopted and asking for government approval. The government took the view that a decision on this matter must depend upon the military plans for the coming year which were then under consideration, and that meanwhile no action should be taken.

While these considerations were occupying the minds of ministers in London, Germany struck a devastating blow on the Italian front. We know from Ludendorff's memoirs that if it had not been for the Passchendaele offensive the blow would have been yet heavier, for at least two divisions which were destined for Italy were diverted to Flanders. Nevertheless the effect of the Italian retreat at Caporetto was sufficiently serious, and both the French and British governments decided that substantial reinforcements must be transferred to the Italian front without delay. Haig was compelled to part with first two divisions, then two more, and finally with a fifth, and also with General Plumer who took command of them. This was a severe strain on the Expeditionary Force, and Haig believed it to be an error. In his opinion far more practical help could be given to Italy by attacking on the Western Front than by sending reinforcements. His next attack in France, which he already had in contemplation, might have proved far more effective if he had had in reserve, to follow it up, those divisions which had been sent to Italy.

On November the fourth he met Lloyd George in Paris.

The prime minister first made a few remarks regarding the necessity for forming an interallied Supreme War Council and Staff, and asked my views. I told him that the proposal had been considered for three years, and each time had been rejected as unworkable. I gave several reasons why it could not work, and that it would add to our difficulties having such a body. The prime minister then said that the two governments had desired to form it—so I said that there was no need to say any more then. The Supreme War Staff is to consist of the government with a general: in the case of France, Foch; in the case of Britain it is to be Henry Wilson.

We then discussed the Italian situation. I urged strongly that no more troops be sent from my command in France. We could give more effective help by attacking here. L.G. said he would not decide to send more troops until he had seen what the situation is in Italy.

Incidentally he complained about attacks being made on him in the press, which he said were "evidently inspired by the military." He intended to make a speech and tell the public what courses he had proposed, and how, if he had had his way, the military situation would have been much better today, but that the military advisers had prevented him from carrying out his intentions. He took special exception to articles in the *Morning Post, Spectator, Nation, Globe*—and he said one editor had come back from my headquarters and said that I had complained that he (L.G.) had interfered with my tactics. I at once said, "What is his name, because it is not true." He said, "Spender of the *Westminster Gazette*." I said, "I will write to him." But L.G. at once said, "Oh, please do not do that."

I thought L.G. is like our German enemy, who, whenever he proposes to do something frightful, first of all complains that the British or French have committed the enormity which he is meditating. L.G. is feeling that his position as prime minister is shaky and means to try to vindicate his conduct of the war in the eyes of the public and try to put the people against the soldiers. In fact, to pose as the saviour of his country, who has been hampered by bad advice given by the general staff.

One important point to bear in mind is that he has never taken the soldier's advice, namely, *to concentrate all our resources* on the Western Front.

I gave Lloyd George a good talking-to on several of the questions he raised, and I felt I got the best of the arguments. He seemed quite rattled on the subject of Italy.

About twelve o'clock he asked me to go for a walk and I went with him up the Champs Elysées to the Arc de Triomphe. Quite a pleasant little man when one has him alone, but I should think most unreliable. When in Paris I saw no French minister.

General Pershing came to lunch and I had a long talk with him afterward. He is a fine type of man, honest, and apparently determined to do what he believes to be right. He spoke most openly to me and we are in full accord on the situation.

In the afternoon I called on Marshal Joffre at 4.30 in his little house in Passy near Auteuil. A little suburban residence so different to his big mansion at Chantilly, when French commander in chief. The old man was immensely pleased at my calling on him. He said he dared not dine or lunch out as the government were afraid of him. . . . I thought he looked older, softer and his stomach bigger and more wobbly than ever. He has really nothing in the nature of *work* to do. Lord Bertie told me that among the bourgeoisie and "the world" of Paris, "père Joffre" is the only popular figure. In my opinion the old man is past his work.

The creation of the interallied Supreme War Council, which from the beginning of December was to function from Versailles, was only one symptom of the British prime minister's profound dissatisfaction with the conduct of the war. He always believed that political problems could be solved by the manufacture of some new form of political machinery, and he saw no reason why military problems should not admit of the same solution. To Haig, who had no doubts as to what the true solution was, the creation of a new body seemed an unnecessary and dangerous experiment. At best it could only support him in the policy to which he was determined to adhere. At worst it might interfere with him and, by withdrawing troops from the Western Front, render impossible the performance of his task.

On November the twelfth, in a speech at a public luncheon in Paris, Lloyd George thought fit to proclaim to the world his fear that the allies were proceeding upon wrong principles, and his disappointment at the achievements of the British Army. He announced that there was an "absence of real unity in the war direction of the allied countries", which he hoped the new interallied Council would supply. In point of fact the unity secured between independent and equally powerful allies had been remarkable, for not a single important decision had been taken in the war without complete agreement having been first attained. Nor did the interallied Council accomplish anything to improve relations between the allies.

He went on to say, "We have won great victories. When I look at the appalling casualty lists I sometimes wish it had not been necessary to win so many." This bitter sarcasm was nothing less than an accusation against the High Command of having butchered their men unnecessarily. He went on to refer to the Western Front as "that impenetrable barrier" and sneered at such success as had been achieved.

German agents were busy in every allied and neutral country spreading propaganda in words that were almost identical. Nor could they have invented anything more poisonous, or better calculated to break the spirit of war-weary men, who had been fighting for three years, than to tell them that their leaders were unworthy of their confidence, that their military achievements amounted to nothing, and that the front which they were still being encouraged to attack was, in fact, impregnable. We have seen how in the past Haig had been ready to forgive treatment at the hands of the prime minister which he had justly resented at the time. But this was no longer a personal matter. It was an attack upon the army, and that was something which Haig could not forgive.

That the prime minister's opinion was not shared by his

colleagues and that the unity which he was so anxious to establish between the allies did not exist in the War Cabinet was demonstrated by Sir Edward Carson, who took the first opportunity of saying in a public speech, "I have met in the course of my work as a member of H.M. Government three great men—I say that advisedly—Field Marshal Haig, Sir William Robertson and Sir J. Jellicoe. They have my absolute confidence, and it is really difficult to understand the different trends of thought which have appeared in the last fortnight in relation to these men, who morning, noon and night go through anxieties which words cannot picture, who are burdened with orders and commands which involve hundreds of thousands of lives, and who see themselves held up from time to time to the odium of their countrymen as though in some way they were betraying their country, if not by their corruption at least by their incompetence."

The secretary of state for war, Lord Derby, joined with Sir Edward Carson in repudiating the prime minister's speech. "I feel that it is a speech which you will possibly think reflects on you and your men," he wrote to Haig. "I want you to allow me again to express my entire confidence in you—and I shall probably have to show that confidence in an outward and visible way. You know what I mean."

Before the Italian collapse and before the end of the Flanders campaign, Haig had already in preparation on another part of the front a fresh attack of a novel quality. This was to be entrusted to General Byng, who had succeeded Allenby in command of the Third Army. Its main distinctive feature was the lack of a preliminary artillery bombardment. This had become so inseparable a part of every offensive that few soldiers then engaged in the war could imagine the one taking place without the other. By this method and by observing the profoundest secrecy a complete surprise was effected. The following is a part of Haig's account of the first day's fighting:

Our troops rapidly passed the first two systems of trenches and occupied the third line about Masnières and Marcoing with the canal crossings. Havrincourt, Ribecourt and La Vacquerie were taken early in the day; all were found carefully prepared for defence. The Twelfth Division captured the ridge on which is Lateau wood, and formed a defensive flank to the right. After the Hindenburg support line had been taken, the Twenty-ninth Division (De Lisle) passed through and occupied the reserve line, including Marcoing and Masnières. A brigade of the Twentieth continued the defensive flank southeastward from Masnières on the Twelfth Division's left.

The Fifty-first Division was checked in front of Flesquières, but the Sixty-second pressed on and took Graincourt and Anneux before nightfall, and extended north to beyond the Bapaume-Cambrai main road.

To withdraw the enemy's attention from the main attack and to keep him in doubt as to our intentions, two subsidiary attacks were made (*a*) east of Epéhy (Fifty-fifth Division—Jeudwine); (*b*) between Bullecourt and Fontaine les Croiselles. These had limited objectives and all were gained.

Further progress was made on the following day. Flesquières was captured in the early morning. Noyelles, Cantaing, and Fontaine Notre Dame fell later and a counterattack from Rumilly was beaten off. On the twenty-second, however, German reinforcements began to appear and progress was seriously checked. Fontaine Notre Dame was reoccupied by the enemy and fierce fighting began for the mastery of Bourlon wood, which furnished the key to the situation. The battle continued with varying fortunes for a week. On November the thirtieth the full force of the German counterattack was launched and met with considerable success. If it had not been for the presence of the

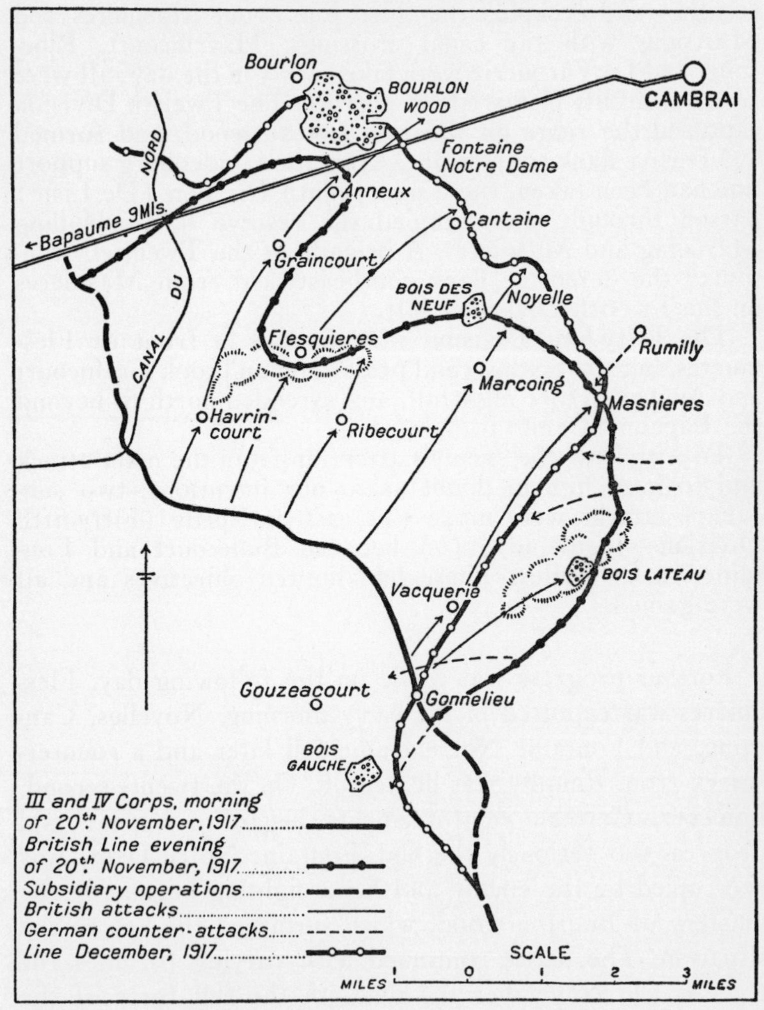
CAMBRAI
20TH NOVEMBER - 1ST DECEMBER, 1917
Bourlon
BOURLON WOOD
CAMBRAI
Fontaine Notre Dame
NORD
Anneux
Bapaume 9 Mls.
Cantaine
Graincourt
DU
BOIS DES NEUF
Noyelle
CANAL
Flesquieres
Rumilly
Marcoing
Masnieres
Havrincourt
Ribecourt
BOIS LATEAU
Vacquerie
Gouzeacourt
Gonnelieu
BOIS GAUCHE
III and IV Corps, morning of 20th November, 1917
British Line evening of 20th November, 1917
Subsidiary operations
British attacks
German counter-attacks
Line December, 1917
SCALE
MILES 1 0 1 2 3 MILES

Guards Division the situation near Gouzeaucourt might have proved very serious.

The sudden reversal of fortune created consternation in London, where the first news of the battle had been received with excessive and premature jubilation. An official court of enquiry was set up in order to provide an explanation, with the result that blame was thrown upon the troops, especially upon junior officers and noncommissioned officers who, it was alleged, had not taken necessary precautions. Haig, characteristically, would have nothing to do with any such attempts to evade responsibility. In his dispatch recording the battle he ignored the findings of the court of enquiry and was content that any blame to be attributed should rest solely on the shoulders of the commander in chief.

During the days following the counterattack of November the thirtieth, the British achieved various successes in many parts of the field. The weakness of their position, however, lay in the fact that their success had created a dangerous salient from which they must either go forward or retire. If fresh troops had been available they might have gone forward from the ground already gained, consolidated their position in Bourlon wood and threatened Cambrai, but Haig had not sufficient reinforcements at his disposal and so was reluctantly compelled to order a withdrawal, which was carried out with complete success.

It would, however, be a mistake to think that the battle had accomplished nothing. Besides coming as a shock to the enemy, who were beginning to hope that the Flanders offensive had exhausted British powers of attack for the year, and besides inflicting heavy casualties, it had had another satisfactory effect of the very type that Haig had anticipated. "Enemy divisions destined for the Italian front were diverted to Cambrai and at a most critical period in the stand on the Piave the German concentration against Italy was suspended for at least a fortnight," says John Buchan in his war history. This was a signal proof of the theory, to which Haig clung so tenaciously, that it was easier to defeat the Austrians in France than to defeat the Germans in Italy.

On the fifteenth of November he had addressed a serious warning to the government with regard to the situation on the Western Front, and he had protested against the weakening of his forces by the dispatch of reinforcements to Italy.

"In view of the advanced season," he had written to Robertson, "and the existing state of the enemy's infantry on this front his attacks are, for the present, unlikely to aim at more than local and limited objectives. . . .

"The situation next year, however, may give cause for more serious anxiety if the measures outlined in your letter are carried out. . . . The increased expenditure of energy and man power on this front and in Italy during the winter will render impossible any serious offensive by the allies on this front next spring, and under the conditions the enemy is not unlikely to seize the initiative in attack, the power of the British and French armies to resist which will be comparatively low."

This was the first warning that Haig addressed to the government with regard to the great German offensive, which he accurately foretold would come in the spring and which he already feared that the British and French armies would find considerable difficulty in resisting.

Lenin had recently succeeded Kerensky in Russia, and it was now plain that Russia would play no further part in the war. Looking forward, therefore, into 1918, Haig had little doubt that it would be the policy of the German government to force an issue on the Western Front before the full weight of the United States could make itself felt. From his diary on December the seventh:

". . . Reports normal—impossible to tell if enemy is going to renew his attacks near Cambrai—*we must be prepared for a strong hostile offensive in the spring.* There are many signs of this."

Henceforward Haig's main efforts were concentrated toward preparing to receive the attack which he knew must come, and all army commanders were instructed to devote their attention to the same subject. So far as the government were concerned his persistent demand was for increase of man power. Even now the powers of conscription were not fully exerted. Commerce and industry were still protesting that they could not carry on if they were not allowed to retain a certain proportion of their key men; Ireland remained unconscripted and the trade unions did nothing to ease the situation. Great Britain was much criticized by the French for not having thrown her whole male population into the fighting line.

Unfortunately the efforts of Haig and Robertson to secure every available man for the army were not enthusiastically supported by the prime minister. Not only was he naturally more inclined than they were to listen with due deference to the views of the trade unions, but also his doubts as to the wisdom of fighting on the Western Front and as to the efficiency of his commander in chief had been revived and intensified by the unfortunate events of November the thirtieth. The prime minister's influence over his colleagues was very great and, if he could not at present persuade them to join him in getting rid of the commander in chief, he could at least take them with him in demanding alterations in the personnel of the commander in chief's staff.

Aptitude to delegate authority and judgment in the selection of subordinates are two of the most important gifts which a man of action should possess. The charge has been brought against Haig that he was too fond of keeping control in his own hands and that he was not always wise in those whom he selected to serve him. It is true that he was himself so admirable a staff officer with so much experience of staff work that he naturally relied less upon his staff than other commanders have done. It is also true that loyalty was so much of the very fibre of his nature that he could not bring himself to part with anyone to whom he had once given his confidence, unless he was convinced that the individual had proved himself unworthy of it. To throw an unpopular subordinate to the wolves in order to placate public opinion would have appeared to him nothing less than a crime.

His intelligence officer, General Charteris, had for some time been the centre of attack from many quarters. It was alleged that his reports were misleading. He was certainly optimistic, a good fault, but he must have known the character of his chief too well to have been guilty of the methods that were imputed to him, namely, of reporting only such intelligence as he knew would be welcome. Moreover, all information that has subsequently come to light from enemy sources and elsewhere has gone to prove that Charteris' reports were extraordinarily accurate. However, he was unpopular and while he retained Haig's confidence he had lost that of others. Lord Derby wrote to Haig, not for the first time, urging his replacement. Haig's reply is a model of how a chief should behave with regard to an attack made on his subordinate.

My Dear Derby—In reply to your secret and personal letter of the 7th inst. I regret that the War Cabinet consider the views put forward by me have not been borne out by events. However that may be, I cannot agree that Charteris should be made "whipping boy" for the charge of undue optimism brought against myself.

His duty is to collect, collate and place before me all evidence obtainable in regard to the enemy. He has unusually high qualifications for that duty and I am quite satisfied with the manner in which he has performed it since I have been in command. The responsibility for the judgment formed on the evidence obtained and for the views put forward to the War Cabinet rests on me and not on him; and if the War Cabinet are not satisfied with the views put forward by me it is I, and not Charteris, who must answer for those views.

My judgment is not formed on the information collected by him alone, but on the views of commanders under me, who are in close daily touch with the troops and the situation on the battle fronts, and on my own experience of the German forces from the commencement of the war until now. I must presume that the dissatisfaction you mention, which I had heard of before, has been brought to a head by the local success gained by the Germans on the thirtieth of November; but Charteris is in no way to blame for that and to connect his name with it by removing him now would be particularly unjust.

Having heard from other sources of the existence of dissatisfaction Charteris has informed me that if I wish it he is prepared to resign as soon as I can replace him satisfactorily. I cannot accept his resignation at present for many reasons. No charge has been made against him beyond that mentioned in your letter which, as I have already said, is based entirely on matters for which, if the charge is justified at all, I am responsible and not Charteris.

If there are other charges, those making them should put them forward for proper investigation before any decision can be formed. Over and beyond this question of personal justice to a subordinate who, in my judgment, has done excellent service, this is a bad time to choose for replacing a very important member of my staff; when all indications point to our being on the verge of a great crisis in the war.

If the War Cabinet desire to leave the chief command in this theatre in my hands through the difficult months which lie before us, I am entitled to ask that their confidence may be extended to my capacity to choose my own staff, and I certainly do not desire at the present juncture to change the head of my intelligence branch.

I trust from the above that you will recognize that I

have received your letter in the same spirit as that in which you wrote it, and I have replied with equal frankness.

General Kiggell was also one who had not escaped criticism. It was said that his health was giving way under the strain of his duties. Haig thereupon caused him to be medically examined by Colonel Ryan and Sir W. Herringham, who reported that he was suffering from "nervous exhaustion due to the very exacting nature of the work he has had to perform". Haig was skeptical. "Personally", he wrote, "I think Kiggell is much better than he was two years ago when I took over from Field Marshal French. I spoke to him. He goes on leave tomorrow and returns the twenty-eighth of December. We agreed together that if either he feels that he is not up to the work, or, having regard to the very serious situation now developing, viz. great increase of German divisions on Western Front, I think he is not fit for the work, I will ask him to go home. But at present he seems better than he has been for some time, and I am very loath to part with Kigg's help and sound advice. Butler, too, is here as deputy C.G.S. and is at hand to take his place if anything happens, or Kigg's health goes. No one could possibly have discharged the duties of C.G.S. during the past two years of great difficulty better than Kiggell has."

Reluctantly also he was compelled at this time to part with other members of his staff. His quartermaster general, General Maxwell, who was sixty-five years of age, was succeeded by General Travers Clarke; his engineer in chief, Sir Robert Rice, was replaced by Sir Gerald Heath, and his director general of medical services, Sir Arthur Sloggett, by Major General C. H. Burtchaell.

Another alteration in his staff at the same period was caused by the replacement of Colonel de Bellaigue by General de Laguiche as head of the French mission.

Relations with the French were now entirely satisfactory. The two commanders in chief dined together at Pétain's headquarters on December the seventeenth, and Haig's final comment on the visit was, "The relations between G.Q.G. and G.H.Q. are better than I have ever known them. . . . We parted both feeling that our meeting today had been most useful for the general cause."

It was not only on Haig's staff that changes were taking place. In the month of December Sir Roger Keyes succeeded Admiral Bacon in command of the Dover patrol. Complete harmony has not in the past always prevailed between naval and military commanders when working together, but fortunately for Great Britain the perfect understanding that had existed between Haig and Bacon was succeeded by understanding and collaboration equally perfect between Haig and Keyes.

The most important change, however, which took place that autumn was the advent of Clemenceau to the premiership of France. Haig had got on well enough, as has been seen, with Painlevé, who had latterly united the offices of prime minister and minister of war. Painlevé had deserved well of his country, if only for having nominated Pétain as commander in chief and Foch as chief of the staff, but a more masterful personality was needed for the last round of the contest. For the next twelve months the formidable figure of Clemenceau was an invaluable asset on the side of the allies. It was felt in all countries that this staunch veteran, who had long ago earned himself the nickname of the Tiger, and who had personal recollections of the defeat of 1870, would never surrender so long as there was a German on French soil and a French soldier capable of bearing arms.

Nor was the will to conquer less determined in his British colleague, but it was not accompanied by the same preparedness to pay the price. Lloyd George was a more emotional man than Clemenceau, one to whom the thought of slaughter was more abhorrent and one who, being younger, was more concerned with what the future had to offer him. He was not a realist and consequently he believed in all sincerity, until the very end and long afterward, that there must be some safe and easy way to win the war.

An amusing proof of the continuance of this belief was brought to Haig's notice in December. "The War Cabinet in London wired through our embassy in Paris to ask for General Pétain's receipt for winning battles without incurring loss. Pétain declined at first to report and treated the matter as ridiculous. Subsequently he was further pressed and so he drafted a memorandum which he sent by a staff officer to London. He gave me a copy of his memorandum. He points out clearly that his object was to organize his army and not to fight. The two attacks which he did make this summer with limited objectives were only possible because the enemy's reserves were held by the British in Flanders and his available divisions greatly weakened by fighting against the British. In fact, Pétain has no 'elixir' for winning battles without losses."

On December the twenty-sixth, "Lord Milner arrived from Versailles and stayed the night. He seems to me a most honest and levelheaded man, and he does very valuable work in steadying Lloyd George. Milner told me that he is more than ever impressed with the latter's ability and power of work. This is no doubt true, and I assured Milner that I as commander in chief in France considered it my duty to assist the prime minister to the fullest extent of my power and not to countenance any criticism of the prime minister's actions. All this I had done, and in fact had stopped criticism in the army. On the other hand, Lloyd George had warned me at my last meeting with him in Paris (end of October last) that he was going to 'retaliate on the soldiers', as he put it, because of attacks made in the press on him, and which he thought were organized by the military. Lloyd George had asked me what my feelings would be 'if the men were told that the attacks in Flanders were useless loss of life and that all the suffering and hardship which they had endured were unnecessary'. I said such action would be most unpatriotic, yet the Lloyd George press at once commenced their attacks on me and other commanders.

"Milner admitted this, and said he had spoken to Lloyd George on the subject. I further said to Milner that if Lloyd George did not wish me to remain as commander in chief in the interests of the country, and in order to obtain success in the war, it would be much better that I should go *at once,* rather than that Lloyd George should proceed with his policy of undermining the confidence which troops now feel in their leaders, and eventually destroying the efficiency of the army as a fighting force. Morale in an army is a very delicate plant. Milner assured me that he believed all these attacks had ceased, and that he knew who had organized them. I said I did not want to know the name, but no patriot should lend himself to such cowardly work at this time of the country's crisis.

"Milner was most pleasant, and we discussed many points most openly.

"He thinks it would be the best thing for the allies that the Germans should attack the Western Front and fail. He thinks, however, that the Germans have all their attention directed on exploiting Russia to the full at the present time. We at the front, however, get a different impression, and expect to be attacked."

Two days later he received a visit from General Pershing. "We discussed his arrangements for training the American forces and my proposals. Briefly, his scheme did not go beyond training a corps of four divisions by June. I pointed out that if peace were not made soon, the crisis of the war would be reached in April, and that he should aim at training an army staff and some corps staff as well as H.Q. of divisions in as short a time as possible. He said that if the situation became critical, he was ready to break up American divisions and employ battalions and regiments as drafts to fill up our divisions.

"My scheme aimed at developing another route from the U.S.A. to France, viz. via Southampton and Havre, and training some higher leaders, staffs and a certain number of divisions. I explained my proposals and asked for one army commander and staff; three ditto corps; six ditto divisions and also the troops of six divisions.

"After dinner I had another talk with Pershing, and we agreed to recommend that Southampton should be developed as a landing place for American troops, and that a training area be organized south of Amiens. By the time the troops begin to arrive we can decide how to employ them. He will also send certain staffs for attachment to our corps and divisional H.Q. for training.

"Pershing's main difficulty, I gather, is that the people in America still want the American Army to support France, while American soldiers now in France want to join the British."

An important recruit joined the ranks of Haig's enemies in the last month of the year. All through the month of November a virulent press campaign against the War Office and the Higher Command had been carried on in papers such as the *Manchester Guardian* and the *Evening Standard,* the inspiration of which originated, as nobody doubted, from Downing Street. Lord Northcliffe, who hitherto had been Haig's firmest friend, was absent in America, and as usual in his absence the newspapers under his control were reluctant to express any strong opinions. On his return he visited Haig at G.H.Q. and some of those who were present thought that he was wounded by Haig's apparent lack of interest in his voluble account of his American experiences.

When the first favourable reports of the battle of Cambrai were received the *Times* came out with exaggerated headlines proclaiming a decisive victory and advocated the ringing of church bells throughout the country in celebration. This display of enthusiasm appeared slightly ridiculous after the events of November the thirtieth. Whether either of these two incidents determined Lord Northcliffe's change of policy, or whether it was due to that lack of balance in his judgment which became increasingly noticeable toward the close of his life, we cannot tell, but it is the fact that all the newspapers under his control henceforward threw in their lot with Haig's bitterest enemies and attacked him as remorselessly as they had formerly attacked Kitchener.

Repington was the military correspondent of the *Times*. He had no love for Haig, nor Haig for him. In the rare interviews which he had been compelled to give him during the war, Haig had never sought to dissemble his personal dislike. It therefore redounds the more to Repington's lasting honour that he alone of the *Times'* staff refused to be a party to a campaign which he did not believe to be in the interest of the country. When, therefore, the editor cut passages out of his articles he protested vociferously, and when the *Times* published false and misleading information he courageously resigned his position. He was shortly afterward employed by the *Morning Post,* and together with Gwynne, Leo Maxse and J. A. Spender formed a rather oddly assorted quartet of journalists who appointed themselves the champions of the commander in chief as against the prime minister.

Lord Northcliffe was promoted to a Viscountcy in the New Year's honours list.

CHAPTER XIII

Calm Before the Storm

At the beginning of the fifth year of the war the allies were faced by the fact that the initiative on the Western Front had now passed to the enemy. Russia had ceased to play any part, and German reinforcements from the eastern frontier were pouring into France and Belgium. The questions whether, and, if so, when the Germans would attack, were occupying the minds of all who held positions of responsibility. Haig believed that if they did so it would be the gambler's last throw, as failure must mean defeat. Meanwhile his whole energies were directed toward preparing his defences.

The new year found him enjoying a short holiday with his family in the house on Kingston Hill. He needed rest, but few days passed without his having to transact some business or to attend an interview at the War Office, at Downing Street or at Buckingham Palace.

Pressure was brought upon Haig to make some of those changes in his staff which everybody except he himself believed to be necessary. With Charteris he had already been compelled to part. General Sir Herbert Lawrence, a Seventeenth Lancer, a contemporary at the staff college, and a companion in arms since South African days, had succeeded him. Haig, who had never lost his faith in Charteris, was much pleased when Lawrence, after having taken over his new duties, "spoke enthusiastically of the efficient state and good organization of the intelligence branch, and gave it as his opinion that Charteris had produced a fine piece of work."

On New Year's day Lord Derby called on Haig in the morning and raised the question of Kiggell's health. Finally Haig made the best terms he could for those who, he believed, had served him so faithfully. Butler was to have a corps and Kiggell was to command in Jersey. Lawrence was to succeed Kiggell and General Cox was to succeed Lawrence.

About the same time Haig was deprived of the assistance of Trenchard, who had served him so long and so successfully in command of the Royal Flying Corps in France. Every week it had been Trenchard's custom to report at G.H.Q. on the situation in the air. Haig had complete confidence in him and fought hard against the government's decision to recall him to London to act as chief of the air staff.

Painlevé has left it upon record that at the meeting which he had with Lloyd George at Boulogne on the twenty-fifth of September, it was secretly agreed between them that they should achieve unity of command on the Western Front in two stages. The first stage was to be the creation of the Supreme War Council which should in fact be controlled by Foch and on which Henry Wilson, the intimate friend of Foch, should be the British representative; and in the second stage, when British public opinion had been properly prepared for it, Foch should openly take over the supreme command of the two armies.

This account seems somewhat at variance with the view subsequently expressed by Lloyd George in the House of Commons on November the nineteenth, when he declared that he was "personally utterly opposed to the suggestion" of the creation of a generalissimo, "for reasons into which it would not be desirable to enter". He went on to say that such a system "would not work. It would produce real friction, and might really produce not only friction between the armies, but friction between the nations and the governments."

Lloyd George may have unintentionally conveyed to Painlevé a wrong impression of his opinion with regard to unity of command, but as to the desirability of the Supreme War Council he entertained no doubts, and the two prime ministers signed at the beginning of November at Rapallo the agreement which brought it into existence. The fact that Foch was at first nominated as the French and Wilson as the British military representative supports the accuracy of Painlevé's statement. On the other hand Lloyd George soon afterward objected to Foch's holding the position on the ground that he was also chief of the French staff. The two positions should not, in Lloyd George's opinion, be held by the same individual, since one of his main objects in supporting the Supreme Council had been to circumvent the influence of Sir William Robertson. Foch was accordingly replaced by Weygand, a change which was not as important as it appeared, for everybody knew that Weygand would never express an opinion that was not the opinion of Foch.

The Supreme War Council first met at Versailles on December 1, 1917. This body, which was designed to coordinate all the efforts of the allies and to exercise a controlling and decisive influence over the fortunes of the war, then adjourned and did not meet again until January 30, 1918.

The government had now two distinct sets of military advisers. On the one hand there was the commander in chief upon whom rested the whole responsibility for the welfare and safety of the troops, and who reported to the government through the chief of the Imperial General Staff. On the other hand, there was the Supreme War Council, upon whom rested no responsibility whatever, and who were independent of the British War Office. What is most surprising in the subsequent history of the Supreme War Council is not that it accomplished so little good, but that it fortunately did not accomplish a great deal of evil. Robertson shared Haig's contempt for it.

Fortunately relations between Haig and Pétain were most friendly. Pétain was, upon the whole, the French general with whom Haig found it the easiest to deal. So long as they understood one another the danger of interference from Versailles could be reduced to a minimum.

As the time approached for the next meeting of the Supreme Council interviews between the two commanders in chief became more frequent, and on the twenty-fourth of January a full-dress conference took place at Compiègne.

Pétain began the meeting by asking Robertson to state what he wanted to discuss because he (Robertson) had called the meeting and no agenda had been issued.

Robertson said that he wished to know for the British government what our arrangements in France are for defence; next the state of the American forces in France; whether a general reserve can be formed; and whether some troops cannot now be withdrawn from Italy.

After Pétain and I had explained our plans, Foch talked most volubly over the advantages of acting offensively. Admirable in theory, but not practical because we have not the forces. Moreover, our defensive plans include several positions prepared for offensive action by way of counterattack.

Much time was wasted in discussing Foch's theories, and also over the American position. It was evident that Pétain thought little of Foch, and that there is considerable friction between them. There is also friction between Pershing and Pétain. And the latter told me that he is tired of the Americans, who are doing very little to fit themselves for battle. We all lunched with Pétain about 12.30 and afterward I took the opportunity of pressing on Pershing the importance of getting well-trained instructors for his troops, and to do all he could to get his units to work well with the French.

Pershing is a good honest fellow, and is quite alive to the need of this, and is doing his best, but he "finds the French very trying", as I know well.

The question of the general reserve was to prove the source of much controversy during the weeks that lay ahead. The two armies were now awaiting attack. The desirability of having a powerful body of troops in reserve which could, at the critical moment, be thrown into the battle wherever needed was obvious. Foch, as the general to whom the command of the reserve would be entrusted, was naturally most insistent upon its creation. Haig's attitude was, as usual, straightforward and easily comprehensible. He recognized that in accordance with sound military principles a general reserve would be highly advantageous, but he also recognized that he had barely sufficient troops at his disposal to protect the length of front that had been committed to his charge. If any more of those troops were taken from him he could no longer bear that responsibility. If, therefore, they desired to form a general reserve, let them, by all means, do so, but they must find the troops in Italy or bring them from the Balkans, for he could not afford to part with a single division.

On January the twenty-ninth "I motored to Versailles with all my party about 11 A.M. The Supreme War Council is housed in a great new hotel building, the Trianon Palace Hotel. An air of unreality prevailed, looking at the place from a war point of view.

"I was shown upstairs and into Sir H. Wilson's room, where Lloyd George, Lord Milner, Wilson, Hankey and Robertson were in consultation with Generals Pershing, Bliss and Captain Boyd (A.D.C.). The arguments seemed heated, and I gathered that Pershing had stated that he was opposed to giving a battalion of Americans to each British brigade. Evidently something had happened to upset him since I saw him at Compiègne. I gathered that the people in America were criticizing their government because there seemed to be no results to show for the money which America has been spending. No troops in the field, no aeroplanes, no guns, no nothing yet in fact. After a time I pointed out that the battalions would come to me for training, and would then be grouped together into American regiments and divisions. At once Pershing's attitude changed, and he said that he was quite agreeable to send one hundred and fifty battalions to the British Army on the lines I had indicated. I also took the opportunity of stating definitely my opinion that the situation of the allies in France would become very serious in September unless steps were at once taken to raise more men for the British Army as well as to bring as many American troops as possible to Europe. Calculating on half a million casualties in the British and French armies respectively, the British would in nine months be reduced by thirty divisions, and the French by fifty-three divisions.

"After the meeting I gave Colonel Hankey a note showing in detail how I arrived at this estimate. He said he would do his best to get the prime minister to give his attention to the matter.

"We had a walk in the park of Versailles Château, then lunched at the Hôtel des Réservoirs, and at 2.30 P.M. attended a conference at the headquarters of the Supreme Council with the prime minister and Lord Milner. We first discussed the demand of the French to extend the British front, and I gave the prime minister detailed reasons why we should not extend our front. Sir H. Wilson insisted that Pétain was 'not playing straight', but said one thing to me and another to his government. I can't believe this, but think Wilson has never forgiven Pétain for having him removed last May from being the head of the British mission at French G.Q.G.

"We also discussed the question of a general reserve for the Western Front. I said that I could not spare troops for that, but recommended that British troops in Italy and elsewhere should be set free for this purpose."

The next day Haig again drove out to Versailles and attended the meeting of the Supreme War Council. "M. Clemenceau presided and Lloyd George was on his left, with the British on *his* left. The French representatives were on the right of the President. Italians sat opposite the latter, and a couple of Americans with them. Clemenceau began by asking us to discuss the allied plans for next year. Foch led off with a speech of generalities; Robertson followed, then I was called upon.

"I pointed out that before we could make plans, we must know what means we had at our disposal. In my opinion, the situation was now serious on the Western Front, and might become grave in September, unless more fighting men were provided.

"I gave an estimate in divisions of our receipts in men for nine months, and, estimating for a loss of half a million if enemy attacked, I showed that the British should be prepared for a reduction of thirty divisions by the autumn unless action were taken at once to get men.

"I pointed out that the American Army could not be trained sufficiently to operate in divisions this year.

"General Pétain followed and supported me in every way. He said that *without* fighting, and allowing only for normal wastage, he must reduce twenty-five divisions by the autumn.

"I was very pleased at the way Pétain backed me up, and this without any preliminary talk or argument. Lloyd

George followed and asked for detailed figures. This, no doubt, to give him time to think over the situation which he admits is serious."

The Supreme War Council sat for three more days. On the thirty-first Haig summarized the work done as follows, "Our shortage of men in the field had been demonstrated and Lloyd George had shown himself anxious to prove by figures that we had ample men on the Western Front."

On the first of February the Council met at 10 A.M. "After some more talk it was agreed to accept the recommendations of the military members of the Supreme War Council to adopt a defensive attitude for the present until the situation developed, with a request that commanders in chief should prepare offensive projects suitable for the forces at their disposal. Nothing should be done to weaken the allied forces on the Western Front, but Lloyd George insisted on going on with his schemes for the destruction of the Turks. Clemenceau said that he could not prevent Great Britain doing what she thought best in this matter, but he got Lloyd George to agree that nothing should be done for two months. After that time Clemenceau hoped to have the situation again discussed by the Versailles Council. On that understanding, the Turkish project was passed. Robertson then put in a minute of dissent to the effect that the military members of this War Council did not know all the factors of the problem on which they had made a recommendation. Robertson considered the scheme was quite unsound, and gave his advice against it. I am strongly of the same opinion, but Lloyd George never asked my opinion.

"I saw Lloyd George was much annoyed with Robertson, but he said nothing at the time. Later he told Robertson that, having given his advice in London, it was not necessary for him to have repeated it here.

"I lunched at the Hôtel des Réservoirs along with Lawrence, Davidson and Philip.

"When we assembled in the afternoon the question of an interallied reserve, how it should be organized, and who should command it, was discussed till after 6 P.M. Finally, it was decided to think the question over and put forward draft proposals on the morrow.

"I got back to Paris at 7.30 P.M., a very long day, and much time wasted due to much talking by civilians on military matters, of the basic principles of which they know nothing."

The next day "we met at Versailles at 10.30 A.M. M. Clemenceau had a private meeting (as usual) with Lloyd George half an hour before, in order to settle privately the decisions at which it was intended to arrive in full conference.

"As the result of the night in which it was possible to think over the problem, several proposals were produced on the question of a general reserve. Among these was one from Lloyd George, which appointed Foch as president of the committee, to deal with the matter, and issue orders to commanders in chief as to when and where the reserve is to be used; to decide (in consultation with commanders in chief) the strength of the general reserve.

"This was the proposal which was accepted after some discussion, and a few amendments. To some extent it makes Foch a generalissimo. But, although Pétain and I get on very well and no co-ordinating authority is necessary for us, on the other hand the Italian front needs a central authority.

"When the four representatives (Clemenceau, Lloyd George, Orlando, Bliss) had approved of the resolution, I asked the following question: 'By what channel am I to receive orders from this new body?' This was rather a poser, because this resolution to appoint an international committee involves a change in constitutional procedure. Finally Lloyd George said, 'Orders would be issued by the members of the body nominated by the Supreme Council.'

I asked that the exact position might be made clear to me in writing.

"The next question discussed was the extension of the British front. Clemenceau had previously told me that he persisted in raising this point on account of the necessity of getting more men from England to make sure of holding the front until the Americans could take their share of the fighting.

"I made a few remarks, and stated that, with my present strength, it was quite out of the question for me to extend my line. Notwithstanding the table of figures compiled for the conference, my statement of Wednesday last holds good, viz. that we must expect to have to reduce thirty divisions in nine months if the enemy attacks us heavily. Eventually it was agreed to accept the proposed extension *in principle,* but it was left to Pétain and myself to decide when to carry it out. After this Pétain came along to me and said that 'he had no intention to worry (taquiner) me over this'."

Pétain proved as good as his word and an amicable arrangement was shortly afterward arrived at between the two commanders in chief whereby the British line was extended as far as Barisis.

Haig's view with regard to the appointment of a generalissimo was plain from the start. So long as he and Pétain saw eye to eye it was unnecessary on the Western Front, but if he and Pétain differed upon an important issue the whole situation would be changed.

The constitutional issue, however, which Haig, with remarkable rapidity for one untrained in constitutional law, had pointed out, was a serious one. He was responsible to the Army Council who, in their turn, were responsible to Parliament and the country for the safety of the troops. He could take orders from the Army Council, or from a senior field marshal, but from nobody else in the world. But now it had been laid down at Versailles that Foch or the executive committee in charge of the general reserve had certain powers to dispose of British troops without the consent of any third party. The Army Council a few days later agreed unanimously "that the constitution of the executive committee as it now stands would not only place commanders in chief in an impossible position, but would also deprive the council of the responsibility entrusted to them under the constitution of the realm, and that any such abrogation of that responsibility would be a violation of the trust reposed in them."

The situation was awkward, but the agile brain of the prime minister saw not only a solution of the difficulty but also an opportunity of accomplishing his most immediate purpose, which was to get rid of his chief of the Imperial General Staff. The first step was to get Haig to come to London. He arrived there on the afternoon of the ninth of February. He was met at the station by Lady Haig and Lord Derby. The latter immediately took possession of him and drove him off to Downing Street—"by a circuitous route, so as to have a talk and explain the situation. Briefly, the Cabinet had decided on the previous day to replace Sir W. Robertson as C.I.G.S. On that my opinion would not be asked. He then produced a copy of draft instructions arranging for the new order of things, on the following lines:

"The secretary of state for war was again to assume full responsibility for the War Office, and the C.I.G.S's position was to return again to what it was before Robertson was appointed in Lord Kitchener's time. The C.I.G.S. is to continue to be the 'supreme military adviser of the government'. 'The military representative at Versailles to be a member of the Army Council', and to be a 'deputy C.I.G.S.' It was proposed that orders should be sent to me regarding the handling of the 'interallied general reserve' by the latter. I told Derby of the draft letter which Henry Wilson had sent to me this morning on the question of forming a 'general reserve', and which clearly shows that he and Foch were practically in the position of a 'generalissimo' commanding all allied armies in France.

"On reaching Downing Street we went straight to the council room and found the prime minister there with Mr Macpherson (the under secretary of state for war). The prime minister then explained his views and difficulties. I pointed out the tremendous powers now given to Versailles, that the military representatives there had full powers to commit the government (*possibly against my opinion*) and take decisions which the British government ought alone to take. He said as prime minister he was anxious to get into more direct touch with me as commander in chief in France, and that under the present system he always felt that in seeing me he was going behind the back of the C.I.G.S. I suggested that Robertson's original proposal, by which he (as C.I.G.S.) after consultation with Foch, should send me orders re reserves was probably the best solution of the difficulty. The prime minister said he had come to the same conclusion, and he proposed to send Robertson to Versailles as military representative, and to make Henry Wilson C.I.G.S.

"This came as a pleasant surprise to Derby, who evidently was much exercised in his mind as to how to get out of his present difficulty with Robertson. The latter had lately become more difficult to deal with, and lost his temper quickly, he told me.

"The draft decision was accordingly revised so as to make the military representative at Versailles 'absolutely free and unfettered in the advice which he gives, but he is to report to C.I.G.S. the nature of advice given for information of the Cabinet, and C.I.G.S. will advise Cabinet thereon'.

"I warned the prime minister and Derby of the distrust

in which Henry Wilson is held by the army. Derby said that he would issue instructions in the War Office to ensure that staff appointments are fairly made.

"The prime minister also said that he considered that the best solution of their present difficulties would be to make me 'generalissimo' of *all* the British forces. Derby concurred and I was asked what I thought of the proposal. I replied that with a serious attack pending in France, I considered that no change should be made in the command there, even though the change might be to my personal advantage. I knew every detail of the situation, and it would not be fair to the army suddenly to appoint a new commander in such a grave emergency. The prime minister agreed, and said he 'ought to have made me generalissimo last September.'

"A copy of the agreement was duly signed by the prime minister and Derby, and I received a copy.

"I met Doris in her mother's house in Seymour Street, and we then motored to Kingston Hill.

"Doris and I dined quietly together."

Haig passed a peaceful Sunday with his wife and on Monday morning, called at the War Office where he learned from Lord Derby that Robertson had refused to accept the suggested arrangement. Robertson was a proud man with a great career behind him. He took the orthodox army point of view with regard to personalities, and it doubtless seemed to him a hard thing that he should have risen from the ranks to the pinnacle of C.I.G.S. in order to end as deputy to Henry Wilson. It is impossible not to sympathize with the rugged old soldier; but Haig, single-minded as ever, was thinking only of the war. After his conversation with Lord Derby he writes: "I then went to Robertson's room. He said he had no intention of accepting the appointment at Versailles. The position would be impossible, for all information was in the hands of the C.I.G.S. in London. I disagreed, and said that as the British member of the Versailles Committee he was in the position of 'generalissimo', and further that this was no time for anyone to question where his services were to be given. It was his *duty* to go to Versailles or anywhere else if the government wished it. I am afraid that in the back of his mind he resents Henry Wilson replacing him in London."

Haig had an interview with the King the same morning and returned to France in the afternoon.

Two days later he visited the Fifth Army, and carefully inspected their system of defence. Believing that an attack was pending and that it was likely to fall upon this sector of the front, he had none the less decided that with the limited, and indeed insufficient, troops at his disposal it was in this sector that he could least afford to concentrate his strength. The armies were now arranged as follows. The northernmost was Rawlinson's, which was for the present called the Fourth Army, but was shortly to resume the name of the Second Army when Plumer once more took command of it. On its right lay the First Army under Horne; then came Byng's Third Army and finally the Fifth Army under Gough. The Second Army covered a front of twenty-three miles; the First Army one of thirty-three miles; the Third Army twenty-eight miles and the Fifth Army forty-two miles.

Two good reasons justified Haig's decision to hold his left more strongly than his right. In the first place defeat on the left might mean the loss of the Channel ports and the cutting off of the British Army from its base. In the second place French reinforcements could reach his right far more rapidly than they could reach his left. He would not put his faith in a general reserve controlled by an executive committee from Versailles, but he had agreed with Pétain that each of them should be ready to support the other in emergency. But if the blow fell on Plumer it could hardly be hoped that Pétain's support would arrive in time, whereas if it fell on Gough the distance that the French troops would have to cover would be the shortest possible.

It was therefore the position of the Fifth Army which was causing Haig most anxiety when he visited it on February the thirteenth. He met Sir Hubert Gough at Jussy and found him "as usual, very fit, active and in the best of spirits". Together they "looked at the crossings of the canal, planned some extra ones and then examined some of the wire and trenches. Everything seemed carefully thought out, and if only we have another month to work, this sector *ought* to be very strong". During that day and the next he inspected the various corps, divisions and brigades. "At the conclusion I said a few words to the brigadiers and commanding officers of battalions and encouraged them to maintain smartness and discipline, esprit de corps, etc. I told them to be ready for *a heavy attack*."

But home politics continually obtruded themselves upon these urgent preparations for the coming battle. Early in the morning of the fifteenth of February, "cipher personal telegram from Lord Derby arrived 1 A.M. It stated that Robertson had been offered choice of Versailles or remaining where he is, but had decided to resign, claiming that it is necessary to be both C.I.G.S. and government representative on the Council at Versailles. Government is now offering position to Plumer. He would like to see me, as he thinks a talk would be an advantage.

I replied that I consider only permanent solution of difficulty is that C.I.G.S. should have his deputy at Versailles in same way that the French have Foch with a subordinate general at Versailles. And I added that I would come to London tomorrow afternoon to see him.

I sent Sassoon to Montreuil to arrange for my journey. Everything arranged when Derby's private secretary states the prime minister would rather that Derby came to Boulogne to see me. I reply that I am coming to London and desire to see the prime minister.

I decide on this course because the latter is stating that I am "in agreement with the government". I am anxious not to embarrass the government at this time, but I am *not* in agreement on all the decisions passed regarding Versailles. For instance, I agree on the need of forming a general reserve, but not on the system of control which has been set up.

Haig arrived at Doullens at eight in the morning of February the sixteenth. At 9.15 he had an interview with Loucheur, the French minister of munitions, and at ten he held a conference of his army commanders. "All were present. General Cox gave a very clear account of the situation of the enemy, emphasized his greatly increased strength and *indicated that we must be prepared to meet a very severe attack at any moment now.* After army commanders had stated their views on the situation on their respective army fronts, and their arrangements for defence, we discussed the handling of reserves and the action of artillery on the defensive. All felt confident of being able to hold their front.

"We finished about 12.30. I then motored to Beaurepaire Château, had lunch and went at once to Boulogne. There a destroyer was waiting for me. I left at 3 P.M. and reached London by special train at 5.30 P.M.

"The secretary of state for war met me at the station and motored with me to Kingston Hill. He told me that Robertson had declined to serve either as C.I.G.S. on the new conditions, or to be military representative at Versailles, so Sir H. Wilson had been appointed C.I.G.S. He would call for me at 11.30 A.M. tomorrow and take me to see the prime minister.

"I found Doris looking very fit and well. How petty all this squabbling in high places is, compared with the great problem of beating Germany, and the present anxiety of commanders in France."

Robertson called on Haig at 9.30 next morning. Haig explained that he had never been asked whether he approved of the new scheme, but only whether he was satisfied with the proposed arrangement whereby he was to receive orders. He had replied that the constitutional difficulty had been got over by the fact that the British representative at Versailles would henceforth be a member of the Army Council and that therefore the Army Council would be responsible for any orders that he gave. He added, however, that he had never approved of the new system, nor of the Foch committee for creating and commanding the general reserve, "nor indeed of the Versailles military organization itself".

Later in the morning he drove down with Lord Derby to the prime minister's country house. "Lloyd George had been ill, and was resting upstairs when we arrived. He came down and saw Derby and myself together. In the course of our talk, I made it quite clear to the prime minister that I had never approved of any of the arrangements now under discussion. When asked, I had stated my reasons for disagreeing, but once the Cabinet had given its decision I had loyally done my best to make the system run. I had only one object in view, viz. to beat the Germans. Lloyd George said that was so, and warmly thanked me. Lloyd George left the room for a moment, and Derby said that I had put my position quite clearly to the prime minister.

"If the latter made any misstatement regarding me in the House of Commons on this subject, he was prepared to get up in the House of Lords and deny it flatly."

Haig returned to Kingston for luncheon and in the afternoon Henry Wilson called on him. Together they agreed that Rawlinson should fill the vacant situation at Versailles on the understanding that he should be immediately replaced by Plumer in command of his army.

The Haig diary records the following incidents during his stay in London:

Field Marshal French then passed me on the stairs. We greeted each other in a very friendly manner; he asked me to call in and see him even for a few minutes whenever I came to London. . . . I . . . went over to the Horse Guards and saw Viscount French. He was very pleased to see me—said he had been afraid that the paper on the military situation in the west which he wrote might have put me against him. He wished our friendship to be as in days gone by. I asked him to come to France when things are quieter. As regards his paper, I held strongly that his plan for sending troops from the Western Front to fight against the Turks might bring about our defeat. . . .

Sir H. Rawlinson arrived from France. I explained the situation, and offered him the post of military representative at Versailles. He accepted it, and assured me that he was only anxious to serve where I thought he could be of most use. He was also prepared to decline the appointment, if I thought that it was in the interest of the Service that he should do so.

Doris and I dined quietly together.

Another air raid, but very little noise heard near this home.

After returning to France, Haig "read Lloyd George's speech in the *Times* of this morning regarding the differences which had arisen between the government and Sir W. Robertson. The prime minister of course makes out an excellent case for himself, which the bulk of the House (not understanding military matters) thoroughly endorses. Indeed, Sir William comes out of the controversy as a 'mulish, irreconciliable individual'. This must, I think, always be the result of controversies between statesmen and soldiers in which the issue is not simple, and when the former tell the story. Sir William would have done better to have resigned when the government rejected his advice regarding the Western Front, and decided on sending an expedition to Syria to fight the Turks."

A few days later Clemenceau came to dinner.

He is most active and alert in mind and body, though seventy-six years of age. He has always drunk water, but eats well. After dinner he came to my room and had a quiet talk for half an hour. His intention was merely to come and pay his respects to me at my headquarters, but after seeing Pétain yesterday he felt in some difficulty. He spoke quite frankly. Some friction had arisen between Foch and Pétain, and he was uncertain how to act over the question of reserves which Foch claimed to control as the result of the decision of the Versailles conference.

As regards interallied reserves, I said that I had told my prime minister that I could not earmark any divisions at the present time as an interallied reserve without upsetting my plans for defence. I only had six divisions under my own hand at the present moment. And that rather than change my plans at a time when, at any moment, the enemy might attack in force, I would prefer to resign my command.

M. Clemenceau at once said that my statement indicated his line of action. He would arrange to "écarter" (set aside) Foch gradually. He personally looked upon a close agreement between Pétain and myself as the surest guarantee of success.

. . . Clemenceau and I parted great friends. He said he had only one object, namely, to beat the Germans.

On the twenty-fifth of the month Henry Wilson arrived at G.H.Q. and Haig was again pressed to earmark certain divisions for the general reserve. He made the same reply that he had made to Clemenceau. On this subject he was as firm as a rock because he believed that the safety of the army was involved. He would resign his command rather than budge an inch. Rawlinson was also on a visit to G.H.Q.

and firmly supported Haig's attitude. The fact that he was now the British representative at Versailles in place of Wilson proved of value to Haig in two ways. In the first place Rawlinson was loyal to him; and in the second place Wilson, being now C.I.G.S. in London, was no longer anxious to magnify the importance or increase the power of the Supreme War Council at Versailles.

Still more fortunate was the fact that Clemenceau preferred Pétain to Foch and was prepared to support Haig in refusing to give way in the matter of the general reserve. If Henry Wilson had remained at Versailles, and if he and Foch working together had had the support of the French prime minister on this issue, Haig might have been driven to resignation, a new commander in chief appointed, and the British front still further denuded of troops in this fateful month of March.

On the fifth Rawlinson arrived from Versailles, having been sent by Foch, with the support of his Italian and American colleagues, to make a further effort to persuade Haig to alter his decision with regard to the general reserve. Seven divisions were this time demanded and the executive committee had decided that, if the request were refused, they would report to their respective governments that owing to the refusal their role was nonexistent and that they had better be dissolved. Haig replied that he could not possibly alter his decision "since the possibilities of having to meet an attack grew greater every day", and Rawlinson, who was in entire agreement, telephoned accordingly to Versailles.

The early days of the month of March were busily occupied in making final preparations to resist the great attack which was now almost hourly expected. On the second a conference of army commanders was held at Doullens, when Cox, the new head of the Intelligence in France, reported that the attack was likely to be delivered on the fronts of the Third and Fifth armies. Further information to the same effect was received the next day, and reports from French G.Q.G. of the movement of German troops and of the postponement of the offensive were disregarded. French sources of information were now considered distinctly inferior to British.

On the fourth Haig addressed a letter of exasperated protest to the secretary of state owing to the War Cabinet's decision to postpone the return of Plumer from Italy. Haig had consented to Rawlinson's going to Versailles only on condition that Plumer should resume command of the Second Army. Now, on the eve of the great battle, he was still deprived of one of his best army commanders. The War Cabinet had acted without consulting the secretary of state for war. Lord Derby lost no time in putting the matter right, telegraphing to Plumer to return to France without delay. At the same time Lord Derby wrote strongly advocating the removal of General Gough from the command of the Fifth Army, a change which he said that the prime minister was anxious to see effected. But Haig had not lost faith in Gough, and would in any case have refused to change an army commander at such a moment.

On the sixth Haig visited Pétain. The two were in complete agreement on the question of the general reserve and were strengthened by the knowledge that they had Clemenceau behind them. They agreed also that the work of the Versailles Council should be of a purely advisory character, and that no council or committee should ever be charged with the disposal of troops. Pétain's suggestion for obtaining greater unity had been to divide the whole of the western European front, including the Italian front, into two parts, giving to Haig supreme command from the sea to Verdun and retaining the remainder himself. Haig thought there was much to be said for the scheme, but it had not found favour and was now abandoned.

On March the fourteenth there took place in London the third meeting of the Supreme War Council.

"I visited Downing Street at 10 A.M. and had a long talk with the prime minister and Mr Bonar Law until nearly 11 A.M. I pointed out that the deficiency of men would make the situation critical by June. If the enemy attacked, our position would be worse. In the month seventh of April to seventh of May last year the Germans ran through forty-seven divisions and they actually had forty-two in reserve when our attacks began. We must expect *at least* to suffer similar losses.

"They did their best to get me to say that the Germans would not attack. The prime minister remarked that I had 'given my opinion that the Germans would only attack against small portions of our front'. I said that 'I had never said that. The question put to me was if I were a German general and confronted by the present situation would I attack'. . . . I now said that the German Army and its leaders seem drunk with their success in Russia and the middle east, so that it is impossible to foretell what they may not attempt. In any case, we must be prepared to meet *a very strong attack indeed on a fifty-mile front, and for this, drafts are urgently required.*

"We then spoke about the question of forming a general reserve. Lloyd George did his best to frighten me into agreeing to earmark certain divisions. He spoke of all the other general commanders in chief having agreed and I alone stood out. He then tried to flatter and wheedle me. I was equally firm. I said among other things that this was a military question of which I was the best judge. I only had eight divisions under my hand; the position of these *may* vary from day to day, and only the commander in chief in close touch with the situation could handle them. Versailles was too distant and not in touch with the actual military situation.

"Finally Lloyd George agreed that it was too late to touch my divisions now, in view of the apparent imminence of a large attack. . . .

"The question of the general reserve was the first point dealt with—Lloyd George opened the discussion and put my case very well. He finally proposed that, although neither I nor Pétain could contribute toward the general reserve at once, the intention to form a reserve should still be maintained, and that as the American troops arrived and set free British and French units, the decision should be given effect to. . . .

"When the resolution on the question of the interallied reserve was formally put to the meeting, in reply to Lloyd George's question if anyone had anything further to say, General Foch asked leave to speak. He stated that he 'objected to the whole resolution'. This led to a wordy altercation between Clemenceau and him, which finally ended by Clemenceau waving his hand and shouting 'silence'.

"Clemenceau then thoroughly sat on Foch! . . . . We adjourned about 6 P.M. When Foch bade me good-night he said in rather bitter chaff, 'only in London can military matters now be regulated'."

Another meeting was held on the following day when the question of air bombing was discussed. Haig throughout the war adhered to the view that the bombing of defenceless towns was as wrong from a military as it was from an ethical standpoint.

"The first question discussed was regarding our policy in the matter of air bombing. M. Clemenceau asked me some questions. I read a few notes which I had had prepared in consultation with Trenchard.

"Briefly I stated that we only bombed objectives of military importance, namely factories, mines, camps and military junctions, that we had three squadrons (bombing) near

Nancy, and these would be increased to eight by June. I also explained how the work was divided between ourselves and the French. Lastly I recommended that the bombing should be continued, notwithstanding that the enemy retaliated on London and Paris.

"M. Clemenceau (who came and sat by me when I was speaking) said that he entirely agreed with all I had said, and recommended that my paper be at once accepted by the War Cabinet. Bonar Law had meantime arrived, and now said that what I had stated was contrary to what he had told the House of Commons. He had there stated that the British now 'by way of retaliation bombed German towns', i.e. we had no military objective. Clemenceau did not wish in any way to interfere with the British government, all he wanted was to assure the French Chamber that British aeroplanes 'only bombed military objects' when they started from the French lines! 'And whatever Mr Bonar Law had told the House of Commons, the result was as stated by the field marshal.' After some further discussion a resolution based on my memorandum was accepted."

On these same ides of March an event occurred of deep importance in the life of Haig. Between eleven o'clock and midnight a son was born to him. Colonel Ryan of the Royal Army Medical Corps, who had been with him during the retreat from Mons and ever since, was in attendance. Haig was now nearly fifty-seven and must have almost given up hope of handing to an heir the ancient name which he had inherited and to which he had added such great renown. When therefore the news was brought that the child was a boy and that all was well, words failed him. He threw his arms round the astonished colonel and, as the latter has described it, "kissed me like a Frenchman". Very seldom was any man privileged to see behind the mask of stern reserve with which Haig concealed from the world a sensitive and intensely human heart.

The next morning, having paid a visit to Buckingham Palace, where he received the warm congratulations of his king and queen, he had barely time to hold his little son for a moment in his arms before he hurried back to the seat of war, there to await the coming of the enemy's desperate thrust.

CHAPTER XIV

The Enemy's Great Attack

IT WAS BEFORE EIGHT O'CLOCK on the morning of March 21, 1918, and the commander in chief had not finished dressing when the chief of staff came into his room to inform him that the great attack had begun. Despite the elaborate precautions that the Germans had taken to conceal their intentions, both the date and the place of the attack had been anticipated by the British Intelligence Service with remarkable accuracy. All possible preparations to meet it had been made, but the reinforcements which Haig had never ceased to demand had been denied him. If he had consented to the further depletion of his force by detaching troops to be sent to Italy or to form part of a general reserve, the very narrow margin which finally divided the allies from complete disaster might have been obliterated.

The story of this battle is therefore one of a defensive force, outnumbered, fighting a series of rearguard actions and offering so stubborn a resistance that in the end the attackers were exhausted and incapable of pressing their advantage home. New methods were employed by the enemy. The German genius for war discovered a fresh device for making the most of their diminishing resources in this final, gigantic effort to obtain a favourable decision before it was too late.

The quality of their fighting forces had deteriorated. Largely they consisted now of middle-aged men, of boys and of those who had been often wounded or previously discarded as unfit. They therefore decided not to confuse the better with the inferior material, but to divide the two. The bravest and best trained were drafted into separate battalions of storm troops, and, while the less formidable units were put merely to holding the line or to meaner tasks, these storm troops were reserved for great occasions and had now been rapidly collected at the vital points to play their part in the greatest occasion of all. These picked troops were given no limit to their objectives, and their success was to depend upon the speed of their advance. "As regards keeping in touch," they were instructed, "infantry which looks to the right or left soon comes to a stop. Touch with the enemy is the desideratum; a uniform advance must in no case be demanded. The fastest, not the slowest, must set the pace." These were the tactics of infiltration—the hammering into the opposing lines of a series of iron wedges, as a man might drive wedges under the closely nailed-down lid of a wooden packing case until finally its resistance is overcome.

The strategy behind these tactics was to divide the English from the French—according to the traditional policy of Germany, in peace as well as in war. For this reason the spot selected for the attack was that where the two armies met. The first objective was to roll up the extreme right of the British Army. This done, the victorious Germans were to strike not southwest at Paris as in 1914, but northwest at the Channel until the British, cut off from their allies, would be swept into the sea. When that was accomplished, or simultaneously with its accomplishment, the remainder of the German Army would be hurled against the isolated French Army which divided them from the capital.

The tactics were novel and the strategy was sound. The former had been experimented with successfully by General von Hutier at Riga, by Otto von Bülow at Caporetto and to some extent by von der Marwitz in the counterattack at Cambrai. These were the three generals who were now in command of the armies playing the principal parts in the offensive. The strategy was Ludendorff's own. In coming to his decision he was guided by three main considerations. The troops at his disposal sufficed for *one* great offensive only. This must take place not later than March, before the arrival of the Americans, and thirdly "We must beat the British".

The British lines of defence were constructed on the principle of three zones. The forward zone was held lightly with a view to resisting raids and with the intention of withdrawing from it in the face of a concentrated attack. The battle zone to which withdrawal was to be made would, it was hoped, present an insurmountable obstacle, but if the worse came to the worst there was still behind it the defensive zone, or "green line" as it came to be called, beyond which there must be no retirement.

Once again the weather fought on the German side. The method of infiltration relied for its success upon the creation of confusion and panic. Fog was most likely to increase both. The British front line, so lightly held with long gaps between small detachments, was penetrated with extreme rapidity. Before those who held it were assured that the enemy had left their trenches, they were already surrounded and found themselves attacked from the rear. As far back as brigade headquarters, while news of the attack was still awaited, the attackers themselves arrived in overwhelming numbers.

Confusion therefore was great, but panic there was none. Telephonic communication had mainly been destroyed by shell fire and what followed became therefore a soldiers' battle. Fighting in the dark, without orders and without knowledge of what was happening, isolated units put up

GERMAN OFFENSIVE
MARCH, 1918

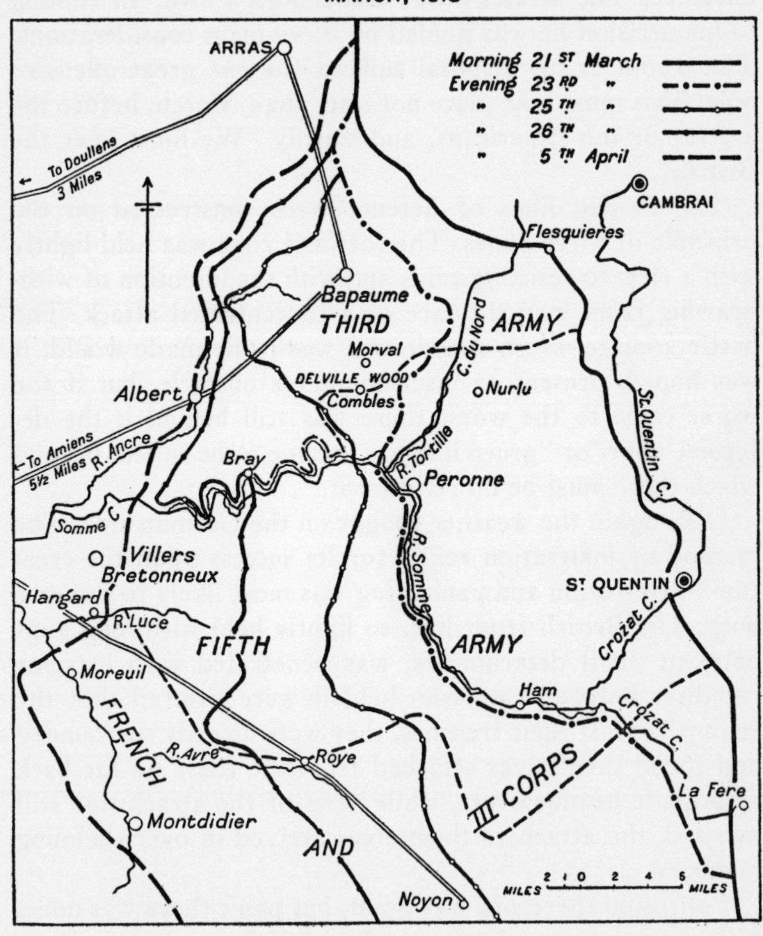

heroic resistance and in many cases died to a man rather than surrender. No troops in the whole history of war ever fought more gallantly than the men of the Third and the Fifth Army.

On March the twenty-second fierce fighting continued. The Germans were able to bring fresh troops into the field against the exhausted and depleted forces of the British. Fog once more assisted the enemy, especially on the right of the Fifth Army, who in accordance with plan retired steadily until they reached the line of the Crozat canal and the Somme. "At 6 P.M.", Haig writes, "Gough* telephoned 'Parties of all arms of the enemy are through our reserve line'. I concurred in his falling back and defending the line of the Somme and to hold Péronne bridgehead in accordance with his orders. I at once sent to tell General Pétain and asked his support to enable us to hold the line of the Somme and Pérrone bridgehead. I expect big attack to develop toward Arras."

Owing to the better visibility in the north, the attack against the Third Army on this day proved much less successful than that against the Fifth and caused acute disappointment to Ludendorff. But none the less Haig considered that the position was growing increasingly serious, and on the morning of the twenty-third he visited the two army commanders.

I then went on to Villers-Bretonneux and saw General Gough commanding Fifth Army. I was surprised to learn that his troops are *now behind* the Somme and the river Tortille. Men very tired after two days' fighting and long march back. On the first day they had to wear gas masks all day, which is very fatiguing, but I cannot make out why the Fifth Army has gone so far back without making some kind of a stand. . . .

General Pétain arrived about 4 P.M. He seems most anxious to do all he can to support me and agrees that the

*General Sir Hubert Gough, commanding the Fifth Army.

only principle which should guide us in our movements is to keep the two armies in touch. In reply to my request to concentrate a large French force (twenty divisions) about Amiens, Pétain said he was most anxious to do all he can to support me, but he expected that the enemy is about to attack him in Champagne. Still, he will do his utmost to keep the two armies in touch. If this is lost and the enemy comes in between us, then probably the British will be rounded up and driven into the sea. This must be prevented even at the cost of drawing back the north flank on the sea coast.

"Pétain struck me as very much upset, almost unbalanced and most anxious," wrote Haig on March the twenty-fourth. "I explained my plans . . . and asked him to concentrate as large a force as possible about Amiens astride the Somme to co-operate on my right. He said he expected every moment to be attacked in Champagne, and he did not believe that the main German blow had yet been delivered. He said he would give Fayolle all his available troops. He also told me that he had seen the latter today at Montdidier, where the French reserves are now collecting, and had directed him (Fayolle) in the event of the German advance being pressed still further, to fall back south-westward to Beauvais in order to cover Paris. It was at once clear to me that the effect of this order must be to separate the French from the British right flank, and so allow the enemy to penetrate between the two armies. I at once asked Pétain if he meant to abandon my right flank. He nodded assent, and added, 'It is the only thing possible, if the enemy compel the allies to fall back still further.' From my talk with Pétain I gathered that he had recently attended a Cabinet meeting in Paris and that his orders from his government are to *'cover Paris at all costs'*. On the other hand to keep in touch with the British Army is no longer the basic principle of French strategy. In my opinion, our army's existence in France depends on keeping the British and French armies united. So I hurried back to my headquarters at Beaurepaire Château to report the serious change in *French strategy* to the C.I.G.S. and secretary of state for war, and ask them to come to France."

Slow of speech, deliberate in council, Haig was nevertheless, like all great soldiers, swift to perceive and to appreciate the importance of a fundamental change in the situation and swift to act. Pétain's decision, communicated at that midnight meeting, meant nothing less than the division of the two armies. It might mean the loss of the war. Haig had a high regard for Pétain. He might have attempted to dissuade him from his decision. But he knew his man, and he was also conscious of his own limitations. Pétain's resolution had not been lightly come to, nor were Haig's powers of persuasion in the French language likely to alter it. Time would have been wasted, and time was now more precious than gold. At all costs the two armies must be kept together. Haig's simple and direct brain saw the only way in which it could be accomplished. Let both armies be put under one general, for no general in the world will voluntarily abandon half his force.

"Monday, March 25, 1918. . . . Lawrence at once left me to telegraph to Wilson requesting him and Lord Milner to come to France at once in order to arrange that General Foch or some other determined general, who would fight, should be given supreme control of the operations in France. I knew Foch's strategical ideas were in conformity with the orders given me by Lord Kitchener when I became commander in chief, and that he was a man of great courage and decision as shown during the fighting at Ypres in October and November, 1914."

Wilson reached Haig's headquarters soon after eleven o'clock the same morning. Haig had not known when he telegraphed that Milner was already in France. His endeavours, therefore, to arrange a meeting for that day,

March the twenty-fifth, at which Lord Milner and the French prime minister should be present, proved abortive. He and Wilson drove to Abbeville that afternoon, but of the authorities that they had invited only Weygand arrived, so everything had to be postponed until the morrow. Haig gave Weygand a note for Clemenceau in which he stated briefly "that in order to prevent a serious disaster it is necessary that the French act at once, and concentrate as large a force as possible north of the Somme near Amiens". On this day the British forces were driven farther back along the whole line of battle and the enemy firmly established himself on the southern and western side of the Somme.

Meanwhile a conference was being held at Pétain's headquarters at Compiègne, where owing to the absence of Haig nothing could be settled, except to hold another conference on the morrow which Haig should attend. This was a desperate evening for the allies, their armies in full retreat, their commanders in chief in disagreement and their political leaders wildly telegraphing to one another across the void.

Some uncertainty still exists as to exactly what was passing through the mind of Pétain at this critical moment. It has been asserted on good authority that he had mistaken Haig's intentions and believed that the British were determined to retreat in a northerly direction, in which case it was obvious that he could not indefinitely keep in touch with them. It is certain that on the following day Clemenceau informed Milner, when they met at Doullens, that Haig had decided to abandon Amiens, an impression which one minute's conversation between Milner and Haig sufficed to dissipate. Haig had only emphasized the urgent need for French reinforcements in front of Amiens, and from the beginning of the war he had been clear in his own mind that, while the loss of the Channel ports would be a fearful blow to the allied cause, the failure of the two armies to keep in contact would be a still graver disaster.

Making, therefore, full allowance for the misunderstandings that may arise in moments of crisis owing to the prevalence of rumour, the brevity of messages, the lack of time for consultation and the necessity for swift decisions, it is still difficult to believe that on so simple and so vital a question as that of the direction in which Haig meant to withdraw Pétain had formed any misconception. No line of written evidence has been produced that would have justified it.

The only alternative explanation of Pétain's attitude is that he had reluctantly arrived at the melancholy conclusion that the British Army was defeated. If that were so, his duty was plainly to preserve the French Army at all costs and to defend the capital. At Doullens he expressed these sentiments to Clemenceau, "The Germans will beat the English in the open field, after which they will beat us too." Clemenceau, who hated the mention of the word defeat, transferred his faith from that moment to Foch, who still spoke bravely, if vaguely, of fighting before Amiens, in Amiens and behind Amiens, and of not yielding an inch.

March the twenty-sixth was a cold, bright day and Haig left early for Doullens. At eleven o'clock he held a conference there with Plumer, Horne and Byng, his three army commanders. Gough was not present. He was fully occupied on his own front, nor was he any longer an independent army commander, for Haig had placed him and all the British troops south of the Somme under the command of the French General Fayolle.

The commander in chief briefly outlined the situation. "Our object", he explained, "was to hold on. It was vitally important to cover Amiens, and troops were to be disposed accordingly, but there must not be a break between the First and Third armies. All available reserves were being sent down to support the Third Army." He then asked the commander of the First Army whether he could spare any more troops to take part in the battle. Horne replied that he could, by taking risks, spare one more Canadian division. Haig decided that the risk must be taken, and greater risks still if the situation of the Third Army again became critical. The opinion of Byng, however, was somewhat reassuring. "In the south near the Somme the enemy is very tired and there is no real fighting taking place there. Friend and foe are, it seems, dead beat and seem to stagger up against each other."

Plumer was then consulted with regard to the general situation. He "said he agreed with the plans made and with the absolute necessity for holding on. He also said that the enemy were obviously milking divisions from the Second Army front, but that he had only seven divisions left to hold his front and did not think he could spare any of them at present."

While Haig and his army commanders were sitting in conference the President of the French Republic, his prime minister and Milner, representing the British War Cabinet, together with Generals Foch and Wilson, were hastening along the road that leads from Paris to Doullens. Wilson was in the same car as Milner. The night before at Versailles he had put forward the suggestion that Clemenceau should be appointed generalissimo and that Foch should act as his deputy. The proposal met with approval nowhere save in the oversubtle mind of its author. That he should have made it is the more remarkable in view of the fact that having paused at G.H.Q. on his way to Versailles he must have been already aware that Haig was in favour of the simpler solution, namely the appointment of Foch to the supreme command. In any case, Wilson had by now abandoned his first idea and during the drive from Paris he strongly advocated to Milner the proposal of Haig without, however, so it seems, making it plain that Haig himself would support it.

The meeting in the little square at Doullens was dramatic. No conference of plenipotentiaries throughout the war took place so near to the firing line. Shells were falling in the vicinity and troops with the marks of battle upon them were marching continually through the town.

While Haig was still in conference with his generals, motorcars bearing the men upon whom so much now depended kept dashing up the narrow street and halting before the small Hôtel de Ville. Poincaré and Clemenceau were the first to arrive, then Foch, then Pétain and lastly Milner and Wilson. As Haig came down the steps to meet them observers noticed that his face was tired and anxious.

During the greetings that followed Clemenceau informed Milner of the rumour that had reached him with regard to Haig's intention of abandoning Amiens. It therefore seemed best to Milner to hold a preliminary conference with the British generals, who in a very few minutes reassured him as to their determination to hold on. There followed a short private conversation with Haig which further enlightened him, for he was still in doubt as to the attitude that Haig would adopt toward the proposal to appoint Foch generalissimo. Very few words sufficed to make this plain. Haig had refused to detach divisions that he could not spare to form part of a general reserve under the control of a committee, but he was willing and eager at this crisis to place himself and all his forces under the command of a fighting general.

"I can deal with a man," he said, "but not with a committee."

The historic conference took place soon after midday, and the following is the brief account of it that Haig wrote in his diary.

"We discussed the situation, and it was decided that

Amiens must be covered at all costs. French troops, we are told, are being hurried up as rapidly as possible. I have ordered Gough to hold on with his left at Bray. It was proposed by Clemenceau that Foch should be appointed to co-ordinate the operations of an allied force to cover Amiens and ensure that the French and British flanks remained united. This proposal seemed to me quite worthless, as Foch would be in a subordinate position to Pétain and myself. In my opinion it was essential to success that Foch should control Pétain, so I at once recommended that Foch should *co-ordinate the action of all the allied armies on the Western Front.* Both governments agreed to this. Foch had chosen Dury for his headquarters (three miles south of Amiens). Foch seemed sound and sensible, but Pétain had a terrible look. He had the appearance of a commander who has lost his nerve.

"I lunched from the lunch box at Doullens, then motored back to Beaurepaire.

"I rode about five P.M.—as I was going out I met Milner and Wilson. They spoke to me about Gough. I said that whatever the opinion at home might be, and no matter what Foch might have said, I considered that he (Gough) had dealt with a most difficult situation very well. He had never lost his head, was always cheery and fought hard."

Wilson also recounts in his diary this brief encounter. "I saw Douglas Haig just going out for a ride and he told me he was greatly pleased with the new arrangements. . . . Douglas Haig is ten years younger tonight than he was yesterday afternoon." The causes of his rejuvenation were that his plan had been adopted, that a great weight of responsibility had been lifted from his shoulders and that he felt confidence in his new commander.

When many minds are travelling in the same direction and ultimately arrive at one conclusion, genuine doubt must always exist as to when, where and with whom the idea originated. It was so with the invention of the tanks, and it is so with the appointment of the generalissimo. It has been seen that Haig was opposed to such an appointment earlier in the war, and reasons have been given for believing that he was right to oppose it. It has been seen also that he resented the temporary appointment of Nivelle, and the facts have shown that that appointment was a mistake. That Lloyd George had worked for greater unity of direction in his negotiations with Painlevé and by the setting up of the Council at Versailles, has been admitted, but he had subsequently, in November, expressly dissociated himself from the proposal to appoint a supreme commander. Nor had Milner any authority to go back upon that very definite declaration. It is to Milner's credit that he took upon himself the responsibility of committing the British government to so important a step which was endorsed by the War Cabinet two days later.

But wherever the idea originated, and many people had long been thinking of it, it can hardly be denied that its realization at that time and in that way was due more to Haig than to any individual. From the night when, having grasped the intentions of Pétain, he telegraphed to London for Milner and Wilson, to the last moment of the Doullens conference when he corrected the first draft of Clemenceau and gave to Foch the full powers he needed, there had been only one definite plan in his mind, and it was because he had been able to put that plan into action that he looked ten years younger when Henry Wilson met him riding out from the Château of Beaurepaire.

Satisfied as he was with that day's work Haig would have been the last to exaggerate its importance. In suggesting that Foch should be given supreme command he had had one definite object in view, to prevent the withdrawal of the French in a southwesterly direction on Paris and the separation of the two armies. That was the immediate danger which the policy of Pétain, communicated to Haig on the night of March the twenty-fourth at Dury, had revealed. That danger had been averted by the appointment of Foch, but that appointment had not sufficed to win the war or even to stave off defeat in the battle that was still raging.

Nobody knew this better than Foch. He, the intrepid apostle of victory, in the hour of his triumph at Doullens allowed to escape him the only words of pessimism which history has to his record. At luncheon after the conference Clemenceau, who never liked him, rather bitterly congratulated him on having at last obtained what he had always desired.

"A fine gift," was Foch's retort; "you give me a lost battle and tell me to win it."

It seemed indeed during the days and weeks that followed that this statement was hardly an exaggeration. March the twenty-seventh was another day of hard fighting when the exhausted remains of the Fifth Army were almost surrounded owing to the right of the Third Army having uncovered their flank and allowed the enemy to cross the Somme in their rear.

On the following morning the Germans delivered, with terrific energy and fresh troops, a new attack in another part of the line. The objective was Arras and the brunt of the attack was borne by the Third and the First armies. On this day the enemy's most formidable ally failed him. There was no fog. The result was that after having gained a few yards at the price of fearful casualties the attack failed, Arras was saved, and, so far as this particular stage of the long battle was concerned, the worst was over. The credit was principally due to Horne and the men of the First Army, who fought in blissful ignorance of the fact that the great principle of unity of command had been established and that Foch was the generalissimo.

On March the twenty-ninth the King, prompted by his unfailing instinct for making the right gesture in every public emergency, arrived at the headquarters of his commander in chief. In the account that Haig gave him of recent happenings he laid stress on three outstanding facts. First that the British infantry in France were less numerous by one hundred thousand than they had been a year before; secondly that they were now opposed by three times as many Germans as they had had against them then; and thirdly that they had been compelled to extend the length of their line by at least one fifth of the front they had held in the previous autumn.

That same day Haig met Foch at Abbeville. The generalissimo arrived "about twenty minutes late as usual, and full of apologies. He tells me that he is doing all he can to expedite the arrival of French divisions, and until they come we can only do our best to hold on to our present positions. It is most important to prevent the enemy from placing guns near enough to shell the great railway depot and troops sidings near Amiens (Longueau)—on the east of the town. By the second of April I gather that the French should have sufficient troops concentrated to admit of their starting an offensive. But will they?

"I think Foch has brought great energy to bear on the present situation, and has, instead of permitting French troops to retire southwest from Amiens, insisted on some of them relieving our tired troops and on covering Amiens at all costs. He and I are quite in agreement as to the general plan of operations."

Haig has been often unjustly accused of failing to maintain friendly relations with his French allies, and it is true that he was by temperament a man who did not easily cooperate with foreigners. The greater credit is therefore due to him for the fact that at this crisis, and henceforward among the many difficulties that still divided the allies from victory, such satisfactory relations existed between the British commander in chief and the French generalissimo, and that although no love was lost between the French generalissimo and his own prime minister, Haig succeeded in remaining on good terms with both.

On the day after his meeting with Foch at Abbeville he met Clemenceau at Dury. "Clemenceau is in full accord with me and gave orders for the French to support us energetically and cross the Avre river so as to hold the high ground where the Canadian cavalry now is. I sincerely hope that Clemenceau will get his order carried out. Clemenceau spoke most freely about Foch's position. He had no fears about my loyally doing my best to co-operate. It was Pétain and Foch who, he feared, would squabble. 'Pétain', he said, 'is a very nervous man, and sometimes may not carry out all he has promised.' Personally, I have found Pétain anxious to help and straightforward, but in the present operations he has been slow to decide and slower still in acting. At times his nerve seems to have gone—and he imagines that he is to be attacked in force. Hence the troubled position of affairs about Amiens."

Haig said afterward that during these early days of the new system it was Clemenceau who really played the generalissimo's part. Curiously unforeseen in their developments are the most carefully constructed of men's devices. Wilson had thought to make Clemenceau the figurehead, giving to Foch the real executive power. And now it appeared that exactly the opposite, a proposition which nobody would ever have put forward, had been accomplished.

At the Beauvais Conference on April the third, which Haig, with Lloyd George and Wilson, attended, together with Clemenceau, Foch and Pétain, "M. Clemenceau proposed to modify the agreement come to at Doullens, which gave Foch authority to 'co-ordinate the action of *all* allied armies on the Western Front'. After considerable discussion, it was agreed to entrust to Foch 'the strategical direction of military operations. The commanders in chief of the British, French and American armies will each have full control of the tactical action of his respective army. Each commander in chief will have the right of appeal to his government, if in his opinion his army is endangered by reason of any order received from General Foch.'

"I was in full agreement and explained that this new arrangement did not in any way alter my attitude toward Foch, or the commander in chief of the French Army. I had always, in accordance with Lord Kitchener's orders to me, regarded the latter as being responsible for indicating *the general strategical policy* and, as far as possible, I tried to fall in with his strategical plan of operations.

"Before the meeting broke up, I asked the governments to state that it is their desire that a French offensive should be started *as soon as possible* in order to attract the enemy's reserves and so prevent him from continuing his pressure against the British. Foch and Pétain both stated their determination to start attacking '*as soon as possible.*' But will they ever attack? I doubt whether the French Army as a whole is now fit for an offensive."

With tactical control of his army, and with right of appeal to his own government, Haig held now very much the same position with regard to Foch as he had formerly held with regard to Nivelle. In practice, as the sequel will show, there proved to be little difference in his relations with Foch from his previous relations with Joffre and Pétain. From the very beginning of the war he had plainly understood that in all matters of strategy the final decision must rest with the French, and he had loyally attempted to fall in with their views except when he believed that the safety of his own troops was endangered. Henceforward he continued to maintain the same attitude. Much exaggerated are the claims that have been put forward on behalf of the principle of unity of command. That its adoption on March the twenty-sixth, 1918, saved the cause, as Haig had foreseen that it would, may be admitted, but it would be difficult to point to any subsequent occasion during the next eight months when it seriously affected the conduct of the war.

The result of the conference at Beauvais was apparently the opposite to what had been intended. Clemenceau, according to Henry Wilson's diary, had called the conference in order to strengthen Foch's position "principally to allow him to coerce Pétain, and not Haig who is working smoothly". The actual result, as Wilson saw, was to weaken Foch's position rather than to strengthen it.

Haig drove part of the way from Montreuil to Beauvais that day with Lloyd George, whom he found "a fatiguing companion in a motor. He talks and argues so". Nor was the principal subject of conversation an agreeable one. It concerned the future of General Gough.

"I gather that Lloyd George expects to be attacked in the House of Commons for not tackling the man-power problem before, also for personally ordering divisions to the east at a critical time against the advice of his military adviser, viz. the C.I.G.S. (Robertson). He is looking out for a scapegoat for the retreat of the Fifth Army. I pointed out that 'fewer men, extended front and increased hostile forces' were the main causes to which the retreat may be attributed. He was much down upon Gough. I championed the latter's cause. 'He had few reserves, a very big front entirely without defensive works recently taken over from the French and the weight of the enemy's attack fell on him', I said. Also that in spite of a most difficult situation he had never really lost his head. Lloyd George said he had not held the Somme bridges, nor destroyed them, and that Gough must not be employed. To this I said I could not condemn an officer unheard, and that if Lloyd George wishes him suspended he must send me an order to that effect."

Now it must be admitted that grave doubts with regard to Gough's competence as an army commander had existed before March the twenty-first and had not been confined to civilian circles. They had been brought to Haig's notice both officially and unofficially. Lord Derby as secretary of state had written to him more than once on the subject, and divisional commanders had expressed their reluctance to serve with the Fifth Army. There are no scales for weighing the qualities of generals. Contemporaries are inclined to rely upon rumour, and historians can only judge by performance, paying at the same time due respect to the recorded opinion of accredited contemporaries. In the conduct of this great battle, from March the twenty-first to March the twenty-eighth, it is impossible to prove that Gough, fighting against tremendous odds, made a single mistake. Had he retreated less rapidly his whole force might have been annihilated, the link between the French and British armies would have been broken and the object of the enemy would have been achieved.

A despot can behave magnanimously in the hour of defeat. After Blenheim Louis XIV addressed not a word of reproach to Tallard. But magnanimity is not among the many virtues that belong to popular government. Democracy demands its victims. There had been a spectacular retreat, there had been terrible casualties, there had been days of the gravest anxiety, and the general who seemed to be responsible was the very one against whom whispers had already been percolating the masses. Fiercely the cry went up for his head on a charger, and the prime minister was only too willing to make such an offering to public opinion, especially if it was likely to prevent a demand for more.

Haig took a different view. In his mind popular opinion

counted for nothing against the demands of justice. He had thought it wise after the conference of Doullens to replace Gough by Rawlinson in command of the Fifth, or as it was henceforth called, the Fourth Army, because he knew that Foch, who had been personally rude to Gough, thought that he was to blame. But Gough was still in France, and Haig would condemn no officer unheard. On the day after his conversation with the prime minister, however, he received a telegram from the secretary of state for war conveying the decision of the War Cabinet that Gough should return home at once. Haig could only bow to that decision. He naturally supposed, as he told Gough before they parted, that an enquiry would be held. He did not believe that such a gallant officer with so fine a record would be disgraced without being allowed to say a word in his own defence or to produce one out of a cloud of witnesses. He should perhaps have anticipated that the government would not dare to institute an enquiry which might so easily have ended by the prosecutor finding himself in the dock.

After two more days of fierce fighting, the fourth and fifth of April, the attack upon this particular section of the front died away. From the enemy's point of view it had accomplished much, but it had failed in its main objective. The allies' front had been driven back for many miles, but the line was still unbroken, the Channel ports had not changed hands and Paris was preserved.

Haig knew that the battle was not yet over. He alone had fully appreciated that this must be Germany's final effort, and he was therefore convinced that it would not be abandoned after a fortnight. Once again his military instinct, guided by his admirable Intelligence Service, led him to form a fairly accurate forecast of the direction in which the next blow was to be delivered. On April the sixth he wrote in his diary, "The enemy's intentions seem still to be the capture of the Vimy position by turning it on both flanks by mass attacks on the south of Arras as well as on the north, south of the La Bassée canal. At the same time a surprise attack by three or four divisions against the Portuguese front is also to be expected. The First Army is quite alive to these possibilities and is prepared to meet them."

That evening he wrote to Foch:

> All information points to the enemy's intention to continue its efforts to destroy the British Army. . . . In view of this threatening situation, I submit that one of the three following courses should be given effect to without delay, viz.—either
>
> 1. A vigorous offensive in the next five or six days by the French armies on a considerable scale,
>
> or
>
> 2. The French to relieve the British troops south of the Somme (a total of four divisions),
>
> or
>
> 3. A group of four French divisions to be located in the neighbourhood of St Pol as a reserve to the British front.

He concluded his letter by asking Foch to meet him on the following day, which Foch agreed to do, and the meeting accordingly took place at Aumale on April the seventh.

Haig began by stating his reasons for believing that the next German attack would be delivered further north on the British front.

"Foch quite agreed that the British must be prepared for a very heavy attack. His plan was first to block the door to Amiens. To this end the French were going to attack from Moreuil southward, and he wished the British Fourth Army to co-operate. I pointed out the very limited means at Rawlinson's disposal. When the door to Amiens was barred, then he (Foch) would consider the advisability of putting in a large attack from the south toward Roye. Personally, I do not believe that either Foch or Pétain has any intention of putting French divisions into the battle.

"As regards my requests for either taking over British front south of Somme, or placing a French reserve near St Pol, Foch said he was unable to do either; but he had ordered a reserve of four divisions and three cavalry divisions of the French army to be located southwest of Amiens (i.e. in a very safe place).

"This was, he said, the best that he could do at present, and he thought that the presence of the French reserves near Amiens would enable me to move my own reserves from the right flank if the battle required them further north. I wired to the C.I.G.S. result of my meeting with Foch, and suggested that he (Wilson) should come out to discuss the situation, and try to get better arrangements from Foch."

On the following day a German aviator captured by the French gave the valuable information that the mass of the German reserves were in the Tournai-Douai-Cambrai area. On learning this Haig realized that the attack was likely to come further north than he had at first anticipated. He immediately sent for General de Laguiche, the head of the French mission, "and asked him to request General Foch to arrange to relieve six British divisions in the Ypres sector, i.e. as far south as the Ypres-Comines canal. This would enable me to form an effective reserve on my left." Later in the day General Weygand arrived at G.H.Q. to explain that Foch was unable to agree to this proposal.

Henry Wilson arrived early next morning, but did not prove an effective ally to Haig in his efforts to persuade Foch. Wilson did not approve of Haig's suggestion that French troops should be sent to the Ypres sector because he still failed to appreciate the likelihood of the attack being delivered in the north. Yet even while they were talking the blow had fallen.

It was on the north, not on the south, of the La Bassée canal that the attack was delivered, and the weight of it fell upon the Portuguese troops as Haig had foreseen. The discipline of the Portuguese had lately given cause for anxiety. Of the two divisions one had already been relieved, and it had been arranged that the relief of the other should take place on the following night. But the attack came too soon, the Portuguese were unable to meet it, and although the divisions on either side formed defensive flanks a huge gap was created which there were no troops immediately available to fill. It would require a volume to recount in detail the events of that disastrous day and of the two that followed. The Germans were attacking with two armies, one under General Sixte von Arnim, who commanded from the sea to the river Lys, and the other under General von Quast, who covered the area from the Lys to the La Bassée canal. Opposite to them respectively were the Second Army under Plumer and the First Army under Horne. It must not, however, be supposed, because the Second and First armies had played a secondary part in the previous battle, that therefore the troops which now composed them were fresh and undepleted. Divisions were continually being moved from one army to another, and many of those which had experienced the worst of the fighting on the Somme had been sent further north to rest and recover, only to find themselves once more in the centre of the battle area.

The British Army in France now consisted of fifty-eight divisions, of which forty-six had already been engaged between March twenty-first and April seventh. Nor were there any reserves in the vicinity. A few French divisions at Ypres or at St Pol would have been invaluable. But once again the battle-weary British Army had to bear unaided the full weight of the attack. Once again Haig's warnings had been disregarded and his demand for reinforcements denied.

The retreat which began on the ninth was continued on the tenth. Haig wrote to Foch as follows:

General Headquarters,
British Armies in France.
Wednesday, April 10, 1918.
Noon.

DEAR GENERAL FOCH,

You will by this time have been informed of the results of the enemy's attack yesterday north of the La Bassée canal. This morning he has extended his attack north of Armentières as far as Messines.

These facts still further confirm me in the opinion which I expressed to you yesterday, viz. that your plan of placing the heads of four French divisions on the Somme, immediately west of Amiens, does not adequately meet the military situation of the British Army.

The enemy will without a doubt continue to strike against my troops until they are exhausted. It is therefore vitally important, in order to enable us to continue the battle for a prolonged period, that the French Army should take immediate steps to relieve *some part* of the British front, and take an active share in the battle.

As to what portion of our front should be taken over by the French, I leave you to decide. But I must emphasize my opinion that the military situation is such that an immediate decision and action, on the lines which I have suggested above, is necessary in the combined interest of the allied armies.

Yours very truly,
D. HAIG.

At ten o'clock that night Foch arrived at G.H.Q. He said that he had carefully considered Haig's letter and that he had at last agreed that the enemy's objective was the British Army. He had therefore decided to move up a large force of French troops so that they would be in readiness to take part in the battle. Plans were at once drawn up and orders issued for the head of a French force to cross the Somme west of Amiens and to reach the lines Molliens-au-Bois-Vigniecourt on the twelfth and Vauchelles-Doullens on the thirteenth. The force was to consist of four infantry and three cavalry divisions. The intention was that as the French force advanced the British reserves would be moved further north. On the fourteenth, however, the promised aid had not materialized. That day a conference was held at Abbeville. At this meeting Foch was at his most abrupt and least comprehensible. To Haig's urgent requests for reliefs on account of the tiredness of his troops he would reply that there must be no relief during a battle; and to the suggestion that the line might be shortened by a withdrawal on the left he answered monotonously that there must be no withdrawal. When he was pressed to send as many troops as he could to the Hazebrouck-Cassel area, he said that he would see what the situation was when the movement of troops then in progress was finished. The fact of the matter was that Foch believed this particular offensive was slackening and that he was determined to economize his reserves, and to retain them so far as possible in a position where they would be readily available wherever the next blow fell.

There had existed for some time a school of thought, more prominent in Paris than elsewhere, that was in favour of a complete amalgamation of the two armies, the French and the English, into one. Such a decision would have rendered the existence of a British commander in chief superfluous, and the British government would have ceased to exercise any control over the direction of the campaign, save such as could be brought to bear by diplomatic pressure.

Haig had always condemned the proposal and was always on his guard against any suggestion which seemed to have a tendency in that direction.

On April nineteenth he wrote:

After lunch Commandant Gemeau brought me a letter from Foch stating that he was anxious to maintain fifteen

French divisions in reserve behind the British Army. To enable him to obtain these divisions it would be necessary to put tired British divisions in the positions now held by the French divisions which he wants.

I at once replied that I would do anything necessary to help to win the battle, but it was desirable to tell Foch that any idea of a permanent "amalgam" must be dismissed from his mind at once, because that would never work. I also reminded Gemeau of the proposals made at the Calais conference in February, 1917, by which the British G.H.Q. was to disappear. He assured me that I could implicitly depend on Foch's good faith. So I told Gemeau I would send a favourable reply and have the question studied at once.

Lord Milner arrived about 3 P.M. on his way to London to take up his duties as secretary of state for war. He expressed his intention of doing his best to guard the interests of the army, and he hoped that the army would treat him in a kindly spirit.

I showed him Foch's letter. He agreed that it was necessary to meet his request, but only as a temporary measure. He was entirely opposed to mixing up units of the French and British. The needs of this great battle had made intermingling of units for a time necessary, but he would never approve of a permanent "amalgam."

Lord Milner had been appointed to the War Office in succession to Lord Derby, who was taking over the post of British ambassador in Paris. Haig regretted the change. There had been from the first no rift in his harmonious relations with Derby, to whom he telegraphed on this occasion: "We shall miss you very much at the War Office but feel convinced you will be of great assistance to the army in your new post."

After his conversation with Milner recounted above, Haig wrote to Foch and undertook to send the four divisions which had been asked for. When he had done so, and the letter had been dispatched, he received an excited telegram from the War Office, who had been informed of the proposal by the British liaison officer at Foch's headquarters. The War Office had realized, as had Haig, the possibilities which such a suggestion might involve. "As this would eventually result in the complete intermixture of French and British armies", so ran the telegram, "destruction of identity of British Army, and is contrary to instructions contained in first five lines of paragraph three of Lord Kitchener's memorandum No. 121/7711 December 28, 1915, to you which has not been altered by the recent arrangements for command of allied forces on the main front, I presume that you are refusing."

Haig's reply was brief—"Your telegram 56739. I explained proposal to Lord Milner yesterday. I consider military situation requires me to meet Foch's wishes to a limited degree. Am writing."

There was a certain irony in the situation. Within a month of the introduction of unity of command, for which the authorities at home had endeavoured to secure the credit, those same authorities are found telegraphing to Haig "presuming" that he has refused to obey the wishes of the generalissimo.

The fierce fighting still continued, and none knew when or where the next blow would fall. On April twenty-fifth a great German attack was delivered in the north. Kemmel was the main objective—both Kemmel village and Mount Kemmel to the southwest of it. This part of the British line was then held by French troops, who were unable to maintain their position. Kemmel had been considered impregnable, and the loss of it was a severe blow, necessitating a withdrawal of the whole line in that sector. Further assaults on the twenty-seventh and the twenty-ninth proved less effective, and may be taken as marking the end of the last stage of the battle that started on March twenty-first.

As April ended and as May began, there was no man in France from the commander in chief down to the latest landed private soldier who could be aware of the fact that for the British Army the bitterness of death was past. Much fighting yet remained to do and heavy losses to be suffered, but there were to be no more surprises, no more headlong retreats, no more backs to the wall with anxious eyes turning to the left and to the right, to the Channel ports and the French Army.

None knew so well as Haig how near his army had come to disaster, but none had felt greater confidence than he, even in the darkest days, that disaster would be avoided. In the diary that he wrote from hour to hour can be found the deep anxiety that he often experienced, but from first to last there is not one note of pessimism, not one hint of despair. To General Edmunds, who dined with him on March twenty-second, he had said that the Germans had enough men to make three big attacks, and that if the French played up the attacks would be beaten off and that the allies would win the war in the autumn. It was the first time that he had committed himself to so definite a prophecy, and he never wavered from it.

On April twenty-eighth he wrote in his diary:

"I gave Lord Milner a note with reference to a statement by Mr Bonar Law in the House of Commons in which he declared that the extension of the British lines had been *arranged between the commanders in France* without interference by the British government. My note showed clearly how on twenty-fifth September last a conference (at which I was not present) was held at Boulogne, and the British and French governments decided *on the principle* that the British should take over more line. Against this I protested. Today I told Lord Milner I did not wish to embarrass the government at this time, but I must ask that a true statement of the facts be filed in the War Office. Milner said he would be glad to do this, and that he recollected very well how all along I had objected to any extension. He (Milner) wishes to throw blame on no one, but is quite ready to accept all blame himself. 'Unfortunately', he said, 'some of the members of the Cabinet are not so constituted!'

"Milner has given me a very favourable impression as secretary of state for war. He spent all yesterday afternoon and morning in the offices of G.H.Q. learning all he can; his one idea is to be as helpful as possible."

There was nothing military about Lord Milner, yet Haig found no difficulty in understanding him. His relations with Lord Kitchener and with Lord Derby, when they were at the War Office, had always been perfectly satisfactory, just as they had been with Haldane and with Asquith. Equally so were his relations with Lord Milner. It is impossible to pretend that Haig was a difficult man for politicians to deal with.

The private soldier was another man whom Haig understood, and who understood him though they had little to say to one another. When he did speak, he used words which the men could understand, and which stirred their souls to that supreme effort with which they answered. Throughout these battles, as survivors testify, there was a high spirit of hope and gaiety among the British troops which had been lacking at Passchendaele and even on the Somme. Even retreat did not depress them unduly, for retreat meant movement, good-bye to the trenches; and they remembered how the retreat from Mons had been followed by the battle of the Marne.

The Germans, on the other hand, were aware that this was their supreme effort for victory, and when they realized that it had failed their hearts failed too.

The long battle which now drew to its end has been referred to often enough as a great defeat for the British Army. Nor can we quarrel with the word defeat, where there has been rapid retreat in accordance with no previous plan, fortified positions hastily abandoned, artillery, stores and equipment lost. Yet where there is defeat there should be victory, and what kind of a victory had the Germans won? Not a single main objective had been taken. Paris and the Channel ports were intact, the solidarity of the French and British armies was unbroken. In return for far greater casualties than they had inflicted, and for the destruction of the flower of their last army, the enemy had won a few miles of devastated territory.

As the spring days of 1918 led on to summer hope grew in the hearts of the allied armies and belief turned to certainty in the mind of the British commander in chief.

CHAPTER XV

The Turn of the Tide

THE THREE MONTHS that followed the collapse of the great German attack proved a period of comparative calm so far as the British front was concerned. Before the end of the summer the majority of the troops were eagerly expecting the next battle.

And the Americans were arriving. Haig's first impressions of Pershing were wholly favourable.

"I was much struck", he wrote on July 20, 1917, "with his quiet gentlemanly bearing. Most anxious to learn and fully realizes the greatness of the task before him."

It was natural that Pershing should, as Haig put it, "hanker after a great self-contained American Army", but he had the good sense to realize that the most rapid and satisfactory method of creating such an army was to give the men who were to form it the opportunity of learning their profession on the battlefield, and that they could find no better teachers than the veteran soldiers of their ally, who spoke the same language as themselves. An agreement was made that 120,000 American infantry should join the British Army during the month of May. Haig's view of the manner in which they should be treated is revealed in the following passage from his diary, written on May seventh:

"General Bonham Carter (director of training) reported on the arrangements made to receive and train the Americans. We are using the cadres of our Thirty-ninth, Sixty-sixth, Thirtieth and Thirty-fourth Divisions to help in the training of the infantry of four American divisions. I impressed on Bonham Carter that our officers are not to command and order the Americans about, but must only help American officers by their advice and experience to become both leaders in the field and also instructors. For the moment training as leaders should take first place."

Not only had the Americans as much to learn as had the earliest battalions of Kitchener's armies in 1914, but they lacked such advantages as those armies possessed. They were without the trained noncommissioned officers to assist them, without a certain nucleus who had had some experience with the Territorials, and without the presence of a few veterans who had seen service in the South African War. The wonder was not how little they knew, but rather the rapidity with which they acquired knowledge.

At the end of the month Haig inspected the American troops that had already arrived, and recorded his impressions:

"I left by motor about 10 A.M. with Major Bacon of the American Army, who is attached to my personal staff now as A.D.C. for American troops. Major Heseltine also accompanied me. I spent the day with certain American divisions which are now training with the British Army.

"At Frivelle-Escarbotin, headquarters Sixty-sixth Division, I saw Major General Bethell commanding and his staff. General Burnham, commanding the American Eighty-second Division, was also present. After a short talk over the general arrangements for training, we motored to the neighbourhood of Tilloy Fleriville, where we got on some horses, and I spent a couple of hours riding about with one of the brigades which was training in a valley by companies.

Shooting, bayonet practice, drill of platoons, etc., were all going on. I spoke a few words with each of the company commanders and as dinner time approached I went round most of the kitchens, examined the dinners and spoke to the cooks. All were quite happy, but some had nothing but canned meat, others had ample fresh meat, some had no salt, etc. I arrived at the conclusion that the fault with the American regiments is in the distribution of the supplies. The regimental and battalion staffs seem quite ignorant of how to look after their men.

"It was past 2 P.M. before I left this division. The men and young officers are active and keen to learn. The older officers are ignorant of their duties, but seem anxious to profit by our instruction—and get on well with their instructors.

"We lunched on the roadside after passing Gamach. I then visited headquarters Thirtieth Division at Eu, where General Williams received me, also General Wright commanding Thirty-fifth American Division, which is attached for training. I liked what I saw of Wright; he seemed a modest man, anxious that he should do what was best for his men, and that he should not fail in his command in battle. I thought that he had grounded the rank and file well in first principles. I saw two battalions on parade at Château la Hare, Bois l'Epine. These men came from Kansas and Missouri, twelve hundred miles west of New York. Fine big men, reminded me of tall Australians. Their drill was extremely good, very quick and smart. I was greatly pleased.

"Also went round the kitchens. Cooks complained of too much meat and no oatmeal, no hominy and no vegetables.

"I then motored to Huppy, headquarters American Thirty-third Division, and saw General Bell, commanding. This is a regular division. Bell is an old type of general, with moustaches and imperial on his chin, but ready for anything. He had a numerous staff including a dentist, a sanitary officer, a judge advocate, etc. This division is only now arriving from Brest.

"Summing up my impression of what I saw today, I was much pleased with what I saw of the men and young officers. The latter are a very keen and capable lot of young fellows, but all are very ignorant of military ways and arrangements and tactics.

"My scheme of using our 'cadre' divisions for training is working well."

The French had at one time been inclined to object to the attachment of so large a body of American troops to the British Army, but they had come to recognize the common sense of an arrangement whereby the Americans received training from men who spoke their language, it being well understood that as soon as they could be employed as independent units they would be at the disposal of the generalissimo.

The system of unity of command was working satisfactorily. In normal times it differed very little, as has been already stated, from the system that preceded it. Tact was required on both sides, and tact was seldom lacking. If the correspondence which passed between Haig and Foch is examined, it will not be found to differ in tone from the correspondence which passed between Haig and Joffre, or between Haig and Pétain.

The following two letters are typical of many others:

Headquarters—May 3, 1918.

MY DEAR FIELD MARSHAL,

The enemy attacks on the front Bailleul-Ypres have been stopped for the moment by our resistance. But they may begin again any day if the enemy is left free to act.

He would be deprived of such freedom by a British offensive which, starting from the line Robecq-Festubert, would advance in the direction of Merville and Estaires. As soon as such an offensive could bring under its fire the lines of communication which cross at Estaires, the German attack north of the Lys in a westerly or northwesterly direction would be much interfered with and perhaps rendered impossible.

These extremely important results could be obtained by a limited advance, and in a sector which seems to provide a favourable starting point, especially from the point of view of artillery.

The British Army should have at its disposal the necessary troops for such an offensive. The Canadian Corps, for instance, which is well up to strength, might be employed.

A similar French offensive is now in course of preparation. Like the above, it will give the allied armies the means of re-establishing their moral ascendancy over the enemy.

I have the honour to request the field marshal commander in chief of the British Army to be good enough to let me knew whether he can without delay undertake the study and then the preparation of the offensive outlined above.

Yours very sincerely

F. FOCH.

To which the following reply was returned:

In reply to your letter No. 564, dated May 3, I beg to inform you that an offensive operation as described by you is in course of preparation at the present moment by the general officer commanding British First Army, and could be carried out at comparatively short notice.

The Canadian Corps, less one division, has been withdrawn from the line for this purpose.

I am, however, of opinion that the present moment is not a suitable time for the delivery of a small offensive operation of this nature. The enemy is evidently making preparations for an attack on a considerable scale on the British front, and I shall require all my available reserves in order to withstand such an attack.

Meanwhile, as stated above, I am pressing forward with preparations for the offensive operation outlined by you, and shall be prepared to launch it when a favourable opportunity arises.

I trust that these arrangements will be agreeable to you.

I note with satisfaction that an offensive is about to be delivered by the French Army.

D. HAIG,
FIELD MARSHAL.

It will be seen that there is nothing in the tone of this correspondence which could suggest that the writers are superior and subordinate officers. It is the correspondence of two allies who are collaborating, on the clear understanding that it is the duty of the Frenchman to take the initiative in laying down the main lines of military policy and of strategy, and that it is the duty of the British commander in chief to do everything possible to meet his wishes.

It has been seen how when the principle of a generalissimo was accepted one of the advantages appeared to be that Foch had the French as well as the British commander in chief under his control, and that it was therefore no more derogatory to Haig than it was to Pétain. If such a consideration had ever been present to Haig's mind—and there is no indication in his diary that it had been—it is plain that it no longer carried any weight with him. On May second there was a conference at Abbeville. After certain preliminary matters had been discussed the soldiers withdrew.

"M. Clemenceau, Lloyd George and Lord Milner were to discuss privately who was to succeed Foch if anything happened to him. I told Milner that the best arrangement would be to decide that the commander in chief of the French Army would be *ipso facto* 'generalissimo' (because the latter must be a Frenchman in France). Foch then would be commander in chief French Army as well as 'generalissimo', and have the G.Q.G. under him. At present he lacks a staff and in consequence he and Weygand are overworked.

Having given Foch 'a staff', we get continuity. Then the French government should be asked to nominate (privately) either Anthoine or Pétain to be Foch's successor in case of necessity. Milner agreed, and said he would express my views."

Haig's attitude with regard to the whole question was determined by characteristic common sense and by characteristic selflessness. He had proposed unity of command for a definite purpose—to prevent a breach between the two armies. He had carried his proposal and his purpose had been accomplished. But the principle of unity of command once accepted could not be dropped. It had assumed too important a position in the minds and imaginations of the allied nations. Haig realized that this was so and never suggested going back on the agreement.

It was not Haig, but Henry Wilson, the admirer of all things French and the idolater of Foch, who now began to fear lest the French should obtain too great an ascendancy. Haig had no illusions. He had seen the danger long before Wilson had, and he was confident of his ability to avoid it.

Foch and Haig began to make preparations for the great advance which was to win the war. Haig motored all along the British front, visiting each headquarters and familiarizing himself with conditions.

If proof were needed, and it hardly can be by anyone who had read this book so far, that Haig was above personal intrigue and took no interest in political squabbles even when they affected his own position, such proof should be provided by the perusal of his diary during this month of May. For while there was calm in France there were storms in the House of Commons, and the intriguers were busy at their work. Henry Wilson, while writing Haig friendly, almost affectionate letters, was secretly advising the politicians to dismiss him, and the prime minister was fighting against a formidable array of facts to prove that the reverses of March and April had been due to the incompetence of the soldiers in France and not to his own policy in refusing to send reinforcements and insisting upon an extension of the British line.

It has been seen that when Mr Bonar Law made an inaccurate statement with regard to the extension of the line Haig, unwilling to embarrass the government, had merely written to the War Office asking that for purposes of historical accuracy the true facts should be put upon record. Others took a more serious view of the false information with which the government at this time was assiduously flooding the press and misleading the public. On May seventh Major General Sir Frederick Maurice, who had been director of military operations in the previous month, published a letter in the press categorically contradicting the above statement of Bonar Law, and describing as untrue the prime minister's assertion that "the army in France was considerably stronger on January 1, 1918, than on January 1, 1917".

When questioned on the matter in the House of Commons, Bonar Law replied that as these allegations affected the honour of ministers it was proposed to invite two judges to enquire into their accuracy; but when two days later Mr Asquith moved that the matter should be referred to a select committee the government opposed and defeated the motion and no enquiry was ever held.

To these events, which profoundly interested the army, not even a passing reference is made in the well-filled pages of the commander in chief's diary. He was not interested. He knew the facts, and he knew that they would become known to posterity. For the present his sole concern was to win the war. A correspondence which took place at this time exemplifies his attitude. Repington, as has already been stated, had left the *Times* rather than be a party to deceiving the public, and had since been writing for the *Morning*

Post. In February he had been prosecuted and punished for warning the country of what was about to happen in March. The question how far a man is justified during a war in criticizing his own government and thereby giving encouragement and possibly information to the enemy is a difficult one to determine. Lady Bathurst, the owner of the *Morning Post,* had not unjustifiable doubts as to the usefulness of Repington's activities and therefore adopted the sensible course of addressing an enquiry direct to the commander in chief.

Pinbury Park,
Cirencester,
May 24, 1918.

DEAR SIR DOUGLAS,

I have never had the pleasure of meeting you, though I know Lady Haig, but I am writing now to ask you a question, in my capacity of newspaper proprietor. It is this. Can you tell me whether you consider Colonel Repington's articles in the *Morning Post* are of any use or service to the army? It is a matter upon which I am not competent to judge. I rely upon Mr Gwynne's judgment but I think that he has never asked you for an opinion on this subject. I want you to believe, as I am sure you do, that both my husband and I and Mr Gwynne have only one wish, and that is to serve in any way we can the interests of the British Army. I have had grave doubts lately as to whether our military correspondent was not doing more harm than good. That is why I should be grateful for your opinion on the subject and you may rest assured that the matter will go no further than between Bathurst, myself and Mr Gwynne. If you consider that Colonel Repington is doing good service to the army, well and good, I have no more to say; but if not I shall know what course to adopt. Please forgive me for troubling you at a time when you must have so great a weight of anxiety and responsibility, but the matter is rather important.

Yours sincerely
LILIAS BATHURST.

Haig replied as follows:

Personal and Private.

General Headquarters,
British armies in France.
Monday, May 27, '18.

DEAR LADY BATHURST,

In reply to your letter of 24th inst. owing to stress of work since the battle began in March, I have not been able to read Colonel Repington's recent articles very carefully, but I have no hesitation in saying that in the past Colonel Repington has rendered very great service not only to the army but to our country. And I am confident that he is capable of doing so now. I venture however to make one suggestion and that is that in his articles Colonel Repington be urged to deal as seldom as possible with persons, but to devote his energies to enlightening the public as to what success in war depends on, and to set his pen firmly against any departure from sound principle which he may notice either at home, out here or indeed anywhere! At the present crisis in our country's history, it is of all things necessary that our fellow citizens be united and show a firm front everywhere to the enemy. Hence no matter how much one may dislike the methods of some of our rulers we must sink personal feelings for the time being, and do our duty as best we can.

I hope these remarks may be of some help. I am only sorry that I am not able to answer your question more fully, and with kind regards,

Believe me,
Yours v. truly
D. HAIG.

An attack on the Aisne was delivered May twenty-seventh and for several days caused the generalissimo the keenest anxiety. On the first day the enemy crossed the Aisne, on the second he was beyond the river Vesle, and on the third the French Army found themselves once more on the banks of the Marne. On the last day of the month Haig lunched with Foch at Sarcus.

"After lunch I had a talk with Foch. Present were Lawrence, Weygand and Du Cane. We spoke of the possibility of supporting the French with some divisions. I said it all depended on the situation on my front and read a translation of my note on the question. Foch also said that Pétain had asked for American divisions to be sent him (no matter how untrained), to hold long fronts (twenty-five kilo) on the Swiss frontier, and release French divisions. I gave some good reasons against the proposal, but said I would consider the matter and reply on Saturday (tomorrow). I also promised to go into the possibilities of forming a corps of three divisions as a reserve to support the French in case of grave emergency. While we were talking a message came from Pétain asking Foch to meet him near Meaux, and stating that M. Clemenceau, the French prime minister, would be there too. Foch told me that the situation was anxious; the reserves which had been sent forward had 'melted away very quickly'. Foch and Weygand started at once. I thought Foch looked more anxious that I have ever seen him."

These were indeed days of grave anxiety for the generalissimo. His faith in victory was unshaken. He saw, as Haig had seen, that once the spring offensive was exhausted every factor in the situation would favour the allies' cause. But now there seemed to be a real danger lest this last effort of the enemy should prove disastrous to his plans. There were those in England who now believed that the French Army was beaten, just as there had been some in France two months before who believed the same of the British Army; and serious enquiry was held as to whether it would be possible for the British and Americans to continue fighting in France with the French Army no longer in the field, and Paris in the hands of the enemy.

Haig never took this gloomy view, but as the French retreat continued and the demands for assistance increased he began to grow concerned for the safety of his own forces. Opposite to him was the army of the Crown Prince Rupprecht with powerful reserves, which, information showed, had not been drawn upon. All evidence from every source pointed to the imminence of an attack, and subsequent knowledge has confirmed that such an attack was intended, although it was never delivered. It was in these circumstances that there arose one of the two disagreements which, during the whole period of their collaboration, divided Haig and Foch.

At a meeting at Versailles on June first, when Clemenceau, Lloyd George and Milner were present, Foch repeated the proposal made at Sarcus that the American divisions at present training with the British should take over a quiet portion of the French front in order to relieve a similar number of French troops to take part in the battle. Haig was strongly opposed to the proposal. He was prepared to expedite the training of the Americans and hoped to have some of them ready by the middle of the month. Meanwhile it would be waste of such valuable material to send them, half trained, to a sector where they would see no fighting. Moreover, it was his private conviction, to which he could hardly give utterance, that these fresh troops, full of enthusiasm, the flower of American manhood, would prove more formidable fighters than the weary, war-worn veterans of France.

No settlement of this question was reached at Versailles and subsequently Foch obtained Pershing's consent to his proposal. With Foch and Pershing in agreement with regard to the disposal of American troops, there was nothing left for Haig but to bow to the decision.

On June fourth Foch telegraphed to Haig asking him to place three divisions astride the Somme in order to protect what both believed to be the most vital link in the chain, the point of contact between the two armies. But Haig considered that he could not move so many troops without endangering his whole army. He replied, therefore, that he was complying with Foch's orders immediately, but that he wished to make a formal protest against any troops leaving his command until the bulk of the reserves of Prince Rupprecht's armies had become involved in the battle. At the same time Haig sent copies of both telegrams to the secretary of state for war for the information of the War Cabinet.

It has been seen how at Beauvais on April third it was agreed that each commander in chief should have the right of appeal to his government in certain circumstances. Milner appears to have considered that Haig's protest, and the fact that he had sent a copy of it to the War Office, constituted such an appeal. Haig had not intended it to do so. A man does not make the final appeal to Caesar by merely forwarding copies of correspondence without even a covering letter.

However, a meeting was arranged to take place in Paris on June seventh. Lord Milner and Sir Henry Wilson were present, as well as Haig, Lawrence and Du Cane, Clemenceau, Foch and Weygand.

Lord Milner explained why the British prime minister has asked for this meeting; briefly Foch had moved many reserves (French and American divisions) from behind the British front and, in view of the large number of enemy reserves still available for action against the British, the government had become genuinely anxious.

I then read my memorandum stating I was in full accord with Foch as to the necessity for making all *preparations* for moving British troops to support the French in case of necessity. But I asked that I should be consulted before a definite order to move any divisions from the British area was given. I had repeated to London the telegram which I had sent to Foch, in order to warn the British government that the situation was quickly reaching a stage in which circumstances might compel me to appeal to them (the British Cabinet) under the Beauvais agreement. In my opinion the order about to be issued by Foch imperilled the British Army in France. I hoped that everything that forethought could do would be done now, and in the immediate future, to prevent circumstances arising which would necessitate such an appeal. Foch stuck out for full powers as generalissimo, to order troops of any nationality wherever he thought fit and at shortest notice. Milner and Clemenceau agreed that he must have these powers, and the latter urged Foch and myself to meet more frequently. Clemenceau strongly forbade any orders being sent direct from French headquarters moving French or any unit in my area, without passing through my hands first of all. This was with reference to the departure of certain French divisions and guns from the détachment de l'armée du nord, which had been ordered direct, without even notifying General Plumer or G.H.Q. on the subject.

The effect of the Beauvais agreement is now becoming clearer in practice. This effect I had realized from the beginning, namely that the responsibility for the safety of the British Army in France could no longer rest with me, because the generalissimo can do what *he* thinks right with *my* troops. On the other hand, the British government is only now beginning to understand what Foch's powers as generalissimo amount to. This delegation of power to Foch is inevitable, but I intend to ask that the British government should in a document modify my responsibility for the safety of the British Army under these altered conditions.

The C.I.G.S. asked Foch if he still adhered to the same strategical policy as he enunciated at Abbeville on second of May. Foch replied that he did, namely first to secure the connection of the British and French armies—second to cover both Paris and the Channel ports. And in reply to Foch I said that I agreed with these principles.

After the meeting Haig and Foch left together for the latter's office at the Invalides and had a perfectly amicable discussion with regard to certain military matters. The incident had in no way impaired their good understanding.

It was the general opinion of all concerned that the meeting had been useful. It had cleared the air and clarified the situation. Tact and good humour had been displayed on all sides. Milner had supported Foch, and Clemenceau had stood up for Haig. No real difference of opinion had been revealed and for the next four months no cloud disturbed the harmonious relations of the two great soldiers.

Haig continued to watch closely the development of the American Army, and his impressions continued to grow more favourable. On June twelfth, "I visited the 326th Regiment of the Sixty-second Division (American)—General Burnham. I saw a battalion attacking, others shooting on the seashore, etc., General Bethell and our sixty-sixth divisional staff are training this division.

"Near St Valéry I saw more machine gunners of the American Eighty-second Division under a Major Pike. Fine-looking fellows and all very keen. The Eighty-second Division leaves on the fifteenth of June for the French area. Several American officers said how sorry they were to leave the British.

"We then motored across the Somme via Noyelles to La Bassée (near Rue), where the 107th Regiment and fourteen machine-gun companies of the American Twenty-seventh Division were drawn up in line for my inspection. General Pierce commands the brigade and O'Ryan the division. The men stood well on parade and presented a fine appearance. This is a division of the National Guard of the New York State. It has been in camp training on the Mexican border for the last year, and seemed much better disciplined than any other American troops I have yet inspected. After I had walked down the line, the troops marched past by companies. This was done extremely well. Companies were 250 strong, and a machine-gun battalion 742. So that there were nearly six thousand troops on parade. The men carried huge packs on their backs, yet they marched well, and kept their dressing admirably. They were evidently much pleased at my inspection. I complimented General O'Ryan on his fine command.

"We had tea with General Pierce in a château close to Rue. Pierce has recently taken command of the brigade; before that he was on the general staff at Washington. He told me of the tremendous efforts now being made by America to equip and organize a large army. Both Generals Pierce and O'Ryan struck me as capable men, but without much experience of command. I expect that the Americans will soon produce fairly good staff officers, but the difficulties are greater in the production of commanders. This will be difficult to overcome."

On June fourteenth, "I breakfasted early and motored to Nordausques (between St Omer and Calais) and spent the morning (10.30 to one o'clock) riding about looking at the work of the Thirtieth American Division. I was accompanied by Thompson and Fletcher; and Major Robert Bacon (American Army) attached to my personal staff, Major General Blacklock and the staff of our Thirty-fifth Division are helping this lot of Americans to train. Major General George Read commands the American Thirtieth Division. He was yesterday appointed to command the American Second Corps. I think he should do this satisfactorily. He seemed to me too old for the duties of a G.O.C. *division,* but he knows the fundamental principles of war, and should do well as a *corps* commander to start with. I saw companies of the 119th, 118th and 117th Regiments at work. The men looked in fine form, and very keen; these remarks apply equally to the officers.

"I next motored to the training area near Lumbres, lunching by the roadside on the way, and spent a couple of hours with the American Seventy-eighth Division (Major General Macree). The troops have only been here two or three days, and only begin their scheme of training on

Monday. Major General Nicholson Thirty-fourth Division is (with his staff) helping these Americans to train. All seem to get on very well together.

"The 312th Regiment (Lieutenant Colonel Anderson) was drawn up on parade for my inspection. I was much impressed; they are a fine body of men, keen, active and athletic looking.

"On the way back to Montreuil, I halted in Samer at the headquarters of the American Eightieth Division and made the acquaintance of Major General Cronkhite, commanding the division. He is a fine hearty fellow ready to go into battle at once if necessary with his division."

Haig's high opinion of the American troops was shared by the French. On June seventeenth he wrote in his diary:

"General de Laguiche, who has just returned from Foch's headquarters and G.Q.G., states that the feeling in the French Army has now changed regarding the Americans. Everyone now says that 'they are splendid fighters' and that it would be 'folly to send them to a quiet sector in the Vosges, where they would only deteriorate'. General Fayolle commanding the G.A. reserve (in which is the French First Army) states that the American First Division, which is under him, is 'the best division which he has in his army group'."

The friendly relations existing between Haig and Foch are illustrated by the diary accounts of interviews during the month of June. These are extracts:

"Foch was in good form. He was pleased with the Italian situation and with the fighting qualities shown by the American divisions. By next April Pershing is to have eighty American divisions in France. The question of providing efficient divisional commanders will be a difficult one for the Americans to solve.

"Foch was anxious about reserves. I showed him how mine were disposed. He was quite satisfied and gave it as his opinion that I should keep strong reserves both on the Somme and also in my northern sector. The centre could then readily be supported. This is practically my present arrangement.

"Foch has to keep strong French reserves to cover Paris. I asked him if he was satisfied that the present French forces on my right were adequate for holding Gentelles and the Villers-Bretonneux ridge. He considered that they were.

"As regards defences he found the British had done well in making new lines, but the switch to connect British and French systems southwest of Amiens, which, by agreement, the French were to make, had not been begun. This he is to see to. We also discussed the principles of defence and how to meet German methods of attack. I found we were in agreement. Foch laid great stress on holding 'the second system' (i.e. our reserve zone) with fresh troops, as soon as the bombardment commences. I told him that was our arrangement also, but sometimes we had not had sufficient troops for the purpose. I am using American troops to hold rear lines in some sectors of my front.

"Altogether the meeting was most friendly. Foch made his apologies for bringing me so far away from G.H.Q. to meet him, but it was unavoidable because he has to see Generals Pétain and Pershing this afternoon. Foch's headquarters at present are about thirty miles east of Paris, but he retains Mouchy and also Sarcus in case the battle breaks out again in the northern sector."

Two days later there was another meeting. "At 9 A.M. I left with General Lawrence and Fletcher by motor for Mouchy-le-Châtel. We got there at twelve o'clock. General Foch had already arrived, and was having his lunch—a sardine and hard-boiled egg, as it was Friday, he told me. . . .

"Foch seemed in the best of spirits owing partly to the delay in the enemy's attack, partly to the success of the

Italians, and largely to the report of a speech recently made by Kühlmann in Berlin, which stated that there was no hope of the Germans ending the war by military means alone and foreshadowing the German government's intention of opening direct communication with the allied governments.

"The first question raised by Foch was the relief of the whole of the détachment de l'armée du nord as soon as possible. He said that the French government was alarmed about Paris, and wished to have adequate reserves to protect the capital. I pointed out that I could only relieve the D.A.N. at once by depleting my reserves on part of my front, that this would mean running extra risks; if, however, Paris were really in danger, the risk must be taken. Foch said that the French government insisted on the D.A.N. being withdrawn *on account of Paris*. I therefore agreed to release the divisions of the D.A.N. as soon as possible, and will let him have the exact dates on my return to G.H.Q.

"I asked Foch to arrange to place one or two good French divisions near Dunkirk so as to be in a position to support the Belgians in case of necessity. He agreed with me that such a disposition was desirable, and he would try and arrange it, but for the moment no French troops could be spared.

"He asked me to arrange for an offensive 'at the end of August'. The French would also carry out an offensive, but not the Montdidier-Noyon project, because it was more important to drive the enemy back elsewhere. I told Foch of two small offensive projects which I contemplated carrying out, if the military situation allowed.

"He was pleased at my holding offensive intentions at the present time.

"We finished our talk about two o'clock, and then he walked with me down the hill from the château to the lake, where I had sent Alan with the lunch box. Foch then left us; I sent him in my motor back to the house, as he is not a great walker, particularly up hill."

The détachment de l'armée du nord, familiarly known as D.A.N., had been under Haig's command since the earliest days of Foch's appointment as generalissimo. On June thirtieth they were withdrawn and Haig said good-bye to General de Mitry who had commanded them. "He is of opinion", wrote Haig, "that the Germans have finished their preparations for an attack against the Mont des Cats and adjoining hills. He was presented yesterday with the K.C.B. by the Duke of Connaught. He expressed himself as very sorry to leave my command."

During the whole of June and July the attack that never came was hourly expected. As the Germans remained quiescent the allies became active; as anxieties with regard to defence diminished, schemes of attack increasingly occupied the minds of Haig and Foch. One of the first of these was carried out by the Australians early in July. On the first of the month, Haig wrote in his diary, "I left about 10 A.M. with General Birch and Heseltine, and visited General Monash, commanding Australian Corps—headquarters at Château de Bertangles. I went about an operation which he is shortly to carry out with the Australian Corps. Monash is a most thorough and capable commander, who thinks out every detail of any operation and leaves nothing to chance. I was greatly impressed with his arrangements. A company of American infantry (Thirty-third Division) will be attached to each of the ten Australian battalions detailed for the attack."

A meeting of the Supreme War Council took place at Versailles on July second. There was much talk about the use of American troops and the allocation of British tonnage. Mr Lloyd George and M. Tardieu argued with some heat, but very little was agreed upon and nothing accomplished.

"So far as I was concerned," wrote Haig, "it was a complete waste of a couple of hours."

Then next morning he visited "General Pershing at his house 73 rue de Varennes. A fine old mansion with large garden in the Faubourg St Germain, which has been modernized by some wealthy American.

"I was with him for well over an hour and we got on very well indeed. We agreed about the necessity of Foch's having an adequate staff with headquarters located in a central position, say at Chantilly. Also that Foch should have periodical meetings with his three commanders in chief to discuss future plans. Pershing is most anxious that I should visit him at his headquarters at Chaumont; I promised to do so when things are quieter. He said the French are always buzzing about and he wished that the British commander in chief would come and see him. As regards his troops' taking part in operations with Australians tomorrow morning, he thought them insufficiently trained, and had told Rawlinson yesterday that he did not wish them used. I asked him if he wished me to interfere in the matter, but he said 'no, that all has been settled between him and Rawlinson'.

"I left Paris about 12.15 and motored via Beauvais and lunched in the wood by the roadside to the north of the town. Horses met us at Nampont, and I reached Beaurepaire about 6.30 P.M.

"Before dinner and again at 11 P.M. Lawrence spoke to me regarding the Americans taking part in the Australian operations. . . . Some six companies had been withdrawn, about four could not be withdrawn; were the operations to be stopped in order to do so? I said, No. 'The first essential is to improve our position east of Amiens as soon as possible. The attack must therefore be launched as prepared, even if a few American detachments cannot be got out before zero hour.'

"Mr Sargent, the painter, came to dinner and stayed the night."

The following morning was the fourth of July—a suitable date for the Americans to receive their baptism of fire, and together with the Australians they acquitted themselves nobly. The attack was completely successful. The British line was advanced on a front of four miles to a distance of a mile and a half. The village of Hamel and the ridge to the east of it were captured. Over fifteen hundred prisoners were taken and 103 machine guns, twelve trench mortars and seventy-seven field guns.

After the brilliant success of July fourth and as no counterattack from the enemy seemed likely, Haig considered that he was entitled to a short holiday such as he had not enjoyed since the middle of March. He had left England on the day after the birth of his son who was now nearly four months old. On July sixth he crossed the Channel and found himself that evening at Kingston Hill. "I found everything looking so peaceful and well cared for. The baby is in splendid fettle and all seemed very pleased to see me." It was a modest comment.

His week's holiday passed quickly. He played tennis or golf daily with his wife and with General Davidson, who had travelled with him from France. Although living in the suburbs, he only went into London for the obligatory interviews with the King, with Queen Alexandra, with the secretary of state for war and the prime minister.

The last-mentioned he found "annoyed with the French, because, although the British had carried in their ships fifteen American divisions since April, only five were now in the British zone and in a position to support the British Army in case of attack. There are nine American divisions with the French Army, and another nine or ten divisions training in rear. Wilson had accordingly been ordered to draft a letter to Foch pointing this out, and asking him to replace the five American divisions which had been equipped by the British and were now in the French area—also asking him to hasten the supply of guns for the five American divisions not with the British. The prime minister stated that he would send a letter himself to Clemenceau on the subject."

It seems a curious process of reasoning which led the prime minister to argue that because American troops had been brought to Europe in British ships they should therefore be employed in that section of the front which was for the time being held by the British Army. Such a point of view seems to differ widely from that which had inspired the principle of unity of command. The fact was that Lloyd George's vigorous but volatile mind was no longer so impressed with the advantages conferred by a generalissimo, and he was beginning to be apprehensive, as was Henry Wilson, lest the French should abuse the authority that had been entrusted to them.

Haig was not therefore surprised when a few days later he received a direct encouragement from his government to resist the orders of Foch. He returned to France on July fourteenth. He reached his château at Beaurepaire about 2 P.M. and found Lawrence waiting for him.

"Apparently, without any definite facts to go on, Foch has made up his mind that the enemy's main attack is about to fall on the French on the east of Rheims. Lawrence saw him at his headquarters at Bombon last Friday and, as a result of their talk, a second British division was moved south of the Somme as a reserve to the left of the French.

"But before Lawrence could get back to G.H.Q., Foch, evidently becoming still more anxious, ordered by cipher wire (about midday Saturday) a first instalment of British reserves to be sent to the Champagne sector. This is to consist of a corps headquarters and four divisions. Two divisions are leaving today and will detrain southeast of Châlons. Foch also asks me to prepare for the dispatch of a second group of four divisions. And all this when there is nothing definite to show that the enemy means to attack in Champagne. Indeed, Prince Rupprecht still retains twenty-five divisions in reserve on the British front.

"But Foch has completely changed his view of the situation and strategical plan. On the first of July he issued 'Directive Générale No. 4'. In this he stated that Paris and Abbeville were to be covered before anything else. 'The advance of the enemy must be stopped at all costs in these two directions.

" 'Consequently we must concentrate our force on the front Lens-Château-Thierry.

" 'The allied reserves will be pushed into the battle wherever it takes place.' French reserves to help the British if they are heavily attacked. 'De même, les réserves anglaises au profit des armées françaises, si l'ennemi concentre décidément ses masses dans la direction de Paris.'

"And now we are sending our reserves (of which we have very few) right away to the east of France, by Foch's bidding on Saturday thirteenth.

"I at once arrange to see Foch as soon as possible in order to find out what has happened to him or his government. I also write a letter to General Foch in which I set out the position on the British front and end up by saying that 'I am averse to dispatching any troops to Champagne at the present moment. I adhere to my previous opinion that we ought to be prepared to meet minor operations in Champagne and Flanders to disperse and absorb allies' reserves, and subsequently the main blow in the centre, i.e. between Lens and Château-Thierry.' "

Late on the night of the fourteenth—or strictly speaking at 12.35 A.M. on the morning of the fifteenth, the following message was conveyed to Haig by telephone from the chief of the Imperial General Staff.

"Members of the Imperial War Cabinet have tonight discussed with the prime minister the latest orders by General Foch for moving British reserves southward. As information hitherto has pointed to an attack on your front by Rupprecht's forces as well as an attack by the Crown Prince on the French, they feel considerable anxiety.

"They wish me to tell you that if you consider the British Army is endangered or if you think that General Foch is not acting solely on military considerations, they rely on the exercise of your judgment under the Beauvais agreement as to the security of the British front after the removal of these troops. General Smuts on behalf of the Imperial War Cabinet will proceed to G.H.Q. today Monday to confer with you on your return from Beauvais."

The curious phrase, "if you think that General Foch is not acting solely on military considerations", shows how suspicious of their generalissimo the British government had grown. Fortunately the personal interview between Haig and Foch which took place on the following day restored complete harmony, as such interviews seldom failed to do.

"Gemeau translates my letter to Foch into French, and about 10 A.M. I leave with Lawrence for Mouchy-le-Châtel. We get there just after one o'clock and lunch with Foch, who had sent on a special meal from his headquarters at Bombon for us. Foch was in the best of spirits. He told me that after three hours' bombardment the enemy had attacked at 4 A.M. this morning on two fronts east and west of Rheims. East of Rheims on a front of twenty-six miles, and west of Rheims on a front of twenty-nine miles. A front of sixteen miles about Rheims itself was not attacked. The total front attacked seems therefore to be about fifty-five miles. East of Rheims the attack was held and the enemy only gained the outpost zone. Southwest of Rheims the enemy crossed the Marne, and had advanced three to five miles in places.

"Château-Thierry was strongly held by Americans, and further eastward an American division had counterattacked and driven enemy back into the river, taking one thousand prisoners.

"So altogether the situation was satisfactory, and a weight was taken off Foch's mind, who feared an attack as far east as Verdun, where he had no reserves. The British four divisions had first of all been ordered to detrain near Châlons; now that the enemy's attack had been defined, the divisions were ordered to detrain further west, at Rouille and Pont sur Seine. I put my case strongly to Foch why I was averse to moving my reserves from my front until I knew that Rupprecht's reserves had been moved to the new battle front. I mentioned that eighty-eight additional heavy batteries had come against the British front from Liége in June. 'Marskmen machine-gun detachments' were still training northwest of Liége; prisoners and deserters stated that an attack on the Lys salient was to be ready mounted by the eighteenth instant, while the front from La Bassée canal to the Somme was ready to receive troops. Some new shelters northeast of Bapaume large enough for twenty thousand men had been discovered. All these facts and many others pointed to the intention of the enemy to attack the British front at some time soon.

"Foch agreed with me, but said his first object was to hold up the present attack at all costs as soon as possible. He only wanted my divisions as a reserve in case of necessity and they would be in a position *ready to return to me at once* in case the British front was threatened. Under these circumstances I agreed to send the next two divisions, as arranged. I read my letter to Foch and left him a copy, so that he could have my statements on record in writing.

"I got back to Beaurepaire about 7 P.M. General Smuts and Radcliffe arrived from England soon after 8 P.M. After dinner I had a long talk with Smuts. He said the prime minister was very anxious. I explained that after Foch's statements to me today I considered that the situation was satisfactory, but I must expect to be attacked soon, probably on the Kemmel front, and that the main blow would fall between Lens and Château-Thierry if the enemy did not previously break the French front about Rheims."

While Haig and Foch were both expecting to be attacked, and while both had equally good grounds for their expectations, it was natural that their views should differ as to the most suitable location for such reserves as they had at their disposal. On July sixteenth Haig wrote:

"Will the enemy go on with his attacks about Rheims, or will he withdraw such of his reserves as are left and add them to Rupprecht's reserves for a blow against the British? Evidence seems to be accumulating of an attack against the Hazebrouck-Ypres front about the twentieth. A captured officer under examination stated that his trench mortars had to be in position in the Kemmel sector by the sixteenth. Another prisoner stated that an attack is to be launched on that front between the eighteenth and twentieth."

So much depended on the answers to these questions. We now know that it was Ludendorff's intention if the attack in Champagne succeeded to deliver the attack in Flanders a fortnight later. But the attack in Champagne failed. It was Foch's brilliant counterattack that succeeded and began the series of victories which were to end the war.

On July seventeenth General du Cane arrived at Haig's headquarters with a letter and a message from Foch. The letter asked him for full information with regard to the possibilities of an attack on the British front. The message conveyed the information that Mangin's army would attack the next morning at 8 A.M. with twenty divisions. Du Cane had been long enough at Foch's headquarters to become the perfect ambassador—that is to say, he could not only explain the British point of view to the French, but, what was far more difficult, he could truly represent the French point of view to the British. Foch was not an easy man even for his fellow countrymen to understand. He would conceal his thoughts by the gruff enunciation of platitudes. When asked for an opinion on an important military question he would reply with a phrase, such as "One does what one can", "Never relieve troops during a battle", "There must be no retreat", or something of the sort, not calculated to enlighten the anxious enquirer. He had strong likes and dislikes, and there were good generals in the French Army whom he would not work with. He had received Du Cane ungraciously, but he had come to trust him and his trust had been reciprocated by deep admiration.

Du Cane's mission was to smooth away any difficulties that might arise between the French and English. He found that whenever he could get direct access to the British commander in chief difficulties vanished. But the time of a commander in chief is limited and he is closely surrounded. On the occasion of this visit of July seventeenth a letter had already been prepared for Haig's signature which asked Foch to return to him forthwith the four divisions of the Twenty-second Corps which were at that time serving with the French. Du Cane spoke of the attack which was to be delivered the following morning. G.H.Q. were inclined to be skeptical of his success, but as the result of a long conversation which Du Cane had with Haig after dinner Haig, while signing the letter, told him that he could inform Foch that if British troops were wanted to exploit a success they should of course be used.

It was fortunate that Du Cane should have had so friendly a message to deliver when he returned to Foch's headquarters on the morning of July eighteenth. Before he arrived there the blow had been struck that had definitely marked the turn of the tide. Foch, in whom the spirit of attack was incarnate, had entered into his kingdom at last. The four months' vigil was over. The counterattack had begun.

CHAPTER XVI

The Beginning of the End

IT HAS BEEN SEEN how Haig had never doubted that if the Germans attacked in the spring of 1918 the allies would win the war in the autumn of the same year. It is easy to imagine the mood in which he read a lengthy document drawn up at the end of July by the chief of the Imperial General Staff and entitled "British Military Policy, 1918–19". It was dated July twenty-fifth, covered over thirty typewritten foolscap pages, and was signed by Henry Wilson.

"Even when the German armies are soundly beaten in the west", says this remarkable document, "and driven out of France and Belgium, it is difficult to see how we could force such terms on the Central Powers as would loosen their hold on the East or close the road to Egypt and India. Unless by the end of the war democratic Russia can be reconstituted as an independent military power it is only a question of time before most of Asia becomes a German colony, and nothing can impede the enemy's progress toward India."

The simple fact which the writer seems not to have appreciated, or to have temporarily forgotten, was that once the German Army was defeated nobody had anything to fear from Germany in any continent until that army was reconstructed.

On Haig's copy of this document he scribbled the scornful

comment, "Words! Words! Words! lots of words and little else. Theoretical rubbish! Whoever drafted this stuff would never win any campaign." Already he saw victory within his grasp. The weight of anxiety was beginning to diminish, and there is an entry in his diary on July twentieth which is not without significance: "In the afternoon I motored to Le Touquet with Alan Fletcher and played a round of golf on the links. This is the first round I have played in France."

While Wilson was secretly criticizing Haig to Lloyd George, he was equally willing to criticize Lloyd George to Haig. On July twenty-sixth, the date of the memorandum, he wrote to Haig:

"Having for the last four months tried to get the prime minister to realize that the French meant to take us over body and bones, he (the p.m.) now rushes off to the other extreme of suspicion and combativeness and I shall spend the next four months in trying to steady him."

Fortunately soldiers of different nationalities in France co-operated better than soldiers and politicians of the same nationality in England. Foch had realized, as had Haig, that the turning point in the war was already reached, he could appreciate the value of Haig's advice and of the improvements on his own plans that Haig suggested, and he had complete confidence in Haig's ability in the field.

In view of the decisive effect which was to be produced by the next attack on the part of the allies, it is important that the credit for its conception should be justly assigned. On July twelfth Foch wrote to Haig that in his opinion the first offensive to be delivered on the British front should be on the line Festubert-Robecq in order to set free the Bruay minefields and threaten the communication centre at Estaires. He enquired whether Haig shared his view, and pressed him to name a date when the attack could be delivered.

Haig, however, had meanwhile thought out a different plan, which he believed to be a better one. On July sixteenth he explained to Rawlinson, commanding the Fourth Army, what his plan was, because the Fourth Army was to play the principal part in it. "It was my intention," he said, "if the situation became favourable, that the Fourth Army's right should be pushed forward to the river Luce, say near Caix. Thence the lines would run northward through Harbonnières to Chipilly on the Somme. I proposed to ask Foch to order the French Army on our right to co-operate by an attack advancing northeastward on the south of Moreuil, so as to pinch the salient formed by the rivers Luce and Avre between the villages of Caix and Pierrepont."

On the following day, July seventeenth, he replied to Foch's letter of the twelfth. "I see no object", he wrote, "in pushing forward over the flat and wet country between Robecq and Festubert. . . .

". . . The operation which to my mind is of the greatest importance, and which I suggest to you should be carried out as early as possible, is to advance the allied front east and southeast of Amiens so as to disentangle that town and the railway line. This can be carried out by a combined French and British operation, the French attacking south of Moreuil and the British north of the river Luce." He went on to explain the operation to Foch as he had explained it to Rawlinson, and to point out exactly the part that he would require the French to play in it.

Foch, in reply, while refusing to abandon his proposal for the Festubert-Robecq offensive, fully endorsed the plan which Haig had suggested.

In the afternoon of July twenty-third, Haig drove to Paris and dined that evening with Pershing at the Café Foyot. Pershing informed him that he was quite ready to use the American troops in a big offensive in the autumn and that he had gained his point of forming two American armies immediately, to which the French had formerly been opposed.

The next morning Haig proceeded to visit Foch at his headquarters at Bombon.

"I had a talk with Foch for three quarters of an hour; Generals Lawrence and Weygand were present. We agreed to proceed with the operations east of Amiens as soon as possible. Rawlinson and Debeney are meeting to-day, if necessary, to co-ordinate their plans. I am to meet Foch on some day soon, the date of which he will notify me. . . .

"Weygand read out a memorandum which had been prepared under Foch's direction. Its main clauses dealt with:

"(1) Regaining the initiative and passing to the offensive;

"(2) Opening certain main lines of railway, so as to prepare for future operations;

"(3) Clearing the enemy away from the vicinity of the Béthune coal mines.

"We all agreed to the general principles laid down for future plans. Pétain raised some questions as to the sufficiency of the means at his disposal, such as ammunition and guns and tanks available.

"A list of questions to which General Foch asks for an answer was also circulated to each of us. These questions deal with the forces which each of the allies can maintain in the field on first of January and on first of April next year.

"It was past 12.30 before our conference was over. I then took a short walk in the grounds with General Pétain. He mentioned that General Anthoine had been removed from his appointment of chief of staff simply because Foch did not get on with him. Personally I feel that both Pétain and the French Army will feel his absence greatly.

"At lunch I sat on Foch's right, with Weygand next to me on my right. We were given a magnificent lunch. . . . It was rather wasted on me, and I cannot understand how

PÉTAIN, HAIG, FOCH AND PERSHING

anyone can work in the afternoon after such a huge meal. The cost of food is now very high—fifty francs for a chicken in Paris.

"I was photo'd with Foch, Pétain and Pershing. We got away about 2.30 P.M. and visited Fontainebleau on our way to Paris.

"I had not been there since the summer of 1881 or 1882, when I spent a month of the Oxford long vacation with a Pasteur Brand to learn a little French. . . . The château is now being used as a hospital, but the place looks much the same as when I was last there, only today there was no bread to be had with which to feed the carp in the pond. The water looks as dirty as formerly! We got to Paris soon after 6 P.M. and dined quietly in the hotel."

Two days later, July twenty-sixth, another conference took place. Sarcus was the place of meeting, and further arrangements were made for the carrying out of the attack by Rawlinson and Debeney which Haig had suggested.

"Debeney proposed to carry out a small operation south of Hangard on the river Luce. But Foch decided on a larger operation on the lines which I had proposed. Rawlinson and Debeney are to meet at 10 A.M. tomorrow to settle details regarding the area of concentration, etc. Rawlinson was very anxious to carry out his operation alone, without French co-operation, but in view of our limited number of divisions I agreed that Debeney should operate on our right. This is also the more desirable in view of the reserves which Foch is moving to the Beauvais area."

On July twenty-eighth, "General Weygand arrived from Bombon with a letter from Foch to me. In it he asked me to take command of the French First Army (General Debeney) and combine its action with my Fourth Army in the operations which we are now planning. I said, Yes, and sent Foch a letter of thanks. Foch wishes operations hurried on. I said I will try and gain two days if my Twenty-second Corps can be sent back two days earlier than I asked for on Friday last. This will be arranged. I am pleased that Foch should have entrusted me with the directions of these operations."

In view of the fact that the plan had been Haig's from the first, that he had thought out every detail of it and that British forces were to be mainly responsible for its execution, it is impossible not to admire the modesty with which he records his satisfaction that Foch should have entrusted him with its direction.

On the next day, July twenty-ninth, "At noon I received army commanders except Rawlinson, who is preparing for the forthcoming operations. I met the army commanders alone with my C.G.S. and had a general talk for an hour and a half. They appreciated the opportunity of being able to state their views to me personally instead of before a number of staff officers as on one of the regular periodical conferences with army commanders and staffs.

"I explained the policy and future plans of the generalissimo. He intends to keep the initiative, and feels that we allies have 'turned the corner'. As regards tactics, I called attention to divisions being side by side in the line following different principles and ignoring those laid down in my orders. Corps commanders must be held responsible that these principles are followed by all, and army commanders must be responsible for supervising their corps commanders' methods.

"Then, as to offensive tactics, army commanders must do their utmost to get troops out of the influence of trench methods. We are all agreed on the need for the training of battalion commanders, who in their turn must train their company and platoon commanders. This is really a platoon commanders' war.

"Army commanders lunched with me after the conference. All seemed very pleased with the meeting.

"About 2.30 General Rawlinson came to see me. He has had a meeting with his corps commanders. The date would be advanced two days, as requested by me. All his arrangements were being pushed forward satisfactorily. His relations have been most cordial with Debeney since our meeting at Sarcus with Foch last Friday."

The month of August, that was to prove so fateful in the history of the war, brought with it in the year 1918 an almost uninterrupted series of perfect summer days. The nights were cold and the early mornings were often accompanied by thick mists which, as has already been seen, are more favourable to the attackers than the attacked. Had such weather attended the operations of the previous year the history of the battle of Passchendaele would have been very different.

Now a new spirit began to animate all ranks within the lines of the allied armies. Preparations were going busily forward for the next offensive and they were being conducted with cheerful confidence that was continually stimulated by reports of prisoners concerning the dejected state of the enemy.

Relations between the allies were excellent. Clemenceau wrote to Haig on July thirty-first, in reply to an invitation:

MY DEAR FIELD MARSHAL,

I was well aware that you were the most amiable man in the world but I really didn't think you capable of showering all at once so many flattering attentions on a modest creature like myself. Since however good fortune has decided that you should be so kind as to select me as the object of your favours what can I do but tell you how deeply I am touched? I should have paid you a visit a long time ago if I hadn't been stopped by the fear of displeasing certain people. Your invitation breaks the spell and I propose to come and see you as soon as possible in company with Lord Derby who has kindly consented to accompany me. It will be indeed a great pleasure for me, for it will give me the opportunity of telling one of the finest soldiers of this war what the French people think of him.

Yours very cordially,
G. CLEMENCEAU.

On August third Haig had a satisfactory interview with the generalissimo. "Foch was anxious that our operations should begin as soon as possible, because the enemy is falling back from the Marne very quickly. French forces are already over the Vesle and Ardre and soon will have the heights overlooking the Aisne. I told Foch the date on which we would be ready, and he was pleased that all had been done to be ready so soon.

"As regards the objective, Foch wished it to be some place south of Chaulnes. I pointed out that I had given Ham in my orders, fifteen miles beyond Chaulnes and across the river Somme. This he thought satisfactory.

"He was anxious that there should be no delay on the line Mericourt-Caix. I told him that I had ordered that line to be captured and prepared for defence. If we hold that line we disengage Amiens, and we must be prepared to meet a counterattack. But that does not mean that the advance on Chaulnes is to be delayed until the line in question is consolidated. The advance on Chaulnes and Roye will be carried out as soon as the necessary fresh troops can move forward. This will be as quickly as possible.

"We discussed a few points regarding the Americans, and Foch proposed to see Pershing and urge him to form an American corps staff as soon as possible under my orders, and to authorize me to put the American divisions into battle when I thought fit. He will also arrange to have a meeting between Pershing, himself and me.

"We then had lunch. Foch was in very good form. After lunch he and I took a short walk in the grounds. More than once he expressed the opinion that the 'Germans are breaking up', and was anxious lest they should fall back before I could get my blow in."

On August fifth, "I lunched by the roadside on leaving Villers-Bocage and then went on to Mollins (headquarters American Thirty-third Division). General Bell, commanding the division, was expecting me, and had a guard of honour paraded to receive me. Bell looks a typical 'Yankee' with a little goatee beard, and moustache. He was very pleased with the way the English had looked after him and his division, and with our equipment. The Americans had not treated him so well. His two brigadiers were present. One, newly appointed, had just come from the Marne battle.

"On going away we were photographed and cinema'd much to Bell's delight. Bell seemed a capital fellow, and is distressed that General Pershing won't let him take part in our offensive battle."

The King came to luncheon at Haig's headquarters on August seventh. The President of the French Republic was also present. It was a suitable date for such a reunion. When his troops had been fighting with their backs to the wall the King had been with them. Now when they were about to begin the advance that was to end on the Rhine he was once more at their side.

Not only was all in readiness for the next day's attack, but two of the conditions most essential to victory were present. Secrecy had been maintained and the heart of the troops was sound. On the morrow the Germans experienced "the most complete surprise of the war," as Captain Liddell Hart phrased it in his war history.

This is not the place to tell the story of that battle. How in the darkness of the hour before dawn—darkness that was increased by a heavy mist—456 tanks began to creep over the broken ground that divided them from the enemy—how following close upon them the impetuous advance of the Australians and Canadians burst into the enemy's trenches with the first streaks of morning light and sweeping all before them stormed on to their objectives, so that the battle was won before the sun pierced through the mist at ten o'clock.

The commander in chief is spared the physical agony of the trenches. Only in imagination can he suffer the sickening anxiety of the hour before zero, the deadening fatigue of the long day's fighting, and the scorching pain of wounds. But to him also is denied the glory of battle, the thrill of the race across no man's land, the sudden carelessness of life that comes as a revelation, and the heart-filling triumph of standing on the captured position and witnessing the flight of the foe. These emotions are but dimly reflected in the mind of the commander as he sits by the telephone or reads the messages which reach him from hour to hour.

"The enemy was completely surprised, two reliefs of divisions were in progress, very little resistance was offered, and our troops got their objectives quickly with very little loss," wrote Haig on August eighth.

"I told Rawlinson to continue the work on the orders which I had already given, namely, to organize his left strongly; if opportunity offers to advance to line Albert-Bray. With his left strongly held, he will push his defensive front out to line Chaulnes-Roye. Reconnaissance to be pushed forward to the Somme river, while his main effort is directed southeastward on Roye to help the French. The cavalry should work on the outer flank of the infantry and move on Chaulnes-Roye as soon as possible.

"I returned to my train for lunch, and about 4 P.M. I called on headquarters French First Army at Conty. I told Debeney that the British advance would automatically clear his front. Meantime, to do his utmost to join hands with the British at Roye; his cavalry should be sent forward as soon as possible to operate on the right of the British who had already pierced the German line of defence.

OPENING OF FINAL BRITISH OFFENSIVE
8TH AUGUST - 9TH SEPTEMBER, 1918

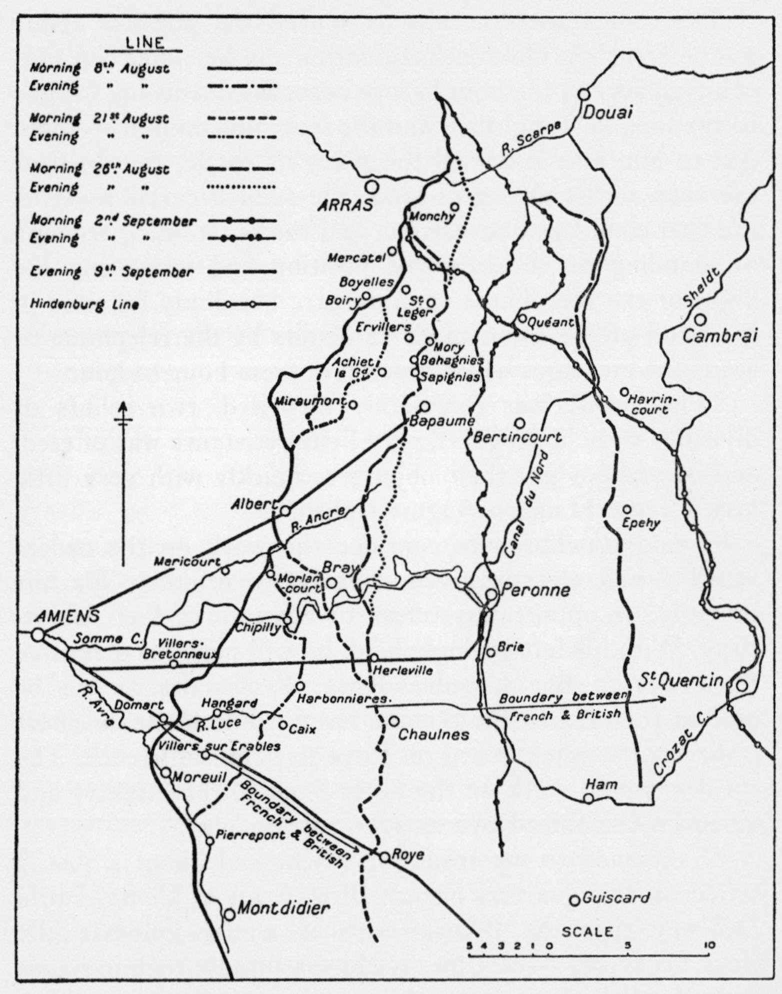

"At 6 P.M. Marshal Foch came to see me. He is very delighted at our success today, and fully concurred in all the arrangements I had made for continuing the battle. His headquarters are at Sarcus tonight.

"Situation reports at 4.30 P.M. stated Canadian Corps had captured Beaucourt, Caix and the Amiens outer defence line east of Caix. Cavalry corps south and east of Caix; Canadians in touch with French at Maison Blanche. Australians on final objective all along their front. Third Corps on ridges northeast of Chipilly.

"Enemy blowing dumps in all directions and streaming eastward. Their transport and limbers offer splendid targets for our aeroplanes."

The victory which, as Haig himself admitted, had exceeded even his most optimistic forecasts, was continued and completed during the two following days. "August eighth", wrote Ludendorff, "was the black day of the German Army in the war. . . . It marked the decline of our fighting power, and, the man-power situation being what it was, it robbed me of the hope of discovering some strategic expedient that might once more stabilize the position in our favour. . . . The war would have to be ended." These words mean nothing less than this: as the outcome of that day's fighting, the man who was responsible for the fate of the German Army recognized defeat. For this result the gratitude of the British Empire and of the allies is due to the men of the Fourth Army, to Rawlinson and his staff, and to Haig the commander in chief, who planned the attack and who persuaded Foch to approve it.

The question now to be decided by the allies was when and where the next blow was to be delivered. Upon one point Haig and Foch were in complete agreement—no time was to be wasted, no breathing space was to be accorded to the enemy. Foch was in favour of continuing to hammer where the dent had already been made. On August tenth:

"General Foch came to see me at 11 A.M. He wishes the advance to continue to the line Noyon-Ham-Péronne, and to try to get the bridgeheads on the Somme. I pointed out the difficulty of the undertaking unless the enemy is quite demoralized, and we can cross the Somme on his heels. At the same time I outlined my proposals for advancing our front on Aubers ridge and so freeing the Béthune coal mines, together with movements against Bapaume and Monchy le Preux. Foch agreed, but said, 'you will be able to carry out the Aubers Ridge plan, all the same'. . . . I agree that some German divisions are demoralized, but not all yet!

"I accordingly issued orders to continue the advance on Guiscard-Ham-Péronne, and occupy passages of the river below Ham. I also ordered General Byng (Third Army) to raid, and if situation favourable to push forward at once strong advance guards to Bapaume."

Haig's expectation that resistance would grow more stubborn on the front already attacked proved correct. Such a development was bound to follow according to the teachings of military science, and according to the laws of common sense. If a man wishing to reach the bottom of a box that is full of cotton wool drives his fist into it he will find that with every blow the resistance of the cotton wool increases until it forms a pad upon which his fist can make no further inpression. It is the same with a purely frontal attack delivered against a large army with strong reinforcements.

That same evening Haig obtained confirmation of his views.

"At the railway station east of Le Quesnel I visited the headquarters of our Thirty-second Division, which had relieved the Third Canadians in the early morning. I met General Lambert (commanding division). He had just returned from visiting the brigades at the front. His opinion was that the enemy's opposition had stiffened up. There were many hostile machine guns, much intact wire and the old battlefield ground between the German and French lines with numerous holes favoured delaying tactics and prevented the action of our cavalry. He had therefore decided to stop the attack till tomorrow morning, when he would put in his remaining brigade, which was fresh, with all available tanks."

The next day, August eleventh, Haig saw General Byng, commanding the Third Army, and told him to be ready to put in an attack. "The objective of the attack will be to break the enemy's front, in order to outflank the enemy's present battle front. The direction of the advance will be Bapaume."

Haig during these days was living in a train at Wiry, and it was there that late that night Foch paid him another visit.

"About 10 P.M. Marshal Foch came to see me with Weygand and Desticker. After a talk, he approved (in view of the increased opposition) of my reducing my front of attack, and aiming at reaching the Somme on the front Brie-Ham (exclusively), instead of Péronne-Ham. The French Third Army had made good progress, as the enemy did not expect an attack in that quarter. He asked me to attack with my Third Army. I told him that three weeks ago I had discussed with Byng the possibility of the Third Army co-operating, and today I had seen Byng and given him definite orders to advance as soon as possible on Bapaume."

On the following afternoon Haig had a further conversation with Byng, explaining his plan in greater detail. Instead of continuing to batter his head against the now hardened resistance in front of the Fourth Army, he aimed at breaking the enemy's front further north, thus threatening the flank of the forces opposing the Fourth Army and compelling them to retire in order to protect themselves and to conform with the remainder of the line.

Foch, while appreciating the design of Haig's strategy, was anxious to combine brute force with subtlety, to make use at the same time both of the rapier and the bludgeon. While therefore approving of the proposed attack by the Third Army, he wanted the Fourth Army and his own First Army to continue to hammer on the dent. Haig was uncertain whether this policy was wise, and the first to protest against it was General Debeney. On the thirteenth he sent a message to the effect that "He wished to postpone the attack twenty-four hours (i.e. until the morning of the sixteenth) because the enemy is now in a strong position covered with much wire—the old German defensive position of 1916. Also there had been some delay in getting up his ammunition. I agreed to the postponement desired.

"Soon after I heard that the Fourth Army commander considered that the attack would be very costly. I sent word to say that if he had any views to express to come and see me in the morning."

At 10 A.M. accordingly, on the morning of the fourteenth, Rawlinson arrived "and brought photos showing the state of the enemy's defences on the front Roye-Chaulnes. He also showed me a letter which he had received from General Currie commanding the Canadian Corps stating that 'to capture the position in question would be a very costly matter'. He (Currie) 'was opposed to attempting it'.

"I accordingly ordered the date of this attack to be postponed, but preparations to be continued with vigour combined with wire cutting and counterbattery work."

The same day he wrote to Foch:

August 14, 1918.

MY DEAR MARSHAL,

During the past forty-eight hours, the enemy artillery fire on the fronts of the British Fourth and French First Army has greatly increased and it is evident that the line Chaulnes-Roye is strongly held, while photographs show that the line is in good order and well wired. Moreover, the ground is broken and difficult for tanks to operate. It is probable that there are at least sixteen German divisions holding the front south of the Somme opposite to the armies under my command.

Under these circumstances, I have directed that the attack be postponed until adequate artillery preparation has been carried out in order to prepare a deliberate attack on the position. This might be carried out in conjunction with the attack from my Third Army front, which is being prepared as rapidly as possible.

Yours very truly
D. HAIG.

Foch immediately replied by telegram that he saw "no necessity for delay Fourth Army and First French Army attack . . . which should be carried out as soon as possible".

But Haig, who was never careless of the lives of his men, refused to order an attack in which neither he nor his subordinate generals had any confidence. He therefore wrote in reply to Foch's telegram that nothing had happened since he came to the decision communicated in his previous letter to cause him to alter his opinion on the situation on the Roye-Chaulnes front. "I therefore", he wrote, "much regret that I cannot alter my orders to the two armies in question."

He followed up his letter with a visit to Foch on the fifteenth. That such differences of opinion should arise were inevitable, but Haig knew that soldiers can settle such matters more easily at a personal interview than by the exchange of notes.

"I visited Foch at Sarcus at 3 P.M.; General Lawrence accompanied me, and Generals Weygand and Du Cane were present at the meeting.

"Foch had pressed me to attack the positions held by the

enemy in the front Chaulnes-Roye. I declined to do so because they could only be taken after heavy casualties in men and tanks. I had ordered the French First and British Fourth armies to postpone their attack, but to keep up pressure on that front so as to make the enemy expect an attack there, while I transferred my reserves to my third army, and also prepared to attack with the First Army on the front Monchy-le-Preux-Miramont. Foch now wanted to know what orders I had issued for attack? when I proposed to attack? where? and with what troops?

"In the course of our talk, Foch admitted that the French First Army was short of ammunition and could not continue counterbattery work for more than one day longer. So the attack must either go in tomorrow or be abandoned.

"I told Foch of my instructions to Byng and Horne; and that Rawlinson would also co-operate with his left between the Somme and Ancre, when my third army had advanced, and when by reason of this some of the hostile pressure (which was still strong on that sector) had lessened.

"I spoke to Foch quite straightly and let him understand that I was responsible to my government and fellow citizens for the handling of the British forces. Foch's attitude at once changed, and he said all he wanted was early information of my intentions so that he might co-ordinate the operations of the other armies, and that he now thought I was quite correct in my decision not to attack the enemy in his prepared position. But, notwithstanding what he now said, Foch and all his staff had been most insistent for the last five days that I should press on along the south bank and capture the Somme bridges above Péronne, regardless of German opposition and British losses."

During the days that divided the two principal attacks of August, the eighth and the twenty-first, Haig was never idle. When more important work did not claim his attention he missed no opportunity of visiting the troops which had taken part in the fighting in order to congratulate them, and those which were about to take part in order to make sure that nothing was lacking that could ensure their success. The former were triumphant, the latter were confident, and all were delighted by a visit from their commander in chief.

One day he visited the Canadian Cavalry Brigade. "I rode round most of the squadrons, horse artillery batteries and machine guns. Fine plucky fellows all, who don't know what fear is—80 per cent are Scotsmen! One young fellow, born in Edinburgh, now a major (by name Strachan) got the V.C. at Cambrai. Was before the war ranching in Alberta. Most are from Winnipeg."

On another occasion he received a reminder of the darkest hour of 1914. "I motored on to the neighbourhood of Marcelcave and inspected some units of the Fourth Tank Brigade under the command of Brigadier General Hankey, late of the Worcester regiment. It was he who launched the counterattack against Gheluvelt on the thirty-first of October, 1914. A fine, bold officer, he did very well on the eighth, especially in carrying out the crossings of the river Luce at Domart and Thennes."

A few days later he was deeply grieved to learn of the death of George Black, who had been badly wounded in action with the tanks. "He was with me from April, 1915, until the beginning of this year in charge of the Seventeenth Lancers troop, my mounted escort. He insisted on going to the Tank Corps, as 'he wanted to fight'. He is a great loss to me and all of us. Always so cheerful and happy even when things looked darkest."

On August eighteenth Haig gave a luncheon party at Amiens which Clemenceau attended. Lord Derby was with him. Foch, Rawlinson and Debeney were also present.

"During lunch M. Clemenceau told me that on the recommendation of Marshal Foch the French government had decided to present me with the Military Medal, and he pinned it on my coat in the drawing room after lunch. The Military Medal is the highest award which can be given to an officer, only very few receive it. It is the same medal as that given to privates."

After luncheon there was a drive through the recently recaptured territory. "M. Clemenceau inspected the Seventh Canadian Brigade on the ground which they had won. Then they filed past by fours. The men looked splendid and the officers looked up to their work in every way. M. Clemenceau then left for Paris. He said he had thoroughly enjoyed his visit, and congratulated us on all that we had accomplished."

On the nineteenth Haig had an important conversation with Byng.

"He explained his plan, which I thought was too limited in its scope. I told him that his objective was to break the enemy's front, and gain Bapaume as soon as possible. . . . Byng had only arranged to use about a brigade of cavalry. I told him that the cavalry corps is now 100 per cent better than it was at Cambrai. He must use the cavalry to the fullest possible extent. Now is the time to act with boldness, and in full confidence that, if we only hit the enemy hard enough, and combine the action of all arms in pressing him, his troops will give way on a very wide front and acknowledge that he is beaten."

On the next day, the twentieth, the eve of the attack, Haig visited the headquarters of no less than seven divisions who were to take part in the fighting on the morrow. "The G.O.C. of each division explained to me the details of his plan. All are most confident. I am told that the enemy divisions on this part of our front are of very poor quality, and do not fight at all when we raid their trenches; on the other hand, our fellows are now on the top of their form as a result of our successes. . . . I came away feeling confident that our troops will reach their objectives."

Haig's confidence was not misplaced. On the following morning, when the Third Army attacked, a heavy mist once more covered the ground and caused a certain amount of confusion in their movements. But the enemy were in no mood for fighting and in many places where the advancing troops expected to meet with stiff resistance they found empty trenches. It was nearly midday before the sun came through, but when it did it found the British forces occupying the greater part of their objectives.

That day Haig entertained Winston Churchill at luncheon. He was now minister of munitions.

"He is most anxious to help us in every way, and is hurrying up the supply of '10-calibre-head' shells, gas, tanks, etc. His schemes are all timed for completion in next June. I told him we ought to do our utmost to get a decision this autumn. We are engaged in a 'wearing-out battle', and are outlasting and beating the enemy. If we allow the enemy a period of quiet, he will recover, and the 'wearing-out' process must be recommenced. In reply, I was told that the general staff in London calculate that the decisive period of the war cannot arrive until next July."

At 10.30 that evening Haig learned that Byng had decided not to continue operations on the morrow. "Troops had suffered much from the heat and were in disorder. Guns too had to be advanced. I expressed the *wish* that the attack should be resumed at the earliest possible moment. The enemy's troops must be suffering more than ours, because we are elated by success while the enemy is feeling that this is the beginning of the end for him."

The next day was one of broiling heat. Haig's view that Byng was wrong to call a halt was shared by some of the troops in the Third Army, who lay on the battered territory that they had captured the day before, exposed to the continuous shell fire of the enemy and the rays of the August sun.

Haig finally issued an order "directing the offensive to be resumed at the earliest possible moment". The attack accordingly took place before dawn on the following morning, the movements of the troops being assisted by the light of a full moon.

"Hard fighting took place; the enemy's losses were most severe, and our troops made considerable progress. The villages of Boiry, Boyelles, Ervillers, Achiet-le-Grand and Bihucourt were captured. We are pushing on toward St Lever and Méry, and our advanced guards are on the eastern outskirts of Behagnies and Sapignies. How different are the conditions today to those of the Somme battle of 1916, when the enemy was organized and we had to advance across this very same country.

". . . This afternoon I visited headquarters Third Army and saw General Byng. He is very pleased with the results of today after yesterday's halt, and he thinks he did right to wait for a day."

On the twenty-second Haig had a meeting with Foch "who was in excellent spirits. He was anxious to know what my plans were, and to ascertain whether I viewed the situation in the same way as he did. I explained in detail my objectives. He was quite pleased. He told me how the French Tenth Army (Mangin) was pressing on. . . . Foch's strategy is a simple straightforward advance by all troops on the Western Front and to keep the enemy on the move. Tonight I issued a note to army commanders asking them to bring to the notice of all subordinate leaders the changed conditions under which operations are now being carried out. 'It is no longer necessary to advance step by step in regular lines as in the 1916–17 battles. All units must go straight for their objectives, while reserves should be pushed in where we are gaining ground.' "

During the remainder of the month of August the triumphant advance of the Third and Fourth armies continued. Every day brought tidings of victory, every hour brought new tasks for the commander in chief, decisions to be taken, advice to be given, positions to be inspected. Daily he visited his army commanders, explaining to each what was required of him, listening to requests, granting them wherever possible, enquiring into details and outlining future strategy on the broadest lines.

Every hour of those long summer days was full. After visiting half a dozen divisional headquarters in succession he writes: "To each one I explained my plan of action. They were all very delighted. Their divisions are soon going into action and it makes such a difference in the way they fight if leaders know the object and scope of operations."

The following passage is also typical. "I learned from General Matheson that the Fourth Division was making a very long march tonight. Some had fifteen miles, others twenty miles to do. I was annoyed at this, because I wanted the divisions to be fresh for battle, and arranged that some lorries should be sent to help the men on the march and to carry their packs."

There has come into existence a legend, the origin of which it is difficult to trace, that the series of British victories in 1918 were planned by the French generalissimo and could not have been carried out unless he had been in possession of the powers conferred upon him under the system known as "unity of command". That such a legend should be believed in France is not surprising, but why it should persist in Great Britain is difficult to explain.

It has been shown how the attack by the Fourth Army on August eighth was of Haig's conception, how he had persuaded Foch to accept it as an alteration to the Festubert-Robecq plan which the generalissimo had himself suggested, how when he believed that the attack had been carried far enough he had successfully resisted the desire of Foch to continue it, and how he had followed it up by the attack of the Third Army on August twenty-first with the most brilliant and far-reaching results. From now onward until the end of the war it was the mind of Haig, and not the mind of Foch, that directed the successive battles on the British front, where the bulk of the German Army was concentrated, and drove that army back, step by step, until it was compelled to surrender. Every move in that magnificent campaign had been thought out beforehand in Haig's council chamber with the assistance of his staff.

Foch himself was frank and generous in his admiration for what was being accomplished. He authorized Du Cane to inform Haig that in his opinion the operations of the British Army during these weeks would serve as a model for all time. He wrote to Haig:

> My Dear Field Marshal,
> Your affairs are going on very well; I can only applaud the resolute manner in which you follow them up, without giving the enemy a respite and always extending the breadth of your operations. It is this increasing breadth of the offensive—an offensive fed from behind and strongly pushed forward on to carefully selected objectives, without bothering about the alignment nor about keeping too closely in touch—which will produce the greatest results with the smallest casualties, as you have perfectly understood.

On August twenty-ninth the two met and found themselves in complete agreement. Haig had already written his views to Foch, who not only accepted them but slightly modified his own plans in accordance with Haig's suggestions.

Ever present in Haig's vision there loomed the vast obstacle of the Hindenburg line, the strongest defensive position ever constructed. Monchy-le-Preux, strongly fortified, fell at the cost of only fifteen hundred casualties, Bapaume fell, Péronne fell, and the retreating enemy streamed back to the shelter of the Hindenburg line behind which they thought to find safety as behind an impregnable barrier. But Haig was determined to smash that barrier. He believed he could do it before autumn turned to winter, and he knew that when he had done it he would have won the war.

CHAPTER XVII

Victory

THE FINAL STAGE of the war was now approaching and gradually generals and statesmen of the allied nations were beginning to accept the view which Haig had formed and expressed six months earlier, that the end was in sight.

Of the many great qualities that Foch displayed during his tenure of the supreme command none deserves greater recognition or has received less than his willingness to be guided by the advice of his subordinate, the British commander in chief. Never was that advice of greater importance than at the end of August and the beginning of September in the final year.

The American Army was now in a position to take the field as an independent force, and at no time since the declaration of 1776 had the United States been more wedded to the principles of independence. As their first objective they had had assigned to them the district of St Mihiel where the German front line protruded in an ugly salient. It was the plan of the generalissimo that the American Army, having fulfilled this task, should press on from St Mihiel in a northeasterly direction to capture the Briey coal fields and the town of Metz. Foch had been a student at Metz when its incorporation in the German Empire had been proclaimed in 1871, so that the reconquest of it meant much to him. The plans of the American staff had been carefully prepared with Briey and Metz as their objectives.

But Haig was now determined to undertake the tremendous task of assaulting the Hindenburg line. While he was confident of his ability to succeed, he realized that success would demand the concentration of all the resources of the allies. To launch at such a moment a divergent attack in a northeasterly direction appeared to him to be a serious error, and he therefore made strong representations to the generalissimo to alter the direction of this offensive, and to request the Americans to proceed northwest from St Mihiel in the direction of Mézières. In this way their advance would converge with his own, and, by threatening the railway line which runs from Mézières to Maubeuge, and thence through Mons to Liége, would endanger the retreat of German troops south of the Ardennes forest.

In the words of Foch's biographer, B. H. Liddell Hart, "Foch lent his ear the more readily to Haig's argument because it accorded with his own predisposition and the enlargement of his horizon. He had now begun to feel" (what Haig had felt and had said for so long) "that the war might be finished in 1918 instead of 1919."

Foch therefore accepted Haig's advice and, although he had some difficulty in persuading Pershing to accept it also, he eventually succeeded. Once again, therefore, the opinion of Haig prevailed and the great advance proceeded in accordance with the plans that Haig had so carefully prepared. It was satisfactory for him to be aware that he possessed the complete confidence of the generalissimo, now, when he was about to undertake the greatest task of the whole war, the assault upon that line of fortifications which many good judges believed to be impregnable.

But if Foch trusted him there were others who did not. On the first of September he received a telegram from Henry Wilson. It was headed "Personal"—and ran: "Just a word of caution in regard to incurring heavy losses in attacks on Hindenburg line as opposed to losses when driving the enemy back to that line. I do not mean to say that you have incurred such losses, but I know the War Cabinet would become anxious if we received heavy punishment in attacking the Hindenburg line without success."

The meaning of the message was obvious. During the last three weeks Haig had scored a series of victories on a scale unprecedented in the history of the war. No word of thanks, no telegram of congratulations had reached him from his own government. Now he was preparing to undertake an even greater task, and all the encouragement that he received from the government was a warning that should he fail he would be called upon to give a strict account for every drop of blood that had been shed in vain. If all went well the government would claim the credit, if aught went ill the commander in chief must bear the blame. The Carthaginians used to crucify an unsuccessful general, but it is not recorded of them that they would send their generals reminders on the eve of battle of the penalties that awaited them in defeat.

It was General Davidson who brought the message to the commander in chief. He had already shown it to General Lawrence and they had both understood its full significance. He remained standing while Haig read it and half expected some sign of indignation or disgust. But when Haig had carefully perused it he laid it aside without a word and raising his eyes calmly enquired what the devil Davidson was waiting for. He would not allow such tactics to alter his plans or disturb his equanimity.

Haig wrote to Wilson the same day:

MY DEAR HENRY,

With reference to your wire re casualties in attacking the Hindenburg line—what a wretched lot! and how well they mean to support me! What confidence! Please call their attention to my action two weeks ago when the

French pressed me to attack the strong lines of defence east of Roye-Chaulnes front. I wrote you at the time and instead of attacking south of the Somme I started Byng's attack. I assure you I watch the drafts most carefully.

Henry Wilson's defence was feeble: "It isn't really want of confidence in you," he wrote, "it is much more the constant—and growing—embarrassment about man power that makes the government uneasy; it is the curiously hostile attitude on several points of both the French and the Americans, it is the uneasy spirit in this country as evinced by the police strike, it is these and other cognate matters whch make the Cabinet sensitive of heavy losses especially if these are incurred against old lines of fortification."

Whatever this may have meant, it seemed a poor excuse for dispatching a warning to a commander in chief about to go into battle that he must be careful not to incur casualties.

But the advance continued.

"The officer examining the prisoners stated that the morale of the German officers was now terribly low," wrote Haig on September second. "He had at no period of the war seen them in such a despicable state. The prisoners I saw seemed well fed, but badly drilled.

"Near Wancourt I visited headquarters of the Fourth Canadian and First Canadian divisions. General Watson commanding. . . . Watson . . . stated that the German private soldiers abused their officers and N.C.O's and would no longer obey their orders. . . . Many of the enemy surrendered without fighting.

"At Bretencourt I saw General Fergusson commanding our Seventeenth Corps. . . . He too said of the prisoners that his provost marshal reported that they would not obey their officers. Discipline in the Germany army seemed to have gone—if this is true, then the end cannot now be far off, I think. Today's battle has truly been a great and glorious success."

On the next day, September third, he wrote:

"During the night Third Army took Rocquigny and occupied Quéant. This morning enemy is said to be retreating on the front of our Third and First armies.

"Our troops have reached (9 A.M.) the line Bertincourt-Doignies-Pronville. First Army is on hill south of Buissy. Thence line passes west of the latter village Dury and Etaing, both inclusive. Advance is continuing to Canal du Nord. I expect that the results of our success in yesterday's great battle should be very far reaching. . . . The enemy seems to be running away. . . . The enemy seems in full retreat today on the whole front from Lens to Péronne. I am inclined to think that the enemy will be unable to remain on the Hindenburg line for any time, but will seek for rest and peace behind the Meuse and the Namur defences, in order to refit his shattered divisions."

Foch told Haig on September fourth that he had had "a great deal of trouble in getting Pershing to agree to attack *at once*. Pershing looks forward to the creation of a great American Army, and will now only allow his American divisions to fight in American corps. However, Foch managed to bring Pétain and Pershing together and fixed up all details for a combined attack under Pétain."

Haig lunched with Foch and after lunch took a little walk with him. "He is most hopeful, and thinks the German is nearing the end. Reports came in that the enemy is in full retreat on the Vesle and Ham fronts."

Meanwhile Haig, with the approval of Foch, had prepared plans and given orders for an advance on the extreme left of his line of battle. This was to be undertaken by Plumer commanding the Second Army in conjunction with the Belgians who held that portion of the front which divided the Second Army from the sea. On September fifth:

"General Plumer came to see me about 11 A.M. regarding the instructions which I sent him for co-operating with the Belgian Army. He was inclined to continue his efforts to press the enemy back between the Yser and Armentières and retake Messines. I told him the most important object was to get the Belgians to advance. With this in view, he was to employ two good divisions on his left with orders to co-operate closely with the Belgians' right. First objective should be Clerken ridge-Forêt d'Houthoulst and the Passchendaele ridge. Then, when the main attacks of the allies have developed, he should be prepared to move a division by sea to Ostend and occupy Bruges, pushing on his left on the Dutch frontier, and connecting with the Anglo-Belgian Army on the line Thourout-Roulers. The first thing, however, was to get the Belgians moving, and for this I authorized him to employ two divisions on the Belgian right. Plumer said he had every confidence that the Belgian troops would do well once they had started."

Haig attended a conference at Cassel where Foch was present, and the Belgian scheme was discussed.

"Foch first of all had a private talk with myself and Weygand. He told me that he saw the King of the Belgians this morning, and that although the Belgian staff opposed any advance by the Belgian Army, the King was all in favour of action. Foch had accordingly made a plan. Practically the same one as Plumer had put forward and I approved. The King of the Belgians would command in person with a French general (de Goutte) as chief of the staff, but under another title. I agreed that Plumer should take orders from the King regarding the operations."

The next morning he received a visit from Winston Churchill:

"I told him that I considered that *the allies should aim at getting a decision as soon as possible*. This month or next, not next spring or summer as the Cabinet proposed."

On September ninth Haig crossed to England and the

following morning he, together with his chief of staff, General Lawrence, had an interview with Lord Milner at the War Office.

"I had specially asked for this interview, and I stated that the object of my visit was to explain how greatly the situation in the field had changed to the advantage of the allies. I considered it to be of first importance that the Cabinet should realize how all our plans and methods are at once affected by this change.

"Within the last four weeks we had captured seventy-seven thousand prisoners and nearly six hundred guns. There has never been such a victory in the annals of Britain, and its effects are not yet apparent. The German prisoners now taken will not obey their officers nor the N.C.O's. The same story of indiscipline is told me of the prisoners from our hospitals. The discipline of the German Army is quickly going, and the German officer is no longer what he was. From these and other facts I draw the conclusion that the enemy's troops will not await our attacks in even the strongest position.

"Briefly, in my opinion, the character of the war has changed. What is wanted now at once is to provide the means to exploit our recent great successes to the full. Reserves in England should be regarded as reserves for the French front, and all yeomanry, cyclists and other troops now kept for civil defence should be sent to France at once.

"If we act with energy now, a decision can be obtained in the very near future.

"As regards next year, aim at having all our units full up by first of April. To consider that first of July is 'time enough' is thoroughly unsound. All reserves of ammunition, aeroplanes, etc. should be reviewed in the light of the present situation. These reserves may well be reduced in order to set free men for the army; men already marked for the navy should for the next six months be sent to the army. It is also important to provide the army with infantry drafts and mobile troops to exploit success.

"Lord Milner fully agreed and said he would do his best to help."

The next day Haig returned to France and found his forces still advancing.

"The Americans attacked the St Mihiel salient this morning," he wrote a day later, after briefly outlining the progress of the Third and Fourth armies. "Nine divisions on the east side and one, aided by one of the French colonial division, on the west side. The former attacked on a seventeen-mile front and advanced five miles. About ten thousand prisoners are reported taken. Nonsard, Thiancourt, St Mihiel, Dommethers all captured. Attack was expected, but the violence of the attack was greater apparently than the Germans anticipated."

On September fourteenth:

"At 12.30 General de Goutte, who has recently been attached to the staff of the King of the Belgians, came to see me. He and his chief of staff, as well as General de Laguiche, stayed to lunch.

"I told De Goutte that I was most anxious to help him and the Belgian Army to the utmost of my power, and would provide maps or hand over railways and stations as required.

"De Goutte came to support me last November when the Third Army broke through the Hindenburg line near Cambrai. He has a mongolian type of head, but I think him a first-rate soldier, apparently honest and very keen. I think his selection to help the King of the Belgians is a very good one.

"General du Cane arrived from Foch's headquarters in time for dinner and stayed the night. I told him of my plans with dates, and asked him to arrange for Debeney commanding French First Army on our right to co-operate, and to have his preparations completed in time."

On September fifteenth:

"I held a conference with the three commanders of armies in my right, viz. General Rawlinson on right; Byng next and Horne on the Scarpe with right on Canal du Nord, west of Bourlon wood. Conference took place at Third Army headquarters at Villers l'Hôpital at 11 A.M. Army commanders in turn explained the situation and outlined the general plan. We then went into the actions of each army.

"Rawlinson's army is now in close touch with the enemy's 'outpost zone' of defence in front of the Hindenburg line. Enemy seems to have strengthened his force holding the line of heights from Le Verguier to Epéhy. On the other hand, in all combats which our troops have recently had with the enemy, the latter has not really fought. The First Army (Horne) stated the same thing, but Byng (Third Army) said the fighting at Trescault and Havrincourt had been severe. Enemy had put in five divisions there in the last three days.

"As the result of our discussion, I decided that Rawlinson should attack in force as soon as possible to capture the enemy's outpost zone on the Le Verguier-Epéhy ridges, and if possible push his right forward to get the rising ground about Fayet and Gricourt northwest of St Quentin. The possession of this height is important for gun positions to attack the main Hindenburg line subsequently. Rawlinson stated that the French First Army was unable to support him. General Debeney has done very little during these operations since eighth of August.

"After Rawlinson's attack has taken place (probably on the eighteenth) we should know more about the nature of the Hindenburg line defences and how they are held. My present view, is that main attack will be made by Rawlinson against the canal tunnel with the object of reaching Bussigny. The Third Army will support him and advance on

Soissons. Horne will take Bourlon wood and cover the left of our third army by holding a front on the rivers Scarpe and Scheldt as far as Valenciennes. Kavanagh with our cavalry corps will be ready to pursue."

On September sixteenth there was a meeting with Foch.

"After a general review of the situation on the British front and outlining my plans, I asked that Debeney's French First Army should be reinforced so as to enable it to co-operate with Rawlinson on Wednesday by taking the village of Fayet, northwest of St Quentin. Foch said that Debeney was very weak, and his guns had been taken for other armies, but he would see that Debeney was strengthened sufficiently to enable him to cover Rawlinson's right. The dividing line was moved one thousand yards to the south, thus giving the village of Fayet to Rawlinson. As regards the operations in Flanders, Foch agreed with me that it was not necessary or desirable for Plumer to attack the Messines-Wytschaete position. Plumer's attack with two divisions should be toward Zandvoorde and Gheluvelt, and these divisions should be well supported in order that the flank of the Belgians should be adequately covered, and the exploiting force enabled to move out at once. Foch gave me the details of the movements of the other attacks, dates, etc. He expressed the wish that I should continue my activity for another week. I explained that Rawlinson's attack would commence on Wednesday, and that the rest of the front to Bourlon wood would be pressing the enemy hard all the time."

On the following Wednesday the promised attack was launched, and it proved eminently successful.

"Our front of attack was about eighteen miles in length. We met and defeated thirteen enemy divisions in front line together with three more divisions brought up from reserve—a total of sixteen divisions. . . . The enemy only fought well in a few places, but opposite the Australians he

THE AMERICAN ATTACK
12TH SEPTEMBER, 1918

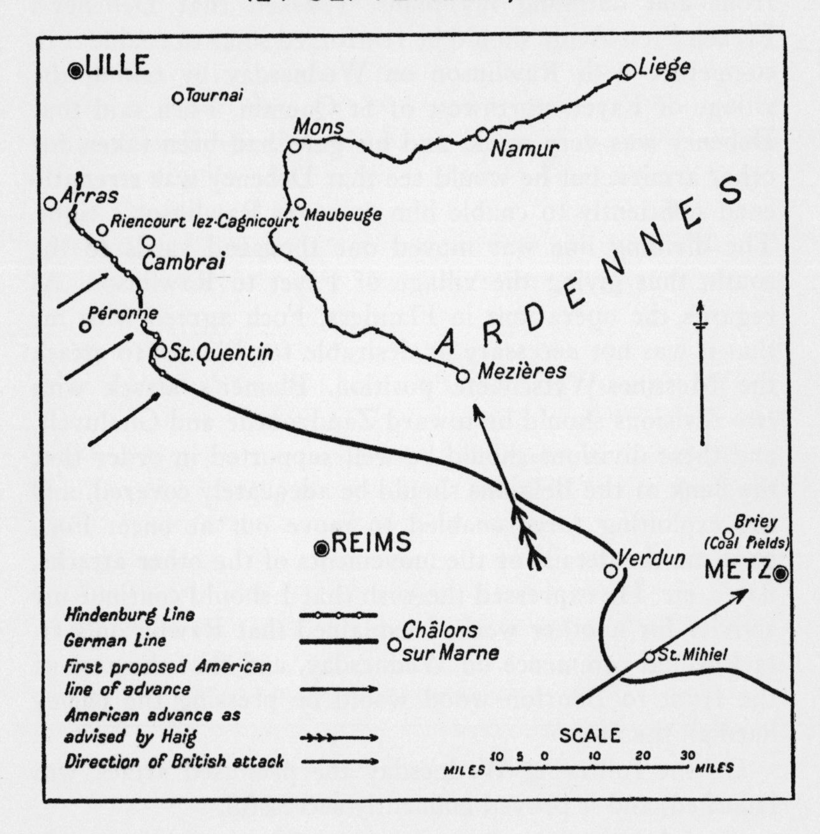

surrendered easily. Over three thousand prisoners were taken by the two Australian divisions engaged, and our losses were very small. The Fourth Army has already passed over six thousand prisoners through their cages, and the Third Army claim over fifteen hundred. So I expect the numbers taken today will be close on ten thousand.

"The enemy launched heavy counterattacks against the front of our third army from Villers Guislain as far north as Moeuvres. All attacks were defeated, and the enemy's losses are stated to be very severe. . . . At 3 P.M. I had a meeting with the King of the Belgians at La Panne. Generals Plumer and Lawrence were present with me. I explained our plan and why I was opposed to attacking Messines. He asked me whether I was satisfied with the general plan. I replied yes, and that I felt no doubt about its being successful provided that the troops were in good heart, because the enemy had no force available with which to stop His Majesty's attack. The King said that the Belgian Army was in the very best spirits and meant to fight well.

"As regards a four-hours' bombardment which the Belgian general staff proposed, I stated that the objection was that it would at once announce to the enemy that an attack was in preparation, and he might be able to organize a counteroperation with gas upon the troops when concentrated for the attack. This might have serious consequences."

In the midst of these continual successes a short correspondence took place between Haig and Henry Wilson which is so characteristic of both men that it is worth preserving. On September nineteenth Henry Wilson wrote:

MY GENERAL,

Well done! you must be a famous general!

HENRY.

To which Haig replied on the following day:

MY DEAR HENRY,

Very many thanks for your kind little note of yesterday. No, certainly not! I am not nor am I likely to be a "famous general." For that must we not have pandered to Repington and the Gutter Press? But we have a surprisingly large number of *very capable* generals. Thanks to these gentlemen and to their "sound military knowledge built up by study and practice until it has become an instinct" and to a steady adherence to the principles of our field service regulations part I are our successes to be chiefly attributed.

At such a moment Haig's anxiety to share all credit with his subordinate generals, his refusal to put forward any claim to inspired leadership and his insistence that his successes were due merely to rigid adherence to sound principles prove surely that he was not, what he has often been called, an ordinary man. If this were the common order of mankind, it would be a different and a better world.

He was above all persistent during these days in his endeavour to impress upon the government the importance of not relaxing their efforts in view of the possible imminence of victory. "Tout le monde à la bataille" was the inspiring slogan of Foch. Haig was incapable of coining a slogan, and would not have done so if he could, but the words expressed his policy in a nutshell.

On September twenty-first:

"I had another talk with Milner. He states recruiting is bad, and that if the British Army is used up now there will be no men for next year. He was quite satisfied that I should do what I deemed best in the matter of attacking or not. I pointed out that the situation was most satisfactory and that in order to take advantage of it every available man should be put into the battle at once. In my opinion, it is possible to get a decision this year; but if we do not, every blow that we deliver now will make the task next year much easier."

According to Henry Wilson's diary of September twenty-third Milner remained unconvinced. "He thinks Haig ridiculously optimistic and is afraid that he may embark on another Passchendaele. He warned Haig that if he knocked his present army about there was nothing to replace it. Milner saw many generals in France and they were all most optimistic. The man power is the trouble, and Douglas Haig and Foch and Du Cane can't understand it."

It seems that all the victories of August and September had not won for Haig the full confidence of even the most reliable members of the government. They argued that he had been optimistic before and his optimism had not been justified. But would they have preferred him to have been pessimistic in the past? A general who goes into battle without the confidence of victory is not fit to command. It was true that Haig had hoped on former occasions for greater results than he had been able to accomplish, but never before had he spoken with certainty of early victory, and never before had he spoken with such a record of success.

On September twenty-third he met Foch when they "discussed the situation and fixed the dates for several attacks".

On September twenty-fourth:

"About noon Admiral Keyes came to see me. He flew over from Dover and flew back to Flanders to see the King of the Belgians. I told Keyes to arrange to get hold of Ostend as soon as the Belgians were round the place on the land side. And I directed Lawrence to keep a good company of infantry ready at Dunkirk to embark if Admiral Keyes asks for them."

On September twenty-fifth Haig visited the Third Army.

I found Byng in an improvised railway train and quite comfortable. He had gutted the inside of an international sleeping car and put his various requirements into two compartments of it. I also saw Vaughan, his C.S.O. I thought that they were unduly afraid that our troops are going to meet strong enemy reserves on the Cambrai-St

Quentin front. In consequence they are desirous for me to wait and do nothing for some days, so as to allow the other attacks time in which to produce an effect and cause the enemy to withdraw some of his reserves from before us. I therefore told Byng of the dates fixed for the various attacks in agreement with Marshal Foch, viz. the Franco-American attack with *right* on Meuse and advancing northwest will be on Thursday twenty-sixth; my attack with our first army and left of Third Army will take place as I arranged last Saturday, namely on Friday twenty-seventh. The Flanders attack will go in on Saturday twenty-eighth, and then my fourth army on Sunday twenty-ninth. The delay in the Flanders attack is due to the lack of reserves behind it; it is therefore desirable to engage the enemy in force elsewhere, and so fix the enemy's reserves before the Flanders attack goes in. I then motored on to Bois du Hennois, headquarters Fifth Corps and had a talk with Lieutenant-General Shute. He said his divisions were full of cheer, but very "sleepy." A few days' rest and they would be as fit as ever again. The Twenty-first Division (David Campbell) had, after the first start, done splendidly. He also spoke about the difficult task which confronted him in attacking Gouzeaucourt and Gonnelieu spur. I told him my plan was to cross the canal at Marcoing, and by the Bellicourt tunnel, and then the centre of the enemy's position (opposite which is his corps) would fall of itself. All he would be wanted to do would be to advance sufficiently to be able to counterbattery the enemy's artillery. Shute had a very comfortable hut made by the Germans. The whole of his hutment is on a hill under trees and is reached by an excellent plank road.

At Grevillers, headquarters Fourth Corps, I saw Lieutenant-General Harper. He was back in the old headquarters which his corps occupied before the enemy's attack in March last. He explained his plans, and said he had no doubts about reaching his objectives on Friday, but expected that the enemy would fight hard, if he was still holding his present front. Today, however, the enemy had fallen back from two trenches.

At Ervillers, headquarters Fourth Corps, Lieutenant-General Haldane stated that he expected to be across the canal near Marcoing on Friday afternoon. He was attacking with the Third Division on the right and the Guards on his left, while the Sixty-second and Second were in second line ready to go through the two leading divisions to the line of the canal east of Marcoing. Noyelles-sur-l'Escaut on the left. All his troops were full of confidence and had been giving the enemy a very hard time of it. Cantaing and Fontaine Notre Dame further north are to be attacked by the Seventeenth Corps. . . .

"This morning reports of a railway strike in England are serious," the diary continues. "Our supply of ammunition would be greatly affected by such a strike. I ordered no change to be made, however, as I have full confidence in the good sense of our railwaymen at home. Some means will be found to keep up our supply of ammunition even if the worst happens. If the strike continues I ordered all leave to be stopped from tomorrow."

Haig's confidence in the workers at home and in the soldiers abroad was justified. On September twenty-seventh was delivered the attack which had been so carefully planned. The Hindenburg line fell before the First and Third armies. This was the beginning of the decisive battle of the war, and it was a military achievement of a magnitude which is seldom realized. This great line of defence had been constructed at leisure and all the engineering talent of Germany had been devoted to the task of rendering it as formidable as possible. Full use had been made of two great canals, the Scheldt Canal and the Canal du Nord. In some places the British infantry carried lifebelts and rafts in addition to their ordinary equipment. So burdened they slid down the steep slope of the canal into deep water, and were faced by an arduous climb upon the further side. Even in the few places where the canal cutting was dry it presented an obstacle which seemed insurmountable if defended by a determined foe. Great indeed was the responsibility of the commander in chief who had ordered the storming of such a stronghold, and who, far from receiving any encouragement from his government, had been warned that if he failed he would be called to account for the casualties.

But he did not fail. The great fortress fell, almost like the walls of Jericho. With clockwork precision companies, battalions, brigades, divisions, army corps and armies advanced as the hour struck and captured the positions that had been assigned to them. Typical of the whole movement was the experience of the officers of one company. On the night of the twenty-sixth they gave their servants the map reference of the exact spot in the German trenches where they were to be met for luncheon on the following day. They attacked before dawn and at 1.30 at the appointed place officers, servants and luncheon were all present.

On the two following days the attack was continued and, the Fourth Army taking part on the right and the Second Army on the left, the advance became general along the whole British line of battle.

On September thirtieth "Marshal Foch came to see me at 9.30 A.M. He was with the King of the Belgians yesterday at La Panne. He said that he is much pleased with the position in Belgium, and the progress made by the allied armies there, as well as on the British front. As regards the American operations west of the Meuse, he says the Americans have employed too many troops on that front, so that they have blocked each other's advance. In fact, they have not been able to feed so many divisions in that area. But they are going on attacking and are 'learning all the time'. Pétain is now using some American troops to push on toward Machault (southeast of Rethel). I asked Foch to send three American divisions to Plumer. Foch said it was not possible at present as 'their amour propre made the Americans determined to press on to Mézières'. But later on 'he would see what could be done when Pershing has learned the difficulty of creating an army'. I explained what my plans were and the direction of the advance of our cavalry corps. Foch said, 'we are in complete agreement'. Lawrence brought me a report that our Ninth corps were now operating northward in co-operation with the Australians, who were relieving the Americans and attacking northward through them, and it was desirable that Debeney should take Thorigny village (north of St Quentin). Foch at once concurred and he himself telephoned to Debeney, telling him to carry out his orders immediately when Debeney began to ask questions.

"Foch told me that the 'Bulgarians had agreed to all our terms of peace'. Foch was of opinion that the Germans cannot much longer resist our attacks against their whole front and that 'soon they will crack'."

When the month of September was ended and the Hindenburg line had fallen, the war in fact was finished, although for six more weeks the fighting continued while the facts were slowly being realized by the soldiers and statesmen on either side.

In the first of the month Haig visited Byng and Rawlinson, who both considered that the enemy had suffered very much, and that it was merely a question of our continuing our pressure to ensure his completely breaking. They agreed that no further orders from me were necessary and both would be able to carry on without difficulty. . . . "All our troops are said to be in the highest spirits."

On October second, "I met Mr Gompers (head of the American Labour Unions) and his friend Mr Fry at one o'clock at Hermies. Gompers accompanied me in my car to see the iron girder road bridge which was in process of being launched across the Canal du Nord to carry the road to Havrincourt. Both Gompers and Fry were much impressed with the magnitude of the engineering works now in hand immediately behind the fighting troops. I also showed him the wooden railway bridge made by the Canadian railway troops, and then took him to lunch in the adjoining valley below Havrincourt. I had the usual lunch in the lunch box, and we had quite a cheery lunch party. Gompers is a fairly old man, and walks slowly, and gets out of the car with some difficulty. I should estimate his age at close on seventy. He seems to have extraordinary power in the United States, where he has complete control over Labour. He is determined to go on until the Germans are beaten. 'There never has been such a just cause for war as we are now fighting for.' He was most complimentary in his remarks about the British Army and of what we had done. He pressed me to visit America after the war. I thanked him, but said I must have a rest from 'propaganda', and that I wished to live my own life quietly with my wife and children."

Daily Haig visited army, corps and divisional commanders to discuss the situation and to give advice as to how the task of harassing the enemy should be continued. He saw that the only danger lay in allowing the Germans time to recover from the series of blows they had received.

When he visited Foch on October sixth he found the generalissimo sitting with a Paris morning paper open on the table in front of him. In large type was printed a note from Germany, Austria and Turkey asking for an armistice. "Here", said Foch, pointing to the paper, "you have the immediate result of the British piercing the Hindenburg line. The enemy has asked for an armistice." It was nobly and generously said.

It is the more to be regretted that there must be recorded an incident which cast a cloud over the relations between the two great soldiers in this month of victory. It has been seen that Haig had consented to the placing of his second army under the command of the King of the Belgians during the operations which were designed to clear the ground on the left flank of the allied line up to the river Lys. This task had now been successfully accomplished, and Haig was anxious that the Second Army should once more be placed under his own command. Foch, for various reasons, resisted this not unreasonable demand.

At a meeting on October twenty-fourth, "I explained the military reasons why my second army must now be under my orders. If there were political reasons requiring the Second Army to remain under King Albert, then the British government must direct me on the subject. Until I was so informed I must continue to view the situation from a military standpoint and insist on the return of the Second Army without delay. Foch asked me to submit my request in writing. He would then let me have his views."

On the following day Haig addressed a formal request to Foch, in writing, for the return of the Second Army. Foch replied on the twenty-sixth to the effect that the Flanders group of armies was now marching on the Scheldt, that he had issued a "directive" on the nineteenth for the guidance of that group's operations, that it was necessary that it should remain under one command, as any alteration of plan at the present juncture would cause considerable difficulties. Haig was in Paris when he received this letter and he asked Lord Derby to speak to Clemenceau on the subject. Clemenceau on being approached "at once said that the French government as well as the British would be behind me in demanding the return of the Second Army to my command. Derby thought the whole matter was settled, but Clemenceau was going to see Foch in the afternoon, and would settle the question if Foch was in a reasonable mood."

That same evening, however, "About 7 P.M. Derby came to see me and stated Clemenceau had seen Foch and had returned much less determined than before about restoring the Second Army to my command. Wilson also came in.

We decided that I should write a letter to Foch which Wilson will take to him tomorrow morning."

Haig accordingly wrote once more to Foch setting forth the reasons why he desired the return of the Second Army. Henry Wilson was his messenger, nor could he in this instance have had a better one, for Wilson not only thought that Haig was in the right, but he was prepared, if necessary, to insist in the name of the British government on Foch's giving way. Moreover, he was a good diplomatist and understood Foch. He told Foch frankly that he was wrong, and Foch agreed to compromise. Haig visited him at Senlis the next afternoon.

"Foch was very pleased to see me, and was evidently anxious to make amends. We agreed that the Second Army should return to me on reaching the line of the Scheldt. This will be after the next operation. . . . Foch was very glad that the Second Army question was settled, because it would have been most unfortunate if the question had had to be settled by our governments, especially at the present time when any report of dissension among the allies would merely play into the enemy's hand."

So ended "with flowers and tea and delights" as Henry Wilson wrote, the last and the most serious difference of opinion that arose between Haig and Foch.

Throughout the months of October and during the first days of November, the fighting continued. On October eighth the Third and Fourth armies attacked and "drove the enemy from his last defensive line east of the St Quentin canal". The next morning General Vaughan, Byng's chief of staff, telephoned that "the Germans appear to have vanished. The Fifth Corps are beyond Selvigny which is full of civilians. The Fourth Corps are approaching the railway, meeting with very little opposition, and picking up a few stragglers. The Sixth Corps are through Wambaix, and on the line of the railway."

On the thirteenth Haig visited, with Clemenceau, the recently recaptured Cambrai.

"We lunched at the back of a ruined house in Rumilly, south of Cambrai, and about 2.30 P.M. met M. Clemenceau who had motored from St Quentin to meet me. I had an open car with me. M. Clemenceau and I got into this near the Faubourg de Paris. He put on General de Laguiche's overcoat, as his was a thin one. A battered-looking old hat surmounted the lot. A queer looking old 'tiger' as he is called.

"In this way we arrived at the city gate where we were received by General Byng and General Horne and a guard of honour of the Leicestershire Regiment.

"An old curé who had been in Cambrai all the time and others were introduced to M. Clemenceau. I then conducted him in my open motor round the town. A great part is in ruins, due to the enemy having set many houses deliberately on fire.

"At 3 P.M. we visited the Mairie. Only the façade was left. The rest was in ruins as the result of a fire, and the whole square was also a mass of burned houses, most of them gutted.

"The enemy has taken away all works of art, and cut to pieces the leather of the furniture and thrown the remains into the street.

"On leaving Cambrai I passed by Marcoing, Ribecourt and Havrincourt to the bridge made by the New Zealanders over the Canal du Nord.

"Clemenceau was much struck with what had been done, especially with the bridge and railway made by our troops.

"We reached his train at Bapaume shortly before 6 P.M. I spoke to him re Foch's proposals for an armistice. I said his demands were too complicated. We ought to say 'hand over Metz and Strassburg as a preliminary sign of your good faith'. Clemenceau quite agreed; then we can proceed at once to frame peace terms.

"I asked for some American divisions. Clemenceau was very keen to send me some and is to try to arrange it. He said France is very short indeed of labour and is anxious for some of our German prisoners of war. I promised to give him ten thousand.

"On leaving he thanked me 'in the name of France' for what I had done. He is evidently fully aware how the recent results obtained are entirely due to the boldness and tenacity of the British Army."

Further attacks were made by the Second Army on October fourteenth and by the Fourth Army on the seventeenth. . . . About 4,000 prisoners have been taken by Fourth Army, and several guns, including two complete batteries. The enemy continued his withdrawal in the Lille sector. Fifth Army is now round Lille. Troops are not allowed to enter the town. The mayor of Lille came to one of our brigade headquarters near Haubourdin, and reported that the enemy had evacuated the town at 4 A.M. and marched to Tournai. Food for eight days was left in Lille. First Army occupied Douai today after pressing enemy's rearguards back from the Haute Deule canal. Opposition ceased at twelve noon, and the enemy went off. Second Army hold the southern bank of the Lys from Wambrecchies to Quesnoy sur Deule, and have troops at La Vigue north of Reckem and south of Lawe."

It was on the same day that Admiral Keyes effected his brilliant landing at Ostend. On the twenty-third the Third and Fourth armies attacked again.

"Our troops drove the enemy from Bois de l'Evêque, Bousies village and Bois de Vendégies; Neuville Salêches and Beaudignies were captured, and the crossings of the Ecaillon river secured at the latter place. At the close of the day the enemy counterattacked vigorously opposite

Vendégies, supporting his infantry with heavy artillery fire, and was repulsed. About five thousand prisoners were taken by the Third Army, and over one thousand by the Fourth Army in today's operations. North of Valenciennes we cleared the enemy out of Forêt de Raismes and captured Thiers, Haute Rive and Thun. Determined fighting took place west of Tournai. The enemy seems to hold a strong bridgehead there."

The last important attack took place on the fourth of November:

"This morning, at time varying from 5.30 to 6.15 our fourth, third and first armies attacked between the Sambre canal at Oisy and the river Scheldt north of Valenciennes. A front of over thirty miles. The First French Army also attacked in co-operation on our right and made satisfactory progress. The French took three thousand prisoners up to 5 P.M.

"At 8 P.M. Fourth Army reported 'Attack is being pressed and progress made along the whole front of the army'. 'Resistance which was stiff all the morning is weakening, except south of Landrecies, where stubborn fighting is still taking place. Our casualties have been light. Prisoners of twenty-one regiments of nine or ten divisions and five battalions of cyclist brigades have been taken today. Attack on so big a scale was not expected. Over four thousand prisoners and thirty guns taken by Fourth Army today.'

"At 8.40 P.M. Third Army reported over eight thousand prisoners and 125 guns. Prisoners taken from forty-three battalions of twenty regiments of eleven divisions. 'There has been considerable opposition on whole army front today.' Thirty-eighth and Seventeenth Divisions advanced over six thousand yards through the Forêt de Mormal. Le Quesnoy surrendered with one thousand prisoners to the New Zealand Division.

"First Army does not report much progress after midday. The troops of the Twenty-second Corps had very hard fighting on the last three days; so this may account for the slowness of their progress.

"The weather has been very favourable—a fog in the valley until 8 A.M. This enabled our troops to get across the Canal de la Sambre without being seen. This part of the country is much enclosed with high hedges which have not been trimmed for at least the period of the war. The barrage only advanced at the rate of six minutes to one hundred yards.

"The enemy seems to have placed all his strength in his front line. Consequently when this was overcome he had no reserves in rear with which to oppose our advance."

From the early days of August onward, throughout these glorious weeks of victory, congratulations had been pouring in from every corner of the Empire, from public bodies and from private individuals, from the King, from Queen Alexandra, from the Lord Mayor of London and from mayors of numerous cities not only in Great Britain, but in every colony and dominion. One of the shortest and simplest ran as follows:

"You will be tired of congratulations but just let me say that as you approach the scene of our former exploits together my heart and thoughts are with you. Don't reply. FRENCH."

It was not, however, until October ninth that a word of official congratulations or thanks was received from the British government. On that date the prime minister telegraphed as follows:

"I have just heard from Marshal Foch of the brilliant victory won by the First, Third and Fourth armies, and I wish to express to yourself, Generals Horne, Byng and Rawlinson, and all the officers and men under your command my sincerest congratulations on the great and significant success which the British armies, with their American brothers-in-arms, have gained during the past two days."

Why the events of the eighth and ninth of October should have been selected for the honour of the prime minister's attention, when the far more important victories gained in August and September had passed unnoticed, was never explained. The suggestion that the prime minister of Great Britain relied exclusively upon the French generalissimo for his information regarding the movements of the British Army was, to say the least of it, infelicitous and, in view of Mr Lloyd George's long experience in the use of words, it could hardly have been unintentional. He wished to make it plain that Foch, not Haig, was winning the war, and that Haig, like other subordinate army commanders and like his American brothers-in-arms, was only to be congratulated when Foch was kind enough to say that he had done well. Haig sent a suitable reply to the prime minister's message and made no reference to the incident in his diary.

It was on October third, less than a week after the attack on the Hindenburg line had been launched, that the German government appealed for an armistice. Their note was addressed to President Wilson, and they referred to the fourteen points which he had laid down as conditions of peace. But an armistice is not a peace treaty, and the terms of an armistice must be decided by the military authorities on the spot.

Haig's views on the subject were definite from the first, nor, as the completeness of the allies' victory became more manifest, did they undergo any alteration. He believed that the one and only way in which the morale of the German Army might be restored would be to insist upon terms so humiliating as to be unacceptable. He believed also that if the German Army could retreat beyond the Rhine they would, fighting in their own country for their own homes and defending a far narrower front, still remain a very formidable adversary. He was further convinced that during the next six months or more the main brunt of the fighting would be borne by the British. It has been seen how he went into the war without any feeling of personal animosity toward Germans. Four years of fighting, with all the propaganda that accompanied it, had not ruffled the serenity of his opinions nor stirred in him a germ of national hatred. He wanted to defeat German militarism, but he had no desire to inflict either misery or humiliation on the German people.

It was on October tenth that Haig first discussed with Foch the possible terms of an armistice. "Foch gave me a paper which he had handed to the allied conference in Paris on the subject of an armistice. He said that his opinion had not been asked, but he had nevertheless given his prime minister his paper. He had now heard that the conference agreed with what he had written and were very pleased to have his paper. His main points were:

"(1) Evacuation of Belgium, France and Alsace-Lorraine;

"(2) Hand over to the allies to administer all the country up to the Rhine with three bridgeheads on the river. The size of each of the latter to be thirty kilometres from the crossing, drawn in a semicircle.

"(3) Germans to leave all material behind, huts, supplies, etc., railway trains, railways in order.

"(4) Enemy to clear out in fifteen days from signing of agreement.

"I remarked that the only difference between his conditions and a 'general unconditional surrender' is that the German Army is allowed to march back with its rifles, and officers with their swords. He is evidently of opinion that the enemy is so desirous of peace that he will agree to any terms of this nature which we impose."

A week later the Cabinet invited Haig to come to London in order to give them his views on this subject. He crossed on the eighteenth and on the following morning—"I visited the War Office soon after 10 A.M. and saw Wilson. He gave me his views on conditions of armistice. He considers that 'the Germans should be ordered to lay down their arms and retire to the east bank of the Rhine'.

"I gave my opinion that our attack on the seventeenth instant met with considerable opposition, and that the enemy was not ready for unconditional surrender. In that case there would be no armistice, and the war continue for at least another year.

"We went over together to 10 Downing Street, and found Mr Lloyd George, Lord Milner and Bonar Law discussing. General Davidson accompanied me.

"The prime minister asked my views on the terms which we should offer the enemy if he asked for an armistice. I replied that they must greatly depend on the answers we gave to two questions:

"(1) Is Germany now so beaten that she will accept whatever terms the allies may offer, i.e. unconditional surrender?

"If she refuses to agree to our terms:

"(2) Can the allies continue to press the enemy sufficiently vigorously during the coming winter months as to cause him to withdraw so quickly that he cannot destroy the railways, road, etc.?

"The answer to both is in the negative. The German Army is capable of retiring to its own frontier, and holding that line if there should be any attempt to touch the *honour* of the German people and make them fight with the courage of despair.

"The situation of the allied armies is as follows:

"French Army: Worn out, and has not been really fighting latterly. It has been freely said that the 'war is over' and 'we don't wish to lose our lives now that peace is in sight'.

"American Army: Is not yet organized; it is ill equipped, half trained, with insufficient supply services. Experienced officers and N.C.O's are lacking.

"British Army: Was never more efficient than it is today, but it has fought hard, and it lacks reinforcements. With diminishing effectives, morale is bound to suffer.

"The French and American armies are not capable of making a serious offensive *now*. The British alone might bring the enemy to his knees. But why expend more British lives? and for what?

"In the coming winter, the enemy will have some months for recuperation and absorption of 1920 class, untouched as yet. He will be in a position to destroy all his communications before he falls back. This will mean serious delay to our advance if war goes on to next year.

"I therefore recommend that the terms of armistice should be:

"(1) Immediate evacuation of Belgium and occupied French territory;

"(2) Metz and Strassburg to be at once occupied by the allied armies and Alsace Lorraine to be vacated by the enemy;

"(3) Belgian and French rolling stock to be returned and inhabitants restored.

"When I had finished my remarks, Hankey (the secretary of the War Cabinet) came in and I had to repeat most of what I had said for him to note down.

"The prime minister seemed in agreement with me. Wilson urged 'laying down arms'. Lord Milner took a middle course between my recommendations and those of Foch, i.e. in addition to what I laid down he would occupy the west bank of the Rhine as a temporary measure until the Germans have complied with our peace terms.

"About noon Mr Balfour (s. of s. for foreign affairs) came in, and the whole story was gone over again.

"I was asked what the attitude of the army would be if we stuck out for stiff terms which enemy then refuses and the war goes on. I reminded the prime minister of the situation a year ago when there were frequent demands for information as to what we were fighting for; he (the prime minister) then made a speech and stated our war aims. The British Army has done most of the fighting latterly, and everyone wants to have done with the war, *provided* we get what we want. I therefore advise that we only ask in the armistice for what we intend to hold, and that we set our face against the French entering Germany to pay off old scores. In my opinion, under the supposed conditions, the British Army would not fight keenly for what is really not its own affair.

"Mr Balfour spoke about deserting the Poles and the people of Eastern Europe, but the prime minister gave the opinion that we cannot expect the British to go on sacrificing their lives for the Poles."

The next day was Sunday. "Doris and I attended the Church of Scotland, Pont Street (St Columba's) at 11 A.M. The Rev. Dr Fleming preached the sermon. He spoke of vengeance and punishment with reference to making peace with Germany. We could not wish to see our armies entering Germany to destroy a German town for a town of France, in conformity with the scriptural passage 'an eye for an eye, a tooth for a tooth'. On the other hand, the punishment must be adequate to the crime committed.

"Afterward we called on Sir W. Robertson at his house in St James's Palace. He knew very little of the military situation on the continent, and seems quite to have dropped out of government circles. He gave the opinion that our present successes are the result of the past two years of hard fighting. I quite agreed with this opinion."

The next morning Haig went early to the War Office where he saw General Macdonogh who was then adjutant general. "I showed him my note on proposals for an armistice. He agreed with me entirely. As regards man power, he stated that our latest figures showed that we are not able to maintain more than thirty-six divisions next year. At present we have sixty-one divisions. I then saw Henry Wilson. We discussed the situation. I gathered that the main reason why he was in favour of a 'complete surrender' for terms of an armistice is on account of Ireland. He is most keen that conscription should be applied to Ireland at once in order to get us more men, and as a means of pacifying Ireland. We went over to 10 Downing Street together and met the prime minister at 11.15 as directed. Lord Milner, Mr Bonar Law and Mr Balfour were present as members of the War Cabinet and Admiral Beatty (commanding the Grand Fleet) and Admiral Wemyss represented the navy.

"We discussed the naval proposals for an armistice. They calculated that if the German High Sea Fleet came out and gave battle, our grand fleet would defeat it entirely but we would lose six or seven ships. So they recommend that all modern ships should now be handed over to the British because they would have been destroyed in the battle if it had taken place.

"Another point discussed was a request by the new Turkish government to make peace. It was sent by General Townshend, a prisoner of war captured at Kut. He had arrived at Mudros. All the Cabinet were agreed that no time should be lost in discussing terms of armistice, and that if we get the Dardanelles open and free passage into the Black Sea for our troops, etc., hostilities with Turkey should be stopped. Delay in making actual peace must occur, as we have to consult our allies.

"We all lunched with the prime minister. I sat on his left at head of table.

"We resumed the Cabinet meeting at 2.45 P.M. and did

not rise till after 6 P.M. The prime minister said it was the longest Cabinet meeting he had known of any Cabinet."

Haig returned to France next day, and on the following one, the twenty-third, General Pershing came to luncheon. He enquired as to Haig's views on the armistice terms and when he had heard them "he said that he agreed with me both as to the state of the enemy and the state of the allied armies and as to what our demands should be. As to the American Army, he also concurred in thinking that it would be next autumn before it could be organized and sufficiently trained to be able to play an important part."

On the following day, at an interview with Foch, Haig repeated his views. "Foch said that he insisted on having bridgeheads across the Rhine, and on occupying all German territory on the left bank as a guarantee to ensure that the enemy carries out the terms of peace which will be imposed upon her. He tried to make out that the enemy on the eastern side of the Rhine, opposed by three allied bridgeheads, is in a less favourable position for battle than if we were astride the river holding the German frontier of 1870. Of course the contrary is the case; indeed the unfavourable frontier was the main reason why Moltke urged the annexation of Metz and district in 1871. On the whole, Foch's reasons were political not military, and Lawrence and I were both struck by the very unpractical way in which he and Weygand regarded the present military situation. He would not ask himself, 'What does the military situation of the allies admit of their demanding?' 'What terms can we really enforce?' "

On October twenty-fifth, "I attended a conference at Marshal Foch's headquarters. There were also present Generals Pétain, Pershing, the latter's chief of the staff and Weygand.

"Foch stated that he had been directed by his government to obtain the views of the commanders in chief on the terms of an armistice. He asked me to give my opinion first of all. I gave practically the same as I had given to the War Cabinet in London last Saturday. Pétain followed and urged the same terms as Foch, viz. the left bank of the Rhine with bridgeheads. Pershing, although two days previously he had acquiesced in my views, now said ditto to Foch. The latter then asked me if I had any further remarks to make. I said that I had no reason to change my opinion. I felt that the enemy might not accept the terms which Foch proposed because of military necessity only—and it would be very costly and take a long time (perhaps two years) to enforce them, unless the internal state of Germany compels the enemy to accept them. We don't know very much about the internal state of Germany—and to try to impose such terms seems to me really a gamble which may come off or it may not. It struck me, too, that the insistence of the two French generals on the left bank of the Rhine means that they now aim at getting hold of the Palatinate as well as of Alsace Lorraine. Pétain spoke of taking a huge indemnity from Germany, so large that she will never be able to pay it. Meantime French troops will hold the left bank of the Rhine as a pledge."

Hearing after this conference that Pershing had resented some of the remarks that he had made concerning the American Army, Haig hastened to correct the false impression:

Paris, Oct. 27, —18

DEAR GENERAL PERSHING,

I have just heard that some of the remarks which I made at the conference at Senlis on Saturday, in French, were misinterpreted so as to give an idea of "failure" to the work of the American Army since it came to France. I write at once to correct this most incorrect impression of what I said. I yield to no one in my admiration for the grand fighting qualities of the American soldier and the manner in which you and your staff have overcome the greatest difficulties during the past year. So such an idea has never entered my head.

[He went on to explain that he had been anxious not to minimize difficulties.]

Foremost among these difficulties is that of creating enough American armies to make up for the rapidly dwindling numbers of the French and British in the field.

Pershing replied:

MY DEAR MARSHAL HAIG,

I thank you for your very courteous note, and for your complimentary remarks about the American Army. I am sure there was no intention of creating the impression that your words as interpreted seemed to convey, and I am more than satisfied with the official correction that you have made.

The very delightful relations that have always existed between us and between British and American officers and men everywhere are most gratifying to all Americans.

With warm personal and official regards,

I remain yours very sincerely,

JOHN J. PERSHING.

With regard to the terms of the armistice it was the view of Foch that prevailed, and no representative of the British Army was present when, in the very early hours of Monday morning, November eleventh, the German delegates surrendered to the French generalissimo in the Forest of Compiègne. Much, however, had happened in the immediately preceding days to strengthen the hand of the allies. The collapse of Bulgaria, Turkey and Austria was complete. The Kaiser had abdicated and Germany was on the brink of revolution. These events had not altered Haig's opinion as to the terms which should be imposed. The milder conditions which he had recommended would have secured to the allies a sufficiently powerful position during the period that divided the armistice from the signature of the peace treaty, and it is possible that if the defeated foe had been spared that first humiliation he might have proved more tractable both at the time and during the years that followed.

But now the war was over, and the soldier's work was done. Haig's diary ends abruptly on November eleventh. There is no trite moralizing, no smug expression of self-satisfaction, no paean of triumph over the great victory. What he had further to say upon the subject was said that night upon his knees.

CHAPTER XVIII

Peace

IT HAS ALREADY BEEN SEEN that Haig's views with regard to the armistice were disregarded; his views with regard to the peace treaty were never asked. International affairs had therefore ceased to concern him, and all his mind was henceforth centred upon those problems that had to be solved at home.

One great convulsion of nature produces another. The earthquake is followed by the tidal wave. In human affairs the same law applies. It is no light thing to turn four million peaceful citizens, occupied only with domestic concerns—the weekly budget and the sporting news—into an army of trained warriors, accustomed to the sight and the expectation of sudden death. Nor is it a simple matter, when the peace is signed, to bid them throw away their weapons, forget their fearful experiences and contentedly revert to the humdrum existence of the past. The red flag of revolution was flying triumphantly in Russia, and during the years that followed the conclusion of the war the tide of revolution rose high in many lands, and the roar of its waves could be heard breaking ominously on the shores of the British Isles. Before 1914 the possibility of European war had been the ever-present skeleton at every feast. After 1918 its place was taken by the fear of revolution, a fear which, in Great Britain, was not dispelled until the collapse of the general strike in 1926.

There is no more promising material for the manufacturer of revolution than soldiers returning from the wars. They have grown careless of danger and accustomed to risks. The peace to which they have so long looked forward is likely to disappoint them. The homes are never worthy of the heroes. They see others who have not endured the same hardships enjoying greater prosperity, and they are easy to persuade that they have much to gain and little to lose from an upheaval of society.

The problem therefore of demobilizing the army in 1918 was one that demanded the most serious study and the most careful handling. It had already engaged the attention both of the British government and the commander in chief.

More than twelve months before a scheme had been drawn up in the War Office and had been submitted to Haig for his approval. The official letter which he wrote upon this occasion affords one of the most striking proofs of his foresight and sagacity.

The government had held the view that the most urgent task to be undertaken at the conclusion of peace would be the reconstruction of British industry. They therefore proposed to release first from the army those men whose places in industry were awaiting their return, places which others without their qualifications could not occupy. These men were called pivotal men, and the system came to be known as "pivotalism". From the first Haig was opposed to it.

On October 3, 1917, he wrote to the War Office: "The procedure outlined in the War Office scheme of demobilization possesses certain serious difficulties, while the principle on which the scheme itself is based is open to grave objection if a well-regulated and disciplined departure from France is to be carried into effect."

He went on to draw a picture of the situation that he

imagined would exist when the war was over. The accuracy of his forecast was remarkable. There would follow, he said, an immediate relaxation of the bonds of discipline. Men's minds no longer occupied with fighting, no longer filled with the engrossing speculation as to their own survival, would immediately turn to more normal preoccupations, to their homes, their business and their future prospects. Competition to get out of the army would be keen. Jealousy of the fortunate ones who were first to leave would be intense. Nerves, already frayed by war, would render men unduly excitable. Unrest would follow.

"The fullest use of the existing military machinery together with the co-operation of all ranks would", he wrote, "be essential if a disciplined demobilization were desired." But the system proposed by the War Office "contemplates the entire breaking up of this organization". He believed that the suggested demobilization of pivotal men, wherever they happened to be and however long they had served, would prove fatal, and he strongly urged that the right principle was "demobilization by complete formations". He recommended that "the departure of the troops be based on the length of service of a formation with an overseas force" rather than according to the War Office scheme, which he said was "based upon the necessity for a rapid reconstruction of the civil and commercial life of the United Kingdom, and hence anticipates the gradual dissolution of military formations into a mass of individuals whose date of repatriation is to be decided solely by trade classifications without any consideration of length of service overseas." He proceeded to enumerate the practical difficulties in the way of the plan and to emphasize his warning as to what he believed would be the consequences.

But his suggestions were treated with contempt, his warnings were completely disregarded, and on November 5, 1917, he was told that "the War Cabinet, who were informed of your views, have now approved the principles of the original scheme of demobilization". The prime minister, who had distrusted his counsel in war, was not likely to listen to his policy in times of peace.

The result was precisely what Haig had anticipated. Men who had been prepared to die for their country were not prepared to watch others with shorter service to their credit getting an unfair start in the race for employment. Before the end of the year 1918 discontent was rife and there were ugly outbreaks among the troops both in France and in England.

In the month of January Winston Churchill succeeded Milner at the War Office and at once dealt vigorously with the situation. He was quick to appreciate that the whole system upon which demobilization was based was unsound, and on further enquiry into the history of the matter he was astonished to find that all that had happened had been foretold by the commander in chief. He hastened to put things right before it was too late, to abolish the obnoxious system and to arrange for demobilization to take place in future on the very lines which Haig had recommended from the first.

"It will be seen", he wrote, referring to Haig's letter of 1917, "that Sir Douglas Haig forecast accurately the state of indiscipline and disorganization which would arise in the army if pivotalism, i.e. favouritism, were to rule in regard to the discharge of men. . . . It is surprising that the commander in chief's prescient warnings were utterly ignored, and the army left to be irritated and almost convulsed by a complicated artificial system open at every point to suspicion of jobbery and humbug."

Owing to the prompt and efficient action that was taken further trouble was avoided and demobilization was carried out with the minimum of friction. But Haig did not consider that the mere process of demobilization terminated the claim that his men had on his care and devotion. Singleness of purpose is the clue to his character and the key to his greatness, and from the moment when the last gun was fired on that November morning, and the main object of his life had been fulfilled, there remained for him one duty only, to see that justice was done to the men who had served him so well. He had never had for them the winning smile, the gay gesture or the light and cheerful words that come so lightly to some men and that win the hearts of subordinates. His stark sincerity made it impossible for him to assume a carelessness he never felt, and the very depth of his emotions made him afraid to display them in a manner which he would have considered unbecoming in a soldier. Only to those who knew him intimately was ever revealed his great tenderness of heart.

General Sir Noel Birch, who had been his artillery adviser since 1916, remembers an occasion when, before returning to England, Haig took leave of all the men and women who had done espionage work for the allies in Belgium during the war. There were some seventy of them collected in one château for the occasion.

"Some of the men," wrote Sir Noel in a letter, "were curés and the women were of every sort and description. He had tea with them and after tea he talked with each one separately, sympathized with them in their troubles and thanked them for all their hard work. Some of their tales made, indeed, sad telling. One woman was the last of a family; the Germans had shot the rest of them. It was pathetic to see how their faces lit up as he spoke words of comfort and sympathy to them. Driving away in the motor afterward the field marshal was visibly upset. . . ."

Another incident occurred a few months later which reveals still more clearly both Haig's wealth of sympathy and his desire to conceal it. During his visit to Oxford in order to receive the honorary degree of LL.D. his old college,

Brasenose, arranged some festivities at which many ex-service men were present. Some of these were private soldiers who had not yet recovered from their wounds and were wearing the light blue hospital uniform which was at that time so familiar a sight. Haig's manner with these men was abrupt and the words he spoke to them were few. When later his old friend and contemporary, Lord Askwith, suggested that he might have shown them more geniality, he confessed that the sight of them had caused such a lump in his throat that he was afraid that if he said more to them he would break down.

This deep concern for the welfare of the demobilized had occupied the mind of the commander in chief long before the conclusion of hostilities. On February 20, 1917, he had written to the War Office:

"I have the honour to bring to the notice of the army council a matter which I consider requires immediate and careful examination and the earliest submission to the government for action. I receive constant communications from private individuals representing the state of poverty and almost destitution to which many of our invalided wounded officers are reduced. A number of them, without any private means of their own, totally and permanently incapacitated by the nature of their wounds from earning a livelihood, are in receipt of a pension which is not sufficient to keep body and soul together, much less to afford them the small comforts which their physical infirmities demand and that their sacrifices in the service of their country have earned.

"In another category are officers invalided from the service partially disabled, and without private means, and months elapse before they receive any pension at all.

"There is no system employed by which such officers who are invalided from the army but who are fitted for sedentary occupation are given opportunities for employment in government and other offices or works. Quite a number of these might be employed and thus release fit men to join the army.

"For every one case that comes to my notice there must be a hundred equally hard cases of officers who suffer in silence.

"In order to deal with these sad and deserving cases, I should suggest that a special government department be formed, which should with tact and discretion devote its energies to the interests of the disabled officer. The following points require special attention:

"(1) The immediate award of pensions on being invalided from the service. The pension should commence on the day on which the officer's army pay ceases.

"(2) The pension awarded to be on a sliding scale ensuring that those officers, who are totally disabled and have no private means or no parents in a position to support them, should receive a pension sufficient to maintain them in reasonable comfort.

"(3) The provision of such remunerative employment for officers as is suitable to their individual physical strength.

"(4) The maintenance of a register of all officers invalided from the service on account of wounds or ill health, with a view to protecting them from want, and providing them with employment. This implies a corresponding register of employers.

"(5) A permanent supervision of the interests of each wounded officer invalided from the service with a view to providing medical benefits and for their welfare.

"I strongly urge that there should be no delay in dealing with this matter, which, if allowed to continue, will constitute a scandal of the greatest magnitude."

A further instance of both his sympathy and his foresight was contained in another letter which he wrote to the War Office in the following year on the subject of the army agents—firms such as those of McGrigors and Cox, who had had an exceptional strain thrown upon them by the great increase in the size of the army.

In this letter he reminded the War Office that officers not only received their pay through these agents, but also banked with them and in many instances kept all their savings and securities with them, and he emphasized what a grave disaster it would be to those officers if any of the army agents proved unequal to their heavy task. He ended by urging the War Office to look into the position and to keep it under continual review in order to ensure that officers' interests in this connection were adequately protected.

The subsequent history of some of the agents concerned proved that Haig's fears were not without foundation.

It was only a few days after the armistice that the first official offer of reward reached him. The prime minister telegraphed suggesting a viscountcy. That this was another attempt to belittle the services of the British commander in chief cannot be doubted. Nobody ever possessed a keener or more exact sense of the value of honours than Lloyd George. A viscountcy had been awarded to French after the battle of Loos. It is the normal reward which the least distinguished secretary of state can claim on retirement. To offer it in the hour of the greatest victory that the British Army had ever achieved to the man who had commanded that army for three years and who had refused a similar offer eighteen months before was an insult both to the man and to the army. There is, however, nothing in Haig's letters or in his recorded utterances to show that he looked upon it in that light. He refused the proffered honour because he had made up his mind that he would accept nothing until he was satisfied that adequate provision had been made for the men and officers who had served under him.

When the offer was increased to an earldom he refused it again, and only gave way when it was pointed out to him that all the other recipients of war honours were about to receive them and that it would be difficult to explain why his name alone was omitted. He therefore accepted because he had no wish to make himself unnecessarily conspicuous, to render the position of others uncomfortable or to court an easy popularity. The earldom was accompanied by a grant of one hundred thousand pounds, which can hardly be considered excessive when it is remembered that Wellington was given two thousand pounds a year for life when the Peninsular War was only half over, and that the sum was made up to half a million together with a dukedom *before* the battle of Waterloo. The purchasing power of money was at that period greater than it is today, taxation was negligible and there were no death duties, under which more than a third of the sum granted to Haig was reclaimed by the Exchequer within ten years.

Another suggestion which the prime minister put forward at this time was that Haig's official return to London should coincide with a great reception which it had been arranged that the British government should give to Foch on December first. In a letter to a cousin Haig wrote, "I may tell you privately that I considered it an insult to be asked by your prime minister to return to London with a crowd of foreigners and on a Sunday too! What would my army have said about the first, and my Scottish friends about the second? So I said I would not come unless I was ordered."

It was arranged therefore that the commander in chief, together with his army commanders, should be welcomed back to England on December nineteenth. Haig was anxious that they should ride from the station to Buckingham Palace, where they were to be entertained at luncheon. It seemed to him ridiculous that soldiers should drive in carriages "like a party of politicians or old women". But his wishes were overruled and he was compelled to drive. At Charing Cross he was officially met by the Duke of Connaught and the prime minister, and also by such old friends as Mr Asquith and Sir Evelyn Wood, and, when his carriage reached the entrance to Marlborough House in Pall Mall, he found Queen Alexandra waiting there with his wife and daughters.

That evening he returned to his house on Kingston Hill, where at night an impromptu torchlight procession took place, some ten thousand people having collected to do spontaneous homage to their victorious commander in chief.

Haig spent Christmas at home with his family for the first time for four years. During the early months of the new year he was busily occupied, his presence being required sometimes in London, sometimes in Paris and sometimes with the army abroad. In March he conducted Lady Haig and her sister, Lady Worsley, over an extensive tour of the battlefields, revisiting many places which he had not seen since the early days of the war.

On April second he handed over his command to Plumer, and having said good-bye to Poincaré, Clemenceau and Pétain in Paris and to Pershing at Chaumont, he finally sailed from Boulogne on April fifth.

He was singularly quiet, even for him, during the passage to Folkestone. And he was not cheerful. The task was accomplished and the work complete, but no man of broad humanity and deep religious feeling could look back upon the events of the last four years without feelings of profound melancholy. He may have remembered at that moment the asperity with which the Duke of Wellington once corrected a lady who was exclaiming what a fine thing a great victory must be—"No, no, madam," said the Duke, "there is no greater tragedy in the world than a victory—except a defeat". And on this last voyage home with his wife beside him he must have reflected on the many soldiers who had never made that voyage, nor seen their wives again.

He was not yet fifty-eight, his health seemed robust and there was no reason for supposing that his career was over. Great posts exist within the British Empire which cannot be filled more worthily than by distinguished soldiers with glorious careers behind them. There was talk of the governor-generalship of Canada and of the viceroyalty of India as suitable positions for the victorious field marshal. But Haig's mind was made up. So long as the army required his services he would continue to render them. While the troops were still returning from France and the work of demobilization was being completed he could be useful as commander in chief of the home forces, but as soon as that work was done he would make way for younger men. Then one task and one only remained for him—to protect the interests of his fellow soldiers, to become the servant of those who had served him.

About this time he began once more to keep a diary, but his postwar diary resembled his prewar ones, rather than the one he had written during the war. It was kept spasmodically and finally, as his work once more increased and his leisure diminished, it faded completely away. He describes how on April eighth he had an interview with the King when the proposal to abolish all full dress for the army came under discussion. His Majesty disliked the suggestion that the Brigade of Guards should be clad permanently in khaki. Haig agreed. "I gave my opinion", he writes, "that so long as we had a voluntary army it would be necessary to clothe troops smartly, pay them well and amuse them with games, etc. Otherwise we won't get the necessary number of recruits."

At the same interview he discussed with the King the future of the Church of England. This was a subject upon which he had always felt strongly. On July 22, 1917, the

Archbishop of York (now Archbishop of Canterbury) had visited his headquarters in France and had spoken to him "about the necessity of opening the doors of the Church of England wider. I agreed and said we ought to aim at organizing a great Imperial Church to which all honest citizens of the Empire could belong. In my opinion Church and State must advance together and hold together against those forces of revolution which threaten to destroy the state."

On this occasion, nearly two years afterward, "I urged the King to press for the formation of a great-minded Imperial Church, to embrace all our churches, except the Roman Catholics. This would be the means of binding the Empire together. In my opinion the Archbishop of Canterbury had missed his opportunity during the war, and not a moment's time should be lost now in getting to work and organizing an imperial body of control, consisting of bishops, moderators, etc. . . . Empires of the past had disappeared because there was no church or religion to bind them together. The British Empire will assuredly share the same fate at no distant date unless an Imperial Church is speedily created to unite us all in the service of God."

The exclusion of the Roman Catholics from this oecumenical ideal was not due to any prejudice against them on his part, but simply to the knowledge, acquired from experience, that no compromise was to be looked for from them. How far he was from being a bigoted Presbyterian was proved by his attitude toward the Prayer Book controversy. He was in Scotland when the matter first came before the House of Lords, but because he believed it to be his duty to be present he travelled to London and sat throughout both days of the debate in order that he might hear the arguments fairly stated. Having heard them he had no doubts as to his own decision and voted in favour of the revised book, although this was not the view of a single

Scottish or Ulster Presbyterian member of the House of Commons.

"On April fifteenth", he writes, "I took over the command of the home forces in Great Britain with G.H.Q. in the Horse Guards.

"I arrived there about 10.30 A.M. and found Sir William Robertson waiting for me. He had nothing to hand over. The army in England was a very heterogeneous affair. His chief anxiety was labour trouble. This for the time being had been settled.

"After Robertson had gone I sent for my C.G.S. (Major General Romer, of the Dublin Fusiliers) and discussed his method of working the command and the office. As regards the latter I urged that the hours of work should be shortened both for staff officers and clerks. He quite agreed and is to lay down that the hours will be 9.30 to 6 P.M. Even this I think can be reduced for a number of them."

In May he was the central figure in what was practically a triumphal tour through Scotland. He received the freedom of the principal cities, honours from the ancient universities, and on May fourteenth delivered his rectorial address to the students of the University of St Andrews. This address began with a comparison between the position of Athens at the height of her power and that of the British Empire. He insisted on the many points of similarity and showed how closely the famous speech of Pericles applied to modern conditions. He went on to make a plea for that broader, imperial church of which he dreamed and concluded by insisting upon the importance of character as the basis of Empire.

"We have won," he concluded, "and if my reading of history and current events is correct we have won because our national character is sound; because it is founded in honesty and love of justice, inspired by comradeship and self-sacrifice, secured by a great capacity for common action in pursuit of high ideals. Let us do our best to keep it so and to hand it on strengthened to our children. So long as our national character remains unchanged we shall always win in all we undertake. It is the sword and buckler of our empire."

These were three weeks of crowded days for Haig. Often he had to make as many as four speeches in a day, but the spontaneous and heartfelt welcome given to him by the people of his native land was reward more than sufficient.

"Everywhere", he wrote afterward, "I was received with the most touching and loving enthusiasm by *all classes*. My countrymen have indeed made me feel that I occupy a warm place in everyone's heart."

In July the peace was signed, and on the nineteenth of that month there took place the great peace procession through the streets of London. Haig was ill that day, he had a high temperature and doubted whether he would have the strength to sit his horse throughout the procession. But Foch was there, Pershing was there, and it would have been a sad thing if the commander in chief of the British Army had been absent. So once more he made the effort that duty demanded of him, and few were aware how much it had cost him, although he had almost to be lifted from his saddle when the procession was over. And even then his day's work was not done.

In the midst of the universal rejoicings on that great day of triumph, when the final victory was being celebrated throughout the land, while rewards and honours were being heaped upon those who had deserved them, one man sat alone, unhonoured, unrewarded and unthanked. From his house in Queen Anne's Gate Lord Haldane could see the crowds that thronged St James's Park and hear the cheers that rent the air as the heroes of the day passed by. Since the beginning of the war he had become the best-hated man in England for no better reason than that he loved German philosophy and had once said, in a phrase which was never forgotten, that Germany was his spiritual home. So violent at times had the feeling grown against him, encouraged by the lowest organs of the press, that he had been insulted in the street, that his house was protected by the police and that his servants had been warned to be careful whom they admitted. So it was that as he sat alone that evening while the shadows were falling in the park and the crowds beginning to disperse, his servant came to inform him that there was an officer below in uniform who wished to see him, but that as he would give no name he had hesitated to let him in. Haldane with a weary shrug told the man to show the officer up, and Haig walked into the room.

He had brought with him as a gift a copy of his recently printed *War Despatches*. He was as tongue-tied and abrupt as ever, never mentioned that he was feeling very ill and left almost immediately. It was only after he had gone that Haldane opened the volume and found that it was inscribed "To the greatest secretary of state for war England ever had".

The incident should silence forever those who have accused Haig of lack of heart or of imagination. Only a man who possessed both those qualities in a high degree could have realized what Haldane would be feeling on that day, and how upon that day the tribute that he wished to pay him would be of greater value than at any other date.

Despite the popular rejoicings at the conclusion of peace, there was ever present during this summer of 1919 the spectre of serious industrial unrest and all that lay beyond it. Soon after Haig's return from Scotland, Sir Basil Thomson, the head of the Intelligence section of the Home Office, had called on him to "discuss arrangements for getting information of internal unrest. As regards the troops I said that I would not authorize any men being used as spies. Officers must act straightforwardly and as Englishmen. Espionage among our own men was hateful to us army men. The position was different during the war when all sorts and kinds of people were sent to France in uniform. They were not all soldiers, nor in fighting units. Now we were going back to the small, professional army. This must be made a happy home for all ranks. Thomson's machinery for getting information of sedition must work independently of the army and its leaders."

When in the autumn the possibility of a general strike became serious he summoned a meeting of the heads of the various commands to discuss the situation. He found all plans were ready to deal with any difficulties that might arise. "I directed", he wrote, "among other matters that troops should be kept concealed as long as possible, and should only appear when the civil authorities required their help. As soon as the necessity for action was over the troops must at once be withdrawn out of sight. Troops must be armed and act as soldiers. It is not their duty to act as policemen as they did in the police strike recently in Liverpool—some men were armed with halves of their entrenching tools."

The view that troops should be used only in the last resort, that they should not be paraded as a menace, which is more likely to prove an irritant, and that when they are employed it should be in their true capacity as soldiers and not as auxiliary policemen, is undoubtedly sound doctrine. Fortunately there was no need to put it into practice that autumn. The railway strike, which appeared at one moment formidable, passed off peacefully, and when in the month of October Haig's family was increased by another daughter he christened her Irene, for it seemed to him that peace had come at last.

Early in the new year, 1920, it was decided to abolish the

post of commander in chief of the home forces, a post which had only existed during the war, a decision which automatically brought Haig's appointment to an end.

The secretary of state wrote to him as follows:

War Office,
January 30, 1920.

My Dear Field Marshal,

As you are giving up your command to-morrow, I write by desire of all my colleagues on the Army Council to express to you on their behalf our enduring sense of the illustrious services which you have rendered to the British Army in the war and of the great assistance which you have given to the War Office and to the government during your tenure of the post of commander in chief, forces in Great Britain. It is a source of keen satisfaction to us, and to me personally, to know that though you will be for the time being enjoying a well-earned period of leisure, your gifts and experience remain at the disposal of the British Army and of the state.

I am giving directions that a special army order, embodying the sense of this letter, shall be read to the troops.

Again, with warm thanks for your many personal kindnesses to me,

Believe me,
Yours very sincerely
Winston S. Churchill.

Henry Wilson, still occupying the position of chief of Imperial General Staff, also wrote:

36 Eaton Place,
S.W.

Saturday night
Jan. 31, 1920.

My General,

It seems so odd your leaving soldiering even though it may be temporarily. The years run by at an alarming pace and at an increasingly alarming pace, and it seems only yesterday that you came to the War Office from Simla, and it seems only last night that we went to France for the Great War.

If any man can be proud and content with the part he played in that final test you most certainly are that man; and whether you serve again or whether you don't you have that supreme comfort for the rest of your time.

And so good-night but please not good-bye.

Ever
HENRY.

This meant for Haig the practical end of his military career. As a field marshal, however, he remained on the active list of the army, and he felt no regret at quitting the post which he had filled during the past year. The possibility of having to use troops in the suppression of civil disorder is always hateful to a soldier. It was doubly hateful to Haig, who knew that if such disorder arose he might be driven to employing force against some of the very men who had fought for him in France, and to whose assistance and protection he intended to devote the remainder of his life.

Now that he no longer occupied an official position his hands were free and his time was at his own disposal. But the task that faced him was not an easy one. It had been considerably complicated by the honest efforts of those who had already tried their hands at it. Before the end of the war there had come into existence more than one organization for the protection of the interests of those who had fought in it. Of these the two principal were the "National Federation of discharged and demobilized soldiers and sailors" and the "Comrades of the Great War". In the uncertain state of national affairs that then existed there was considerable danger that these and similar powerful organizations might be tempted to play an important part in politics and to seek by political pressure to obtain their private ends. The former of the two associations mentioned above had assumed a definitely left-wing outlook, and refused to admit officers to membership. The Comrades had, on the other hand, a predominantly conservative bias.

Haig had already interested himself, together with Sir Frederick Maurice, in the formation of the Officers' Association, which they had determined should be free of any political complexion, and which, it was hoped, might serve as an intermediary to bring the Comrades and the National Federation together. It was on account of this movement that he was obliged, or rather that he obliged himself, to abandon a holiday which he had planned to take on the termination of his appointment. He had hoped to visit his cousin, Mrs. Haig Thomas, who had taken a villa at St Jean de Luz. On January thirtieth, however, he wrote to her:

"Both Doris and I were so looking forward to a trip abroad but we have had to give it up. Tomorrow my appointment as commander in chief, home forces is abolished and I am already very busy organizing an 'Officers' association'. Today I took part in a great meeting at the Mansion House to launch the scheme and raise funds. You will see all about the meeting in the papers of tomorrow, but I enclose a copy of a little pamphlet we issued before the meeting as it summarizes what we are doing. In view of all this I cannot well go off abroad and leave my work to be performed by others.

"I spent last week visiting Manchester, Leeds, Sheffield and Hull. Each place gave me a great reception and I duly rubbed in the shortcomings of many of the employers in not taking on more ex-service men. Some of course have done more than their share and have 20 per cent, whereas we only want them all to take 5 per cent. In the West Riding 25 per cent of the employers have taken on nine thousand ex-service men. There are still four thousand in that area out of work and 75 per cent of the employers still available to do it. Nearly all of them in that part have made great fortunes, so we are not asking very much really."

So it was that, on the abolition of his appointment and the end of his official career, Haig's first act was to postpone a holiday to which he had been looking forward in order to undertake fresh work on behalf of his fellow soldiers. Henceforward that work became unremitting, and it would probably not be an exaggeration to say that at no period of his life did he work harder than during the last years of it. Nor was the work congenial to him. He had loved the profession of arms, and had delighted both in the study and practice of it. But now he was condemned to spend long hours at the writing table, varied by visits of ceremony and the making of speeches. Public speaking is a strain even on those to whom it comes easily; but for those who hate it, as Haig did, it is pain and travail. He had never been fluent either in conversation or on the platform, and he was too old to learn new tricks; but speaking was now demanded of him wherever he went, and during these years he visited every town of importance in the country. He would not spare himself. In France he had kept regular hours throughout the war and taken regular exercise, for he knew it to be his duty to keep himself physically fit for the great task he had to perform. But now he would sit far into the night replying to a host of correspondents—old soldiers and widows of old soldiers who brought their troubles to him with the certain knowledge that they would not be neglected.

His old friend and medical adviser throughout the war, Colonel Ryan, on one occasion warned him solemnly that he was overworking and that the consequences might be serious. He suggested at the same time that his labours would be considerably lightened if he would dictate his letters instead of writing them all with his own hand. Haig replied that he thought people preferred to get letters written in his own hand, that in many cases there was so little he could do for those who appealed to them and that he believed in maintaining the human touch.

The importance of the human touch and the weight of a strong personality were responsible for the great work which he now accomplished. When Colonel Crosfield approached him on behalf of the Comrades of the Great War with the request that he would take over the presidency of that organization, he replied without a moment's hesitation that he would do nothing of the kind. He could not bear to see two bodies of ex-service men in competition, and often in acrimonious competition, with one another. Let them make up their differences, let them unite and he would gladly put himself at the head of the united body.

Colonel Crosfield says that Haig seemed to him at the time to underestimate the difficulties that lay in the way of carrying out his suggestion. When there exist two separate organizations, each possessing branches in many parts of the country, each branch employing its little band of officials and each branch bitterly competing with its rival, it is easy to point out the obvious advantages of amalgamation; but it is as difficult to persuade them to amalgamate as it was to persuade the Capulets to embrace the Montagus.

Haig brought to the task, in addition to his great name and position and his reputation for fair dealing, the fact that he had in July, 1919, given evidence before a House of Commons committee on pensions which had produced a profound impression on ex-service men throughout the country. It had also induced the government to introduce radical changes in the rates and methods of granting pensions which had very materially benefited the recipients.

When, therefore, Haig had to address a meeting of the National Federation at Leicester, the audience, although at first disinclined to accept his advice, were at last convinced both of his sincerity and of his practical sympathy. There are occasions when bad speakers can produce a greater impression than good ones. Parnell seldom spoke well, but seldom failed to produce his effect. The reason generally given is that he meant what he said. The same was certainly true of Haig, and on this occasion he succeeded in a task which it is given to but few orators ever to accomplish—he changed the mind of an audience and won assent to his own views.

So it was that at the end of June, 1921, the British Legion came into being, and united in one body the National Federation, the Comrades of the Great War, the Officers' Association and another organization entitled the National Association. It is not too much to say that without Haig's efforts this great work could not have been accomplished. Ex-service men are aware of how much they owe to the British Legion, but the ordinary citizen hardly realizes how many difficulties and dangers were averted by the unification of these various bodies and the salvation of them all from being dragged into the political arena.

Just as the new organization owed its existence to the strength of Haig's personality, so during the early years of its existence—and the early years of an institution are as important in the formation of its character as are the early years of an individual—was the British Legion moulded into the shape which Haig desired. Unity, comradeship and peace were his watchwords, unity between all ex-service men working in a spirit of comradeship and maintaining peace not only within their own ranks, but in the community at large.

It is interesting to note that he never attempted, as he might easily have done, to assume dictatorial powers in a position where they would probably have been gladly accorded to him. It would not have been surprising if one whose whole career and whole outlook had been so strictly military had allowed something of the regimental tradition to creep into the control and discipline of this new body of which he was the head. But, on the contrary, he was only anxious that in the Legion the old hierarchy should be forgotten and that the constitution should be as democratic as that of any other body of free men who associate together for purposes of mutual advantage. Having, however, secured his first objective in bringing ex-officers and men into the same organization, he realized that, if steps were not taken to prevent it, the control of the different branches and of the organization itself was likely to drift into the hands of those who had held commissions. Therefore to ignore the previous position of men who joined the Legion, which on the face of it appeared the more democratic method, would, in practice, probably defeat the very end that it had in view.

"Really," he wrote to Colonel Crosfield on March 14, 1922, "there *ought* to be no question of 'rank' in the Legion —we are all 'comrades'. That however is not possible and so we must legislate to ensure that the 'other ranks' are adequately represented."

He was above all things anxious that the human sympathy, which his own heart felt so deeply and which his own tongue could so ill express, with those who had fought for their country and had fallen upon evil days should be the prevalent and the abiding spirit in all the activities of the British Legion. On September 23, 1923, he wrote to Colonel Crosfield, with whom up to the day of his death he was in continual correspondence concerning the affairs of the Legion: "As charitable organizations develop and their machinery becomes more systematized, so do they act 'according to regulation' and lose sympathy with the unfortunate who need help. So we must guard against this and I think occasionally change the subordinates who interview the needy ones, replacing them by others who have more recently felt the pinch of poverty and can appreciate more the value of a kindly word."

These are hardly the words of a man who lacked imagination—of a man who was a good soldier and nothing else.

Haig's activities on behalf of ex-service men were not, however, limited to Great Britain or to the British Legion. The army that he had commanded had been, as he had never forgotten, an imperial army, and he was most anxious that the same principles which prevailed among ex-service men at home should extend to those who had come from and returned to the dominions overseas.

Difficulties precisely similar to those which had been encountered at home existed overseas. There, as here, a large number of separate organizations had come into being and had asserted their existence by quarrelling between themselves. Haig's objects were first, to form one single association in each dominion on the lines of the British Legion, and then to unite all such associations in one great British Empire Service League. The first link of this imperial chain was forged in South Africa, which Haig visited at the beginning of 1921. In that country there were already four separate associations in existence, and the obstacles to persuading them to collaborate were considerable; but Haig succeeded in South Africa as he had succeeded at home. His personality, his persistence and his sincerity enabled him to accomplish what it is doubtful whether anybody else could have accomplished. The four South African associations became one, and the British Empire Service League came into existence in the land which Haig had not visited since he left it at the conclusion of the Boer War twenty years before.

He and Lady Haig enjoyed their journey. They visited all the principal towns of South Africa and rode over many of the battlefields. At Bloemfontein he unveiled a war memorial, and he stayed for a few days with General Smuts in the same house where, during the South African War, he had stayed with Cecil Rhodes.

Four years later, in 1925, he paid a similar visit to Canada. Here the difficulties that he encountered were greater even than those that had faced him in South Africa. There, there had been four separate ex-service men's associations—here, there were fourteen. In a series of interviews, however, with the leaders of these different bodies he won them all over to his own view, and at the end of three days a great meeting took place at Ottawa, when these same leaders surrendered into his hands their charters and their seals, "evidence of their desire for unity and as an act of faith in his leadership". Having thus successfully concluded the real object of his visit he was the better able to enjoy a tour across the whole width of the continent, being hospitably entertained wherever he went, and meeting again his old comrade, Lord Byng, who was at that time governor-general of the Dominion.

He fully intended to pay similar visits to Australia and New Zealand, but it was not to be.

Such leisure as Haig allowed himself during the last years of his life was spent, whenever he could so arrange it, at Bemersyde. This ancient house had belonged to a member of the Haig family since time immemorial; and his fellow countrymen, who contributed to purchase it from the Haig who was holding it at the time and to present it to the most distinguished bearer of the name, could have given him nothing that he would have valued so highly.

Years before he had written to a nephew from South Africa: " 'Aim high,' as the Book says, 'perchance ye may attain.' Aim at being worthy of the British Empire and possibly in the evening of your life you may be able to own to yourself that you are fit to settle down in Fife."* He himself had aimed high, he had attained, he had been worthy of the British Empire, and he certainly deserved peace in the evening of his life amid the beloved and legend-haunted

*See vol. i, p. 92.

Haig. F.M.

HAIG FACING THE CAMERAS BEFORE LANDING AT VICTORIA, B. C.,
13 JULY 1925

scenery of the Scottish border. Often he would say during these last years that he demanded nothing more than to be allowed to sit by his "ain fireside".

He had always retained in his speech traces of his Scottish origin, and those who have read closely the extracts from his diary will have noted that he never overcame the Scotsman's difficulty in correctly handling the words "shall" and "will" and "should" and "would". Now the love of his native land became more dominant. Relations, who had seen little of him since he went out into the world and were prepared to regard their great kinsman with awe, found a refreshing simplicity in his conversation. He seemed like one of themselves who had stayed at home, who had never been to Oxford or Sandhurst, or travelled all over the world, or commanded great armies, or moved familiarly in kings' courts.

Wit he had never aspired to, but he was not lacking in the dry humour of his race. One or two instances may be given.

When Lord Trenchard was commanding the Royal Flying Corps in France he was frequently requested to bomb Don Bridge, which was situated in the vicinity of Douai. Although these commands were invariably carried out, the bridge, which was a small one, seemed to continue to serve its purpose, a fact upon which the commander in chief occasionally commented.

During the advance in 1918, when Trenchard was no longer with the British Army but was commanding the Independent Force at Nancy, he received one evening a laconic telegram from Haig—"I rode over Don Bridge today."

There are several charming accounts in Sir William Orpen's *An Onlooker in France* of the impression which the commander in chief made upon the painter. "Whenever it became my honour to be allowed to visit him," he writes,

"I always left feeling happier—feeling more sure that the fighting men being killed were not dying for nothing. One felt he knew, and would never allow them to suffer and die except for final victory. When I started painting him he said 'Why waste your time painting me? Go and paint the men. They're the fellows who are saving the world, and they're getting killed every day.' "

On one occasion after Orpen had been lunching at headquarters and before he had left the building "a most violent explosion went off, all the windows came tumbling in, and there was great excitement, as they thought the Boche had spotted the chief's whereabouts. The explosions went on and out came the chief. He walked straight up to me, laid his hand on my shoulder and said: 'That's the worst of having a fellow like you here, major. I thought the Huns would spot it' and, having had his joke, went back to his work."

Maurice Baring was another temporary officer with whom Haig formed a friendship. As A.D.C. to Trenchard he was a frequent visitor at G.H.Q. and Haig christened him Nicodemus, for what reason Maurice Baring never knew, but suspected some confusion in the commander in chief's mind between the personalities of Nicodemus and Silenus. After the war Maurice Baring once attended a levée at St James's in court dress. Haig was standing beside the throne. After Baring had made his bow, but before he left the palace, a note was handed him which ran—"Nicodemus. Your stocking is coming down. Haig. F.M."

It is curious, but not surprising, that Haig's true character should have been more easily understood by artists and by men of letters than by his fellow soldiers. Recollections of the parade ground are bound to leave a lingering mist of awe between a very highly placed officer and his subordinates, which it is difficult for a shy and untalkative man to dissipate. F. S. Oliver was another writer who came to know Haig during the war, and fortunately he has recorded his first impressions.

Writing to his brother from France during the battle of Passchendaele he says—"Of course the commander in chief is the central figure in the British Army in France, not merely from his position, but also, so far as my experience went, from the sheer greatness of his personality. He is a man of whom, in the earlier stages of his career, I had heard a great deal more harsh criticism than affectionate praise. I think this was partly due to the fact that when he went to India as head of cavalry—about ten years ago, I think—he found officers sunk in a most imcompetent sloth, and didn't hesitate to boot them out right and left, making thereby a large number of personal and hereditary enemies. But I think the chief reason is his obvious difficulty of finding words. Not only the small talk, which may not be supposed to interest him in itself, but also when he has got something very clear and urgent in his mind, and wishes to communicate it. This is a great handicap, as you may imagine, in the task of making the politicians understand his military aims; but it has the indirect effect of making people who meet him casually think him haughty and reserved, neither of which things he seems to me to be in the least. He is certainly shy, and modest also, although as self-confident a man as I ever met—a Scotsman through and through, not only by birth and domicile, but in accent and feature; most of all perhaps, a Scotsman in his manner of thought. He looks you straight in the face with a pleasant, kindly smile, which has at the same time a humourous, slightly ironical twinkle in it.

"I liked him from the first moment I saw him," Oliver writes in *The Anvil of War,* "and after spending a week under his roof, during which time he had both good luck and bad, grounds both for elation and for annoyance, I came away liking him far better than I had done at the beginning. You would like him too. You would like the way he throws back his handsome head and sticks out his chin when he gets at all excited. You would like his fierceness, and his gentleness mixed up with it."

And the following is Oliver's final verdict, written after the armistice:

"You remember what the Mousquetaires said about d'Artagnan—that they loved him more than any of the others. I feel just that about D. H. He isn't the greatest soldier that ever lived. He isn't inventive. He is too slow at getting rid of incompetents. He has old-fashioned ideas about the use of cavalry, etc. But he is a very great character—a perfectly true and simple-minded man, who sees the facts, and can't see the frills and theories. I daresay he often draws wrong conclusions—as even Napoleon did—but his feet are on the ground; he isn't whirling aloft like a withered leaf in the eddies of a theoretic gale.

"People often say that he is cold, stand-offish, self-seeking, etc. I simply don't know what they mean. I think he is about the least self-seeking creature I ever ran across. And certainly, as I see him, he is one of the warmest-hearted and most sympathetic. I've met and known fairly intimately most of the British bigwigs who are engaged in this war. As far as personal affection goes I put D. H. first. And he is perfectly trustworthy."

Happy were the days that Haig now spent at Bemersyde, planning improvements of his new estate and often carrying them out with his own hands. But still the call of duty sounded and so long as there was breath in his body he was bound to obey that call. Everywhere the work of the Legion demanded his presence. His name alone was sufficient to solve problems and to settle disputes—his name which is still reverenced by members of the Legion beyond all others. Wherever he went speeches were demanded, the volume of correspondence did not decrease and he persisted in refusing to employ a secretary.

At the beginning of 1928 he was intending to take a short holiday in the south of France. He travelled from Bemersyde to London in order to attend a scout rally at Richmond on Saturday, January twenty-eighth. As usual a speech was demanded from him and it was noticed that in the middle of it he paused for a moment and turned deathly pale. He recovered immediately and afterward made no complaint of feeling unwell. That day he wrote to Colonel Crosfield about an invitation he had received to become the patron of the Old Contemptibles' Association:

"I think I should reply that as the Old Contemptibles are really part of the Legion, no patron seems necessary, and the Prince of Wales is really the patron of *all* ex-service men —and I hope he will insist on all Old Contemptibles joining the Legion as a section of a Legion branch.

"I hope to see you on Tuesday at 10.30 A.M."

That was the last letter that he wrote. His last business was on behalf of the Legion. The handwriting is as vigorous as ever; there is no trace in it of old age or of infirmity. He was staying in his brother-in-law's house in Prince's Gate, which had been his London home for the greater part of his life. The next day was Sunday and he spent it quietly. After dinner and a game of cards he retired to rest. A little later groans were heard coming from his room, and his brother John, who was staying in the house, found him gasping for breath. In a few minutes all was over. The long strain of the war had told at last. That stout and steadfast heart had ceased to beat. If he knew that the end had come, he had the satisfaction of knowing also that his task was finished and that he had earned his rest.

The depth and the sincerity of the mourning throughout the Empire afforded proof, had any doubted it, of the place that Haig had won in the hearts of his fellow subjects. St

Paul's Cathedral seemed the appropriate burial place for so great a leader, but he had expressed a wish to lie in his own country, and his wish was respected. For two days the coffin lay in the church of St Columba, where he had always worshipped when he was in London, and all day long an uninterrupted flow of mourners passed reverently by, in order to pay their last homage to the dead.

On February third the official funeral took place, the service in Westminster Abbey, accompanied by all the pomp and pageantry that the obsequies of a field marshal demand. The King's three eldest sons walked behind the gun carriage that bore the coffin. Prince Arthur of Connaught represented his father, the senior field marshal. Two Marshals of France, Foch and Pétain, were among the pallbearers, who included those who held the highest rank in the three fighting services.

That night, when the coffin reached Edinburgh, despite the lateness of the hour and the inclemency of the weather, an enormous crowd had assembled to receive it. Here among his own people the sorrow seemed more personal and more poignant. Not only had they been proud of him and of the great honour that he had brought them, but they loved him and understood him. Many were in tears.

The next day the body lay in state in St Giles Cathedral, while from dawn to darkness the sorrowing crowds passed by. When the hour came for the cathedral to be closed at the end of a cold, wet, February day, there was still more than a quarter of a mile of patient mourners, four abreast, waiting for admittance. The cathedral remained open until they had all passed through.

The last scene was the simplest. On a plain farm cart drawn by four farm horses the coffin was carried from the station of St Boswells to the Abbey of Dryburgh—five miles through the country that he knew so well, the valley of the Tweed under the shadow of the Eildon Hills. Finally

there is any whose record would prove as good. The only faults that have ever been attributed to him by reputable writers are merely the defects of the finest qualities. That he was too reluctant to change his advisers, that he was too hopeful on the eve and in the course of battle, and that being once engaged he was too slow to give up the fight—if each of these accusations has a grain of truth in it, they amount only to the fact that he possessed in too great a degree the essential military virtues of loyalty, courage and tenacity.

The differences of opinion on military policy, which during the last two years of the war caused friction between himself and the civil power, were such as are likely to arise in times of crisis between professional soldiers and the popularly elected representatives of a democracy. That Haig's views on strategy were sound it has been the main thesis of this book to prove. Seeing that they were held by the overwhelming majority of those whose lives had been devoted to the study of military science, to decide that they were all wrong and that the truth lay with the civilians would indeed be a melancholy conclusion.

Haig recognized that ministers were entitled to their opinions, and he was fortunate in being able to maintain the most friendly relations with all the politicians who crossed his path, with one exception. In the exceptional case, what he found difficult to forgive were the methods that were employed against him by one whose motives he knew were the same as his own, to win the war. To his straightforward and direct intelligence it seemed incomprehensible that a man who distrusted him should continue to employ him. He was very clear in his own mind as to his constitutional position, and never threatened to resign his command because he considered that he had no right to do so. He was the servant of the state, and so long as the state required his services he was bound to render them. If the state lost confidence in his abilities it was for the state to dismiss him, and we may be certain that he would have taken his dismissal without a word.

To a fellow soldier who thought he had been harshly treated by the government, and with whom Haig sympathized, he wrote: "I strongly recommend you to remain quiet and not stir up an agitation, because, even though an officer has right on his side, it does not in the least mean that he will get what he wants. The government has a perfect right to send any one of us away at a moment's notice without giving us any reason beyond saying that they are not satisfied with us. Indeed, if any authority finds he does not work in sympathy with any of his subordinates, he is perfectly justified, in the interests of the country, in dispensing with the services of that subordinate. I regard the conduct of the government toward you in that light."

How little resentment he bore, how far was any thought of malice from his heart, is shown by the fact that in all the many speeches that he was compelled to make in the years that followed the war, he never allowed one word of recrimination to cross his lips, nor made a single bitter allusion to the past.

Greatness of character is something different from greatness of mind or of intellect. It is a quality that does not dazzle men, and it is one to which few men of genius, especially those who were also men of action, can lay claim. More often than not it must be its own reward, for it seldom leads to fame, or wealth, or power. But when it is possessed by one of those upon whose life the searchlight of history beats, it should command the homage of the historian. In moral stature Haig was a giant. It may be easy to find in history a more brilliant, it would be hard to find a better man. His life was dedicated, from the day that he left Oxford until the day that he died, to the service of his country, and his reward was the firm faith which the majority of his countrymen reposed in so loyal a servant. The nine years that were granted to him after the victory were sufficient to show that his humanity was as deep as his military knowledge, and his fellow countrymen, who, for the most part share and sympathize with his reserve and reticence, learned to understand him as only those people do understand one another who are incapable of giving full expression to their feelings. "The Legion has lost a president," exclaimed one of them on hearing of his death, "but it has gained a patron saint."

If there be a Valhalla, as some of our ancestors liked to believe, where the great captains of the past sit down and feast together and tell again the story of their fights, this modest, quiet Scotsman will have his place there; but very seldom will he be persuaded to tell the story of how for three long years he commanded the greatest armies that his empire ever put into the field, how in the darkest days his faith in their ability to conquer never faltered, and how he led them to victory in the end.

THE END